see pg 234 of B ... above all else ... cons-

The Diary of Dawid Sierakowiak

food - used for status, for favors pg 284
life or death, class structure

Rumors

Library, hospital, clean water, parasites?
pg 239, food, hunger, dulls the senses,
Moral outcry - food rations increased
pg 239

doctors? dentists?
street smart knowledge of ... pg 241-2
pg 242 cholent - ...
food rations go up + down pg 243, vs 239, 248

pg 101
book writing 244
pg 247 - not the head of father to
give up on health for

Rx pg 250?

The only photograph of Dawid Sierakowiak known to have survived, enlarged from his ghetto class photo taken in 1941.

The Diary of Dawid Sierakowiak

Five Notebooks from the Łódź Ghetto

edited and with an introduction by

Alan Adelson

translated from the Polish original by Kamil Turowski

foreword by Lawrence L. Langer

Oxford University Press

New York Oxford

Oxford University Press

Oxford New York
Athens Auckland Bangkok Bogotá Bombay
Buenos Aires Calcutta Cape Town Dar es Salaam
Delhi Florence Hong Kong Istanbul Karachi
Kuala Lumpur Madras Madrid Melbourne
Mexico City Nairobi Paris Singapore
Taipei Tokyo Toronto Warsaw

and associated companies in
Berlin Ibadan

Published by Oxford University Press, Inc.,
198 Madison Avenue, New York, New York 10016

First published by Oxford University Press, Inc., 1996

First issued as an Oxford University Press paperback, 1998

Oxford is a registered trademark of Oxford University Press

Library of Congress Cataloging-in-Publication Data
Sierakowiak, Dawid.
The diary of Dawid Sierakowiak : five notebooks from the Łódź
ghetto / edited by Alan Adelson : translated by Kamil Turowski.

ISBN 13: 978-0-19-512285-5 (Pbk)

1. Jews—Poland—Łódź—Persecutions. 2. Holocaust, Jewish
(1939–1945)—Poland—Łódź—Personal narratives. 3. Sierakowiak,
Dawid—Diaries. 4. Łódź (Poland)—Ethnic relations. I. Adelson,
Alan, 1943– . II. Turowski, Kamil. III. Title.
DS135.P62L4434 1996
940.53'18—dc20   95-49333

Those dying here, the lonely
forgotten by the world,
their tongue becomes for us
the language of an ancient planet.
Until, when all is legend,
and many years have passed on a new Campo dei Fiori
rage will kindle a poet's word.

—Czesław Miłosz
Warsaw, 1943

Foreword

If a primary task of Holocaust literature is to help us imagine the ordeal of those who struggled to stay alive in ghettos and camps, then Dawid Sierakowiak's *Diary* must be hailed as one of the leading texts in the canon. Unlike Anne Frank's *Diary,* with which it is sure to be compared, Sierakowiak's record of diminishing existence in the Łódź Ghetto draws us into the landscape of a savage and incessant oppression from which the young girl hiding in an attic in Amsterdam was lucky enough to be shielded. Although their eventual ends were the same—to die in misery—their routes diverged, and one can only hope that readers will greet Dawid Sierakowiak's sober impressions of Jewish life under the Germans with the same acclaim they gave Anne's *Diary.* It is a milieu Anne herself would grow acquainted with only after she no longer had a chance to write about it.

Dawid's *Diary* begins on June 28, 1939, a few weeks before his fifteenth birthday, and breaks off on April 15, 1943, a few months before he would turn nineteen. He died on August 18 of that year, apparently from tuberculosis. The remaining inhabitants of the Łódź Ghetto, including his younger sister, would have to endure hunger and disease and the illusion of rescue until August 1944, when most of them were deported to Auschwitz. Few returned.

Although there are a few gaps in Dawid Sierakowiak's account because notebooks have been lost, we nonetheless gain from his surviving daily entries a vivid sense of how his own and his community's fate was slowly replaced by its doom. As control of their lives shifted from themselves to the Germans, the future ceased to mean what you might be or do and became instead an issue of how soon you would die. The brutal agents of this doom, the Germans who willfully ignored sanitary conditions in the ghetto and allowed infectious diseases like typhus and tuberculosis, together with hunger, to claim increasing numbers of victims, remain offstage in this drama of a people's gradual slide into the pit of death. The same irony that pervades many Holocaust testimonies and memoirs infiltrates Dawid's text too—the real criminals virtually disappear, and their prey seem to bear the burden of guilt for their own destruction.

This remains one of the most vexing moral dilemmas for Holocaust commentators, and the young Dawid confronts the problem with a mixture of resentment and dismay. As he watches his own family and his neighbors waste away, he is increasingly piqued by the hierarchy of privilege that prevails among Jews in the ghetto. Ghetto head Chaim Rumkowski and his aides, members of the Jewish police, doctors, instructors in the workshops where "ordinary" Jews were employed— those Primo Levi would label the "Prominenten" in a place like Auschwitz—were favored with better living conditions and adequate rations, while the rest of the population fought to stay alive on meager food in sparsely furnished quarters. This inequality of opportunity never ceased to offend the young Dawid, whose political sympathies lay with the Marxist philosophy of the Soviet Union.

Just as readers of Anne Frank's *Diary,* in order to appreciate her full ordeal, must be familiar with the journey of the Frank family to Westerbork, Auschwitz, and Bergen-Belsen after they were arrested, so readers of Dawid Sierakowiak's *Diary* must know the context of his entries in order to respond to their sinister resonance. As the Germans begin to deport those unfit for work, the diarist innocently muses, "Nobody knows what the Germans do with the children and those unable to work." Large numbers of Jews begin to arrive in Łódź from Vienna, Prague, and the Czech Protectorate of Bohemia and Moravia. They are not absorbed into the labor force in the ghetto, but are shipped to work camps in the area of Poznań, according to Dawid. *We* know that they are being sent to Chełmno, where they are murdered in mobile gas vans and buried in mass graves. But when the deportations temporarily cease, Dawid solemnly complains, "Even that chance for getting out of the ghetto has been taken away." By drying up usual sources of information, the Germans found it easy to avoid rousing the suspicions of their victims.

Later, when the Germans reduce the size of the ghetto population (and hence the mouths that need to be fed) by sending off the aged, the ill, and all children younger than ten, illusions begin to fade: "although Rumkowski assures us that he guarantees 'safe conduct' for these children, no one really believes him," Sierakowiak asserts. Parents do what they can to hide their offspring, but the Germans are ruthless and thorough, and few escape. Rumkowski's strategy is to save those he can by surrendering the rest; the text of Dawid's *Diary* makes clear how much anguish he caused for others by his megalomaniacal self-deception.

Some readers may wonder why there was no uprising in Łódź comparable to the one in the Warsaw Ghetto. Dawid's daily observations help us to understand why. By April 1943, the time of the Warsaw rebellion, it was clear that the Germans had decided to liquidate that ghetto and deport its remaining inhabitants. Those involved in the insurrection knew about Treblinka and had no illusions about their fate. But in Łódź, Rumkowski was opening more and more workshops, and Jews lucky enough to be employed in them had some grounds for believing that their labor was of sufficient value to the Third Reich to ensure their survival at least until war's end. Hence, to protect a "safe" future, Rumkowski was determined to stamp out any sign of internal dissent. Moreover, even a stunted hope is a powerful antidote to the "nobility" of collective suicide.

Dawid Sierakowiak himself was a creature of alternating moods. From time to time, rumors spread through the ghetto of various Allied initiatives, and the Jews of Łódź soaked them up like sponges. Such rumors became the lifeblood of a forsaken population, especially as living conditions grew harsher and harsher. Dawid reports them faithfully. But by the time the fourth year of the war arrived, on September 1, 1942, the diarist had little hope that anyone would stay alive to the end, whichever side won. His litany of sorrows reveals a mind resolved to unveil the true plight of his community: "Day after day passes. One buys rations, eats the little food there is in them, starves while eating it, and after that keeps waiting obstinately, continuously and unshakenly until the end of the cursed, devilish war. . . . We're fighting to survive until liberation, a goal as elusive as a phantom."

Those hoping to find in this diary a tribute to the invincible human spirit are bound to be disappointed. Indeed, one of its distinct merits is to convey how powerful a role something as mundane as "40 [dekagrams] of sugar, and 20 [dekagrams] of margarine" could play in the drama of death by starvation unfolding relentlessly in its pages. Dawid is staggered one day by the news that a former neighbor, "an absolute athlete before the war," has died of hunger: "His iron body did not suffer from any disease; it just grew thinner and thinner every day, and finally he fell asleep, not to wake again." Among the many crimes committed by the Germans in the Łódź Ghetto and elsewhere is this: they blithely divorced their victims' deaths from the manner of their lives, leaving a legacy of disrupted achievement that neither logic nor memory can ever reconcile.

For no one is this more true than for Dawid Sierakowiak himself, a talented young man who, had he survived, might have parlayed his intellectual gifts into a promising literary career. He mastered several languages, reading, as he tells us, Galsworthy in English, Thomas Mann's *Buddenbrooks* in the original, the plays of Ibsen and Strindberg in German translation, Romain Rolland in Yiddish, while inaugurating the vocation of author by writing poems and essays in Polish and Yiddish. Not too long before his death, he even began translating one of Lenin's works into Yiddish. But he has few illusions about the ultimate value of these endeavors, inscribing his forays into Schopenhauer with a wry if melancholy wit: "Philosophy and hunger: quite a combination."

If his *Diary* has any hero, it is food, not the human spirit. He is driven to read and write by desire, by habit, by inertia, by the absence of anything else to do, while his greatest source of joy is an extra bowl of soup. His elation seems boundless when he announces gleefully on April 14, 1943, "I will be working in the bakery for three months!" But by August he was dead, of malnutrition and lung disease, his body a victim of what no mind could combat. His final entry here, the day after he learns of his new and much sought-after job, shows how fleeting such turns of fortune might be in a world designed by the Germans to consume all Jews, some sooner, some later: "In politics there's absolutely nothing new. Again, out of impatience I feel myself beginning to fall into melancholy. There is really no way out of this for us."

Of course, he was right: for him and most of the Jews of the Łódź Ghetto the only way "out" was to die or be killed. But his tenacity in writing a few lines or paragraphs in his notebooks almost every day for nearly four years leaves us a remarkable bequest. The Sierakowiak *Diary,* together with documents from other chroniclers of the Łódź Ghetto, gives us a glimpse into the lapsing vitality of a doomed community that would have dwindled into silence without such testimony. While it is important not to exaggerate or sentimentalize this feat—Dawid would gladly have traded each of his journals for 5 kilos of potatoes—his *Diary* is nonetheless a tribute to the power of language to recapture for future generations no small sense of the ordeal of Europe's Jews under the ruthless heel of their murderers. It helps us to imagine what we can never know.

Lawrence L. Langer

Acknowledgments

This volume owes its existence to many individuals, but to two in particular: one a Jewish survivor of the Łódź Ghetto, and the other a conscientious Christian from that city. Together they attempted to publish this book almost thirty years ago, but were defeated by politics and anti-Semitism. The diary of Dawid Sierakowiak was one of the first documents that Lucjan Dobroszycki tried to publish in the course of his highly focused lifetime study of the written remnants of the ghetto where he was held captive with his family. Until his untimely death in 1995, he continued to want to see his schoolmate's full ghetto diary made available to a broad readership.

Konrad Turowski is the Christian who facilitated that goal in the most essential way. As a journalist in Łódź, he made an early and sustained commitment to prevent the historical significance of the city's virtually eradicated Jewish culture from being forgotten. He was instrumental in drawing into the public realm three of Dawid's diary notebooks. He protected and preserved those notebooks through a period in the late 1960s and beyond when such materials were being destroyed under a quasi-official government policy directed at ridding Poland of its few remaining Jews, even denying the existence of the documentary remnants of the Jewish culture that had thrived there. From the moment in 1968 when the publication of the complete diary under Dr. Dobroszycki's oversight was canceled by a government-controlled publishing house until today, Mr. Turowski has continued his efforts to see the complete diary published.

He brought the diary to the attention of this volume's editor more than ten years ago when Alan Adelson went to Łódź to gather materials for the film *Łódź Ghetto* and the compendium of the ghetto's surviving documents, which was published as the film's companion volume. Mr. Turowski assisted tremendously in those efforts, and ultimately made the diary notebooks that he had purchased available for use in the script of the film. Indeed, it is Dawid's description of the invasion of his city that opens the documentary, and his "voice" from the diary provides a continuing narrative thread through the film as the young man's life is progressively extinguished.

We were also assisted in the most essential way by Elizabeth Maguire, who recognized the significance of the diary while she was at Oxford University Press and acted with heartfelt conviction to publish it at last. We could not have asked for a more gracious or more perspicacious editor. Irene Pavitt has brought an enduring disposition and a discerning eye to the editing at Oxford; Adrianne Onderdonk Dudden has designed the book lovingly; and Susan Chang, Elda Rotor, Susan Rotermund, Mary Kate Maco, and Charles Gibbs have all worked conscientiously to see the book published and recognized.

Daniel Grinberg, director of the Jewish Historical Institute in Warsaw, most kindly extended permission for our use of the two Sierakowiak diary notebooks that reside in the collection there, and was always wonderfully responsive to our many inquiries and requests for other assistance. Yitzchak Mais and Yehudit Inbar of the Yad Vashem Museum provided a photocopy of the diary notebook that was lent by the Jewish Historical Institute to Yad Vashem for an exhibition on the Łódź Ghetto.

Marek Web, chief of the archives at YIVO, the Institute for Jewish Research in New York, has been an extraordinarily helpful colleague through the eight years we have been preparing this volume. He was one of the first to commend the book for publication, reviewed an early draft of the translation, and provided his broad-ranging knowledge to the annotation of the text references. Dina Abramowicz, YIVO's always helpful librarian, provided many bibliographical references. Molly Magid Hoagland edited the editor, bringing extensive refinements to strengthen the volume. We are also indebted to Robert Moses Shapiro of the Stern College for Women for sharing his expertise on the writings of the ghetto; to Dr. Daniel Wiener for taking an early interest in seeing the diary published; to Zosia Turowska, the Polish book editor who assisted extensively in her superbly pleasant and diligent manner in the annotation of diary material related to Polish history; and to Raul Hilberg, Madeline Levine of the State University of New York at Buffalo, Karla Schultz at the University of Oregon, Hérica Valadares at Columbia University, Fran Martin, Fernando Moreno, Walter Taverna, Joan Pinaire, Herman Adelson, and Julian Baranowski and Władysław Pohorecki at the Polish National Archives in Łódź—all for their help in reviewing and annotating the text. We are particularly indebted to Magdalena Połujkis, who verified the entire translation, refusing to accept any compensation for her fastidious effort. Her deep compassion for Dawid and his people was engendered, she has said, by her Polish grandmother, Eugenia Socha-Rutkiewicz, who risked her life to smuggle food in a baby carriage into the Warsaw Ghetto before it was closed. The actions of these women from two generations stand as exemplary contradictions to the callousness that Poles are often said to have felt about the destruction of their Jewish population.

As a sustained undertaking by the Jewish Heritage Project, which strives to bring essential works related to Jewish history and culture to a broad audience, we hope this book will stand as one of many memorials to Helen Hauben, whose pragmatic idealism was very much like Dawid Sierakowiak's. She supported our work for over a decade out of her earnest desire to reach out with knowledge of the Holocaust beyond those who suffered to those who might otherwise repeat such horrors in ignorance. We acknowledge with pride and gratitude the ongoing support we have received from her husband, David M. Hauben, and from Bruce M. Hauben, Ellen Liman, and Bernard Stern of the Joe and Emily Lowe Foundation board. We thank as well Suzanne Usdan of the Lemberg Foundation for her generous and continuing support. The Literature Program of the New York Council on the Arts, and its director Jewelle Gomez, provided the initial translation grant that began this endeavor. Her dedication to literature of all ethnicities is unique.

The translator wishes to thank his wife, Kasia Marciniak, for sharing her inspiring enthusiasm and for volunteering her time at all stages of the project. He thanks as well his American family, Kinga and Andrew Zamecki, for sponsoring his work on the diary in the United States.

The editor is deeply grateful to his wife, Kathryn Taverna. The compassion and respect she feels for Dawid Sierakowiak has been an inspiration to see his diary finally published, and with the greatest care. The effort has benefited in the most essential way from her extraordinary generosity of spirit: to support, sustain, and entertain.

Contents

The Diary of
Dawid Sierakowiak

The men of the second-largest Jewish population in Europe fill the streets around the Old Town Synagogue in Łódź for the funeral in 1912 of Elias Haim Meisel, chief rabbi of the Jewish Council.

One Life Lost

Only two months after their invasion of Poland on September 1, 1939, the Nazis began drawing up specific plans for the forced concentration in an urban slave camp of the vast Jewish population that had grown up in the city of Łódź.* Throughout Europe, only Warsaw had a larger Jewish population, and the Jewish community in Łódź was one of Europe's most prosperous. A city of smokestacks like Manchester, England, Łódź was the textile capital of Eastern Europe. Sprawling cloth mills were owned by fabulously wealthy families, some of them Jewish, whose "palaces" remain today as civic buildings, museums, a music conservatory, and the city's renowned film school.

In December 1939, Friedrich Übelhör, *Brigadenführer* of the Kalisz regency,† drafted a secret memorandum estimating that there were 320,000 Jews living in Łódź. He promulgated a plan to force as many as possible into "a closed ghetto." But he left no doubts among the Nazi hierarchy that this was to be "only a transitional measure. . . . The final aim," he asserted, "must be to burn out entirely this pestilent abscess."‡ Meanwhile, every last bit of material worth would be progressively squeezed out of the living Jews, while their strength and energy would be siphoned into the production of goods to arm the German war effort and to improve the quality of life in the Fatherland. The slave colony was assigned to the oversight of a willing young German entrepreneur, Hans Biebow, who had written many letters and exercised all the influence he could from his family's standing in pursuit of the appointment.§

* The stages by which the Nazis carried out the genocidal process in Łódź, including a discussion of the conflicts that persisted in the Third Reich hierarchy over the continued existence of the Jews in Łódź when all other cities in Poland had been "cleansed" of Jews, are detailed in Lucjan Dobroszycki's precise introduction to *The Chronicle of the Łódź Ghetto* (New Haven, Conn., 1984), pp. xxxiv–lxvi.

† Łódź was initially assigned by the Germans to the Kalisz regency, one of three into which the Warthegau section of Poland annexed into the Third Reich was divided. The regency seat was later moved to Łódź.

‡ Übelhör deliberately overestimated the city's Jewish population, according to Dobroszycki, *Chronicle of the Łódź Ghetto*, pp. xxxviii–xxxix. Extending a prewar census to 1939, 230,000 to 250,000 Jews resided in the city immediately prior to the German invasion. Many fled east to Russia, or were voluntarily or forcibly deported into the conquered territory not adopted into the Reich, called the General Gouvernement by the Germans. When the ghetto was closed by the Germans on May 1, 1940, the Nazi-appointed Eldest of the Jews, Mordechai Chaim Rumkowski, reported a population to his German overseers of 163,177.

§ Hans Biebow (1902–1947), the son of the director of an insurance company, was thirty-eight years old, the head of a coffee company in Bremen, and a relative latecomer to the

Delineating its borders in January 1940, the Nazis centered the Łódź Ghetto around the derelict Bałuty neighborhood, where the city's Jewish ghetto had been located in the nineteenth century, a slum area already notorious in Eastern Europe. Until only fourteen years before the war, the district had existed outside all municipal jurisdiction, with no health and safety regulations. A high concentration of the city's poorest Jewish workers lived there in ramshackle huts and houses built in helter-skelter clusters around a catacomb of alleyways, only partially electrified and completely lacking in sanitation and water lines.

But the Nazis also included in the 1.5-square-mile ghetto area a region closer to the center of the city. There, soot-blackened brick and stone apartment blocks had been built around courtyards that would later serve perfectly as discrete enclosures for the forced "selection" of Jews to be deported into the unknown. Once the apparatus for a "Final Solution" was in place, the isolated Jews would be dealt with all the more expeditiously. But they would first be prepared for deportation to the death camps through physical and psychological breakdown. This interim stage of concentration before genocide proved to be one of the cruelest existences ever designed by mankind. With no exaggeration, it was a living hell.*

The Discovery of the Diary

Polish gentiles were ordered to leave the district, to make way for the hundreds of thousands of Jews the Nazis planned to force in from other parts of the city, from outlying districts, and eventually from throughout the conquered territories of Europe. Among those tens of thousands forced to vacate was Wacław Szkudlarek, a gentile man who lived in an apartment that would be occupied for much of the ghetto's existence by the family of a pious, lower-middle-class Jewish cabinetmaker, Majlech Sierakowiak.

Szkudlarek returned to his home in the former ghetto district after

Nazi Party when he was appointed *Amtsleiter* of the German Ghetto Administration. Among the fringe benefits of his office was an exemption from military service. While enhancing his own personal wealth was clearly his motivation in administering the Jewish slave colony, he was known to indulge himself on various occasions in beating ghetto dwellers bloody, including the appointed Jewish ghetto leader Rumkowski. He was tried for war crimes after the war, and hanged.

* For the document appointing Chaim Rumkowski as Eldest of the Jews, see "Announcement," in *Łódź Ghetto: Inside a Community Under Siege*, edited by Alan Adelson and Robert Lapidus (New York, 1989), p. 19. See also Friedrich Übelhör, "Establishment of a Ghetto in the City of Łódź," pp. 23–26; and "Police Order Regarding the Residence of Jews," pp. 31–32. For a meticulous accounting of the establishment of the community, as written in the ghetto by the community's own first historians, see "The History of the Litzmannstadt Ghetto," pp. 43–61.

As seen on a prewar postcard, Jews go about their daily activities in a corner of the New Market Square, later to become a gathering point in the Łódź Ghetto.

the Russians liberated the city almost precisely five years later. There he discovered a remarkable legacy left to humanity by Sierakowiak's only son, Dawid, one of the brightest young men who had lived and died in the Łódź Ghetto.

"A whole pile of notebooks filled with writing was lying on the stove," Szkudlarek told an official committee documenting the history of Nazi crimes in Łódź. "Someone must have been using them to keep their fire burning because some of them were torn up. They contained stories, poems and other notes."*

Five composition books in the pile comprised one of the most detailed accounts ever rendered of modern life in bondage: a fastidiously factual day-by-day record kept by a teenage author who lost both parents in the war against the Jews, whose physical pain and emotional woe had held him constantly at the edge of endurance.

---

* Szkudlarek's testimony describing how he came upon the Sierakowiak diary was recorded at a hearing on May 3, 1966, of the Regional Commission for the Examination of Nazi Crimes in Łódź as its document number OKL 37/67.

The diary provides a detailed and intimate history of how the finest aspects of human nature—intellectual quest, creativity, familial love, and the appreciation of nature—were incidentally stifled during the Holocaust by the most bestial drives of the species: to torment, exploit, oppress, and kill. The struggle between good and evil, the creative versus the destructive, are played out for the reader on every page.

Events conspired for fifty years to keep the diary from being published in its entirety. At least two of the composition books in which Dawid kept his dairy have been lost—very possibly burned by an occupant of the apartment during the bitterly cold winter of 1945 when almost no fuel for heat was left in the depleted city. The first two notebooks that emerged from Szkudlarek's discovery were published in Poland in 1960 in a volume edited by Holocaust scholar Lucjan Dobroszycki, himself a survivor of the ghetto.* A leading Łódź journalist, Konrad Turowski, purchased the remaining three notebooks after they surfaced in 1967. He was preparing them for publication in cooperation with Dobroszycki in 1968 when an anti-Semitic outbreak under the Communist regime in Poland blocked the book's publication. Plates for additional volumes of *The Chronicle of the Łódź Ghetto,* on which Dobroszycki was also working, and various other books on Jewish history and culture, in press at the same time, were withdrawn. Local authorities laid claim to documents that had been collected at the Jewish Historical Institute in Warsaw, and then commonly denied to scholars that the materials even existed.

That five of the notebooks survived beyond the author, his family, and their community is a gift to humanity, just as the author's early death was a loss. The wonder of the diary is that every bit of hardship that Dawid experienced brought out wisdom from his young intellect.

A Brilliant Youth, Climbing Mountains

Dawid Sierakowiak was just fifteen years old in 1939 when he traveled to southern Poland to spend the summer at a Jewish youth camp in the High Tatras. The fleeting glimpses of normalcy in the engaging prewar entries he wrote there introduce us to a spirited young man eager to encounter the world. Even the threatening tensions of approaching war do not dampen his youthful energy.

He comes home to Łódź just before the Germans conquer Poland

---

* *Dziennik* [Diary]. *Dawid Sierakowiak*, edited by Lucjan Dobroszycki (Warsaw, 1960).

with their first blitzkrieg. Dawid enjoys imitating Hitler in the air-raid shelter, to entertain the girls there. "Long live humor," he writes in his diary. "Down with hysteria!"

Innately skeptical, both politically and intellectually, young Sierakowiak holds himself as much apart from mass hysteria as from mass self-deception. Even as the Germans are invading the city, he describes with almost righteous contempt "the psychosis of a crowd going to be slaughtered."

He is seized for forced labor on the way to school, having to fill puddles with sand while Germans and their sympathizers stand and jeer, but the youth never loses his dignity. "It's our oppressors who should be ashamed, not us. Humiliation inflicted by force does not humiliate," he writes. "But anger and helpless rage tear a man apart when he is forced to do such stupid, shameful, abusive work. Only one response remains: revenge!"

On February 28, 1940, storm troopers surrounded a large section of the city, violently rousting Jews from the buildings, killing several hundred, and sending tens of thousands fleeing into the ghetto. On May 1, 1940, the Nazis declared the ghetto officially sealed. For more than 160,000 Łódź Jews who had not fled the city or been forced into early deportation, life began in the most hermetically sealed community in Nazi Europe. Dawid undoubtedly recorded his family's first months in the ghetto in one of the notebooks that was lost.

Barely sustained on 700 to 900 calories a day, the Jews were worked to exhaustion producing munitions, telecommunications equipment, ammunition sacks, *Wehrmacht* helmets lined with fur from the Jewish women's coats, and straw boots for winter battle on the Russian front. Corsets, carpets, and temporary housing—all manufactured in the ghetto—were shipped back to Germany.* Ultimately, as the longest surviving concentration of Jews in Nazi Europe, the Łódź Ghetto proved to be a fabulously profitable slave colony. In reports that are generally considered to have concealed much of the wealth gained from the forced Jewish labor, Hans Biebow's ghetto administration ultimately accounted to Berlin for a net profit of over 50 million Reichsmarks.†

This diary's readers become prisoners in the ghetto with the author and his community, and with discomforting intimacy come to observe

---

* Using excerpts from the ghetto archives, Marek Web, chief archivist at YIVO, the Institute for Jewish Research, compiled "Chronology of the Ghetto's Industry," in *Łódź Ghetto*, edited by Adelson and Lapides, pp. 71–80.
† Adelson and Lapides, *Łódź Ghetto*, p. xix.

the insidious stages of individual diminishment that preceded mass death for a great many of the Jews of Europe. Suppressing the waves of fear and despair that kept welling up in him, Dawid brought stoical discipline to the task of chronicling genocide as it entrapped and stifled his people, his community, his family, his body, spirit, and intellect. A literary figure in the ghetto counsels Dawid to develop his literary skills by writing "only in moments of absolute necessity," but instead the youth almost never fails to record a daily entry in his notebooks. As a result, you feel the daily oppressiveness and agony that the Jews who boarded the trains hoped to be leaving behind.

In the perverse sophistry the Nazis inculcated in the ghetto dwellers' minds, the pain of life in the ghetto turned the threat of deportation into a prospect for survival. For a few, the conviction that the Nazis were essentially murderers was undeniable. But for the masses, volunteering for the transports became a recurring temptation. Wherever the trains are going, it can hardly be worse there, Dawid's own father reasons. If it's for labor, they'll have to feed you. And if you stay in the ghetto, you're going to die of starvation anyway. Majlech Sierakowiak wrestles continually with the question, actually adding his name to a deportation list at one point, then changing his mind and scurrying to have it struck.

With almost clinical dispassion, the young writer chronicles the failing of his own body. He rallies himself against the weakening effects of pessimism and melancholy, taking faint hope from the slightest good fortune—even just receiving an extra bowl of soup. Despite the worst deprivations, he is never demeaned. This is not the work of an innocent youth who is naïve to the forces that are crushing the life out of him. Dawid Sierakowiak does not turn away from expressing anger, and he never fails to assign blame—to the Nazi murderers, to Churchill, Roosevelt, and all the forces of the world that seem to be standing aside while Dawid's people are being annihilated, and to the capitalist system he believes has given birth to the war in the first place.

The population was rapidly being killed off by the syndrome that came to be known simply as "ghetto disease." With fear for his own fate, Dawid marvels when one of the most physically powerful men he knew dies of exhaustion and starvation. No subject inspired such indignation, or such black-humored wit, from the young Communist diarist as the ghetto's tremendous class divisions. He decries the big shots who live off the ghetto, who gorge themselves while the masses starve. Repeatedly, he speculates about how well the whole ghetto population would eat if provisions were not reserved primarily for those with "connections." He visits the homes of the privileged to tutor their children, and in the evenings writes in amazement that they are eating better in the ghetto than his own family did before the war. Yet they serve him watery soup. "I wish I could burn up that whole gang," he writes. "This is the rotten, bourgeois-bureaucratic basis on which the ghetto exists, and on which it will perish."

Sierakowiak is a leader. He is elected president of the *gymnasium* student council and uses that platform to speak out against an uncommonly critical issue: the student body is being starved to death. He tries to prevent the council from turning to any other question until better nourishment is demanded from the ghetto's Jewish Administration. Subservient to Mordechai Chaim Rumkowski's often tyrannical ghetto leadership, the school administrators try to squelch Dawid's effort, but he stands his ground. "I won!" he writes in one of the diary's rare moments of elation after his resolution is adopted.

But there can be no sense of accomplishment for him on graduation when he receives the best grades in his class. "What good are they when I'm still hungry and keep feeling so terribly exhausted?" he acknowledges in the diary. As much as he would love to go to college, he is so physically worn out that he can hardly entertain thoughts of a future beyond the ghetto.

But through it all, incredibly, the youth never surrenders his wish to grow intellectually. Within the ghetto's barbed-wire perimeter, he studies Latin, Hebrew, English, German, and French, always searching out books in which he can engage his mind, to forget the pain of his hunger and leave the confines of the ghetto. In the absence of food, he feeds himself Schopenhauer.

To conceal the genocide, the Nazis impose a total news blackout. To be caught listening to a radio or reading a newspaper means death. Nonetheless, since their survival depends so clearly on the Nazis' quick defeat, the ghetto dwellers struggle to stay abreast of the progress of the most destructive war mankind has waged. But for even so avid a news hound as Dawid Sierakowiak, it is impossible to assess realistically the danger the ghetto dwellers face. In the isolation of the ghetto, the diarist gains access to copies of the city's German newspaper, and hears or has related to him news reports monitored in the ghetto by clandestine radio listeners tuning in the BBC. He reads the account of a speech in which Hitler vows to annihilate all of Europe's Jews. The threat comes alive as the few bereft survivors of decimated neighboring Jewish communities are brought into the ghetto. They tell of the horrors they have just endured, morbid harbingers of the Łódź Jews' own impending doom. "Deportation into scrap metal," Dawid puts it with characteristic black humor.

Against the silence of real facts, rumor builds into a maddening cacophony welling up out of the ghetto dwellers' yearning to live. Bombs heard falling on the city might herald the imminence of liberation. One night in 1942 when the lights went out, Dawid's "heart was racing" because he was so convinced that salvation was coming, "though nothing important happened." He must return to reminding himself to just hold on. And when the ghetto stirs to another rumor that the Allies are advancing, he writes: "I don't believe anything anymore. We have deluded ourselves so many times for nothing."

The Absence of Jewish Resistance: A Case History

Questions of whether there could have been more resistance in the ghettos hinge on whether or not the Jews had knowledge of the genocidal process in which they were trapped. What the Jews in the ghettos knew, and when they knew it, has become focal in studying the Jewish response to the Holocaust. Dawid Sierakowiak was fully aware of the Nazis' intention to annihilate his people. Yet that awareness did not convince him that he would die. He wrestles daily with the reality he calls "pessimism" and fights for the belief that he can survive, for without it he knows he will not.

For anyone who has conscientiously questioned why more Jews did not resist the Nazi Holocaust, Dawid's diary provides a highly illuminating and detailed case history. He has every characteristic one would look for in a would-be resister. He knows what the Nazis are about. "They will probably totally destroy us," he states, nearly prescient. And he is an active member of an organized underground committed to revolutionary Communist ideology. Its leaders persistently try to enlist him in their attempts to organize resistance, arguing with him to pledge his life to a suicide squad of young adults who could strike back against the oppression and annihilation. Dawid is drawn to their cause, but he can't make the blanket pledge the underground requires. In some of the only passages of writing from the Łódź Ghetto revealing that the impulse to resist indeed did exist beneath the ghetto's apparent total submission, Dawid concedes that he simply cannot become "a professional revolutionary." He owes his strength and life to the care of his family. "I understand those people less and less, if what they say is to be believed," he writes. "They show a continual, sober readiness to fight, die, suffer, and so on and on;

quite in the manner of the Middle Ages." He argues for a compromise that will enable him to maintain contact with the underground, not to miss a possible opportunity to exact revenge on his murderous oppressors. But the leaders seek total commitment, and they shun him for a while because of what he mockingly describes as his bourgeois egoism. Not long after that, his strength is gone anyway. "We are in such a state of exhaustion that now I understand what it means not even to have enough strength to complain, let alone protest," he admits.

Chaim Rumkowski's avid and enterprising leadership of the ghetto poses a deep moral conundrum. He is certainly one of the most controversial Jews of modern times. Dawid calls him a "sadist-moron." Rumkowski used his police force to tear children away from their parents, and repeatedly assured his population that they had nothing to fear in getting on the trains, knowing quite the opposite. Never drawing a line based on moral compunctions, Rumkowski strived to sustain the ghetto at any cost, and to come away with having saved at least some. Dawid quotes the report he has heard that of the ghetto population, Rumkowski actually expected to save only 10,000. And, astoundingly, this is indeed about the number of Jews interned in the ghetto who did survive the war.

By using the first waves of deportations from the ghetto to dispose of the ghetto's "troublemakers"—the politically committed leadership that might otherwise have organized resistance in the ghetto—Rumkowski protected his strategy of making the Jews essential through their labor to the Nazis, and he succeeded in holding onto his own position in the process. Indeed, no significant events of organized resistance occurred in Chaim Rumkowski's domain. After the valiant last stand made by the final 10 percent of the population in the nearby Warsaw Ghetto* (after nearly 400,000 Jews had been put to death at Treblinka), after a nine-day fight that ended in the virtual obliteration of that ghetto, the Nazi command inquired of their leadership in Łódź if there was a chance that such an uprising could be repeated there. "Totally impossible," the Łódź German administration responded with utter confidence.†

Little is known what came of Niutek Radzyner's resistance movement. On April 30, 1942, Sierakowiak records having seen Radzyner conferring with his cohorts in a stairwell. "They are apparently up to something . . . serious," he notes in a diary entry that could have

---

* The cities are about 75 miles apart.
† German Document, "Secret Matters of State," in *Łódź Ghetto,* edited by Adelson and Lapides, p. 383.

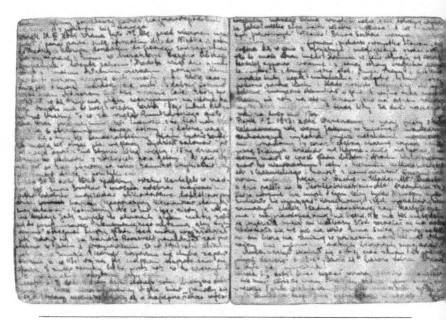

The diary pages for December 29, 1942, to January 2, 1943.

wreaked havoc had it fallen into the Germans' hands. But nothing note-
worthy happens. Then on January 1, 1943, Dawid cautiously notes that
a fire broke out the previous night in the laundry and clothing workshop
(where the clothes from Jews deported from the ghetto were cleaned
and sorted) and that immediately afterward, on New Year's Day, a second fire broke out in one of the textile-fabrication workshops. "My flesh
crawls at the very thought that the Germans may want us to bear the
consequences of these events," he writes.

True to the role of intellectuals throughout history, Dawid Sierakowiak was philosophically committed to a polemical, rather than an activist, political existence. There is no way to know how early in his life he
began keeping his journal; the first of his surviving notebooks certainly
lacks any ceremonious opening. Rather, it feels like part of a continuum
of observant thought established early on by its perceptive young author. Trapped as a victim in history, Dawid seems to take it as his personal duty to record the process of his people's destruction. Never once
does he suggest that he expects the document to be read someday, yet

that assumption seems to underlie many entries. Unlike Anne Frank, Dawid never addresses his diary and barely even refers to the journal in its pages. But the solace it gives him to keep it is evident in an entry he wrote on May 27, 1942. Rejecting the possibility of volunteering for deportation, Dawid admits: "I would miss my books and 'letters,' notes and copybooks. Especially this diary." Already by then, ghetto disease has him. He is finding himself continually overtaken by shortness of breath, feverish sweats, and chills. When the disease took hold of a person, everyone could see it. First came the shrunken "hourglass" look; then a person swelled up, collapsed, and died. "My face is still swollen," Dawid noted that spring when he was seventeen. Like all but the most privileged in his community, his death sentence was on his face.

Dawid's own end is near when exhaustion finally so overtakes him that he no longer has the strength to escape the ghetto through the pages of his beloved great books. Three years of ghetto life have so weakened the young mountain climber that he can barely stand. When there are finally no clean clothes he can change into, when he can no longer combat the scabies and lice infesting his body and he hates the sight of himself, he has still not lost the sharp rage he feels toward his oppressors for forcing those depredations on him. But that rage is helpless.

In retrospect, the underground leaders seem upheld in their argument to Dawid that the choice against resistance that he was making was a doomed strategy. Hunger destroyed Dawid's family, despite his unflagging efforts to support them by tutoring youngsters before and after school, and by toiling in workshops and offices. Hunger turned Dawid's father into a thief unable to stop stealing food from his wife and children.

Nadzia, Too, Must Die

More than 15 percent of the ghetto dwellers died of starvation, exhaustion, and disease in 1942 when those not designated to receive extra rations were deprived of the minimum sustenance to survive. Dawid wrote repeatedly through the crisis that it would be impossible to survive the winter in the ghetto, and he barely made it through.

Despite his constant battle to survive, Dawid Sierakowiak endured through only four of the war's six years. In the spring of 1943, as his life is ebbing from him, his only hope is for the war to end immediately; but he knows that it is far from over. His skin has erupted everywhere with boils from malnutrition, he is so frail that he often cannot get out of bed, and his lungs are so weak that he is constantly faint. But circumstances seem to be offering hope for Dawid finally. People with influence who respect the youth have at last begun acting in his behalf. He's almost sleepless with excitement at being considered for an appointment to the special department police who oversee food distribution in the ghetto. It's "almost the only chance I have," he writes. As the diary breaks off, he's been appointed to work for three months in a bakery, where he will be able to eat his fill. He and his sister have been promised a laundry coupon so they can wash their scabies-ridden clothes. The Allies are finally pushing back the Nazis in Europe. But true to the story of almost all Jews caught in the Holocaust, help for Dawid came too late. He died on August 8, 1943, two weeks after his nineteenth birthday and four months after the last of his surviving notebooks broke off with the recognition, "There is really no way out of this." His death certificate lists the cause of death as tuberculosis; racial hatred destroyed this fine young man.

Dawid Sierakowiak and his father were 2 of the more than 60,000 Jews who died in the Łódź Ghetto. About 130,000 Jews deported from the ghetto were asphyxiated in the gas vans at Chełmno, as was Dawid's mother, or in the gas chambers at Auschwitz. Although her older brother's death must have caused Nadzia Sierakowiak overwhelming grief, she was one of those who apparently survived the hardships of the ghetto until the final wave of deportations in the summer of 1944, only to be sent to Auschwitz, where she, too, is presumed to have been put to death.

Appreciate the Richness of a Life Denied to Dawid

As its author races through his implausibly foreshortened adulthood, the survival of his diary seems to become his readers' sole consolation. But the effect of this rare work need not end there.

With the publication of this volume, Dawid has his say in a fashion that would have made him extraordinarily proud. He succeeded in leaving us a profoundly honest and involving microcosm with which we can begin to contemplate humankind's unfathomable loss in the Holocaust. The Nazis did not care to comprehend that they were killing intellects and spirits, not just pathetically deteriorated bodies. Reading Dawid's diary, and knowing what promise for humanity he had already developed, some realization of the magnitude of the destruction becomes possible.

This one life, Dawid Sierakowiak, this person, this intellect, this author, would have contributed so much more to the world. His diary enables us to embrace that loss intimately, to grieve for one life in the host of lives so deliberately stifled.

What are we to do with the terrible wisdom he has left for us? "If we survive the ghetto," he wrote, "we'll certainly experience a richness of life that we wouldn't have appreciated otherwise."

The luxury of life was never returned to Dawid, but a new awareness of its richness can be our reward for reading the diary of this brilliantly deserving and brutally deprived young human being.

Street map of Łódź Ghetto: (1) Bałuty Market, site of the Jewish and German administration offices; (2) 4 Plac Kościelny (Church Square), the ghetto archives office; (3) 5–7 Spacerowa Street, the Sierakowiaks' first home in the ghetto; (4) hospital on Wesoła Street, brutally evacuated by the Nazis in September 1942; (5, 6) two primary carpenters' workshops, sites of early labor unrest; (7) 3 Krawiecka Street, the House of Culture, an assembly point during the final liquidation of the ghetto in the summer of 1944; (8) old Jewish cemetery, to the south of which was "ghetto field," where tens of thousands of ghetto dwellers were buried in graves marked with only temporary placards; (9) Marysin, the "rural" region of the ghetto, which contained the "villas" of the ghetto elite, the old-age home, the orphanage, the major school buildings, and many communal gardens; (10) 17 Lutomierska (Fire Brigade Square), where Rumkowski delivered many speeches, including the "Give Me Your Children" exhortation; 11 Lutomierska, site of the Arbeitseinsatz; (11) hospital on Drewnowska Street, used as a deportation site; (12, 13) two primary tailors' workshops; (14) 20 Wawelska Street, Dawid's second home in the ghetto; (15) 34–36 Łagiewnicka Street, hospital where Dawid's mother was taken and that was evacuated during the "Nightmarish Days" of September 1942; (16) prison on Czarnieckiego Street; (17) 31 Franciszkańska Street, former movie theater Bajka, which was used as a synagogue; (18) 6 Smugowa Street, *gymnasium* that Dawid attended.

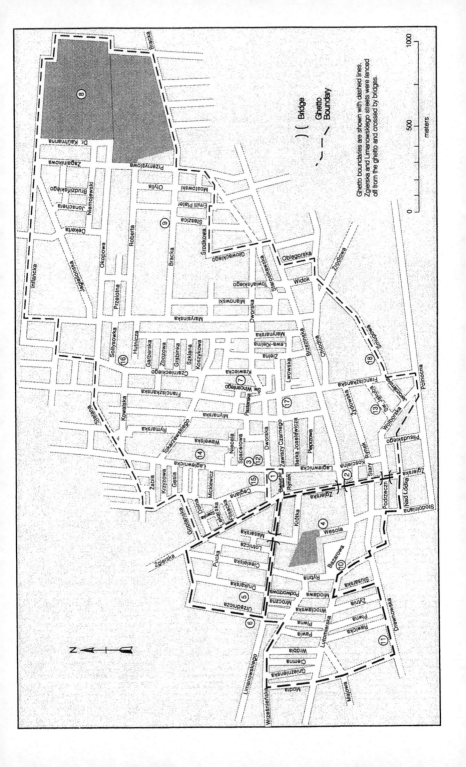

Ghetto boundaries are shown with dashed lines. Zgierska and Limanowskiego streets were fenced off from the ghetto and crossed by bridges.

) (Bridge

- - - Ghetto Boundary

0   500   1000
meters

Łódź is occupied

W*ednesday, June 28, 1939. Krościenko on the Dunajec.*
We arrived safely today at summer camp. After a fourteen-hour train
ride and an hour by bus, dinner was waiting in Krościenko. The food is
excellent, plentiful, and tasty.

We are staying in a small house on a hill. From our room we can see
the Dunajec River and the beautiful Pieniny mountain range rising behind it. We're about to go to sleep now. It's a nuisance standing in line to
wash. There's one basin for every six boys.

Friday, June 30. Krościenko on the Dunajec.   We were examined by a
doctor. I'm fine. I can swim and hike. My dear Mom will be happy. We
had our first swim in the Dunajec. They worry so much at home about
the swimming. I sent them a card immediately after arriving. I wish I
already had an answer. I guess I'm starting to miss them. I got a good
tan; in fact, I think I got burned.

Saturday, July 1. Krościenko on the Dunajec.   It really feels like Saturday. Prayer, Sabbath meals, holiday. We went for a two-hour walk up
the nearest mountain. The view was magnificent. Krościenko was
clearly defined, and the Tatras were visible in the distance.

Sunday, July 2. Krościenko on the Dunajec.   The first rainy day. Ping-
Pong, reading, writing. Today's newspaper is not at all satisfying. The
situation in Gdańsk is becoming more and more complicated. French
and English papers say that tomorrow Hitler will even proclaim the
annexation of Gdańsk to the Third Reich, but I doubt that he'll dare for
now. The French statesmen have again declared that any attack on
Poland means war with France.

Tuesday, July 4. Krościenko on the Dunajec.   We went on a hike rich
with splendid thrills. After breakfast we set out in the direction of the
Pieniny, particularly to Czertezik and Sokolica [peaks]. I had put on
thick winter boots, which really came in handy.

We climb easily. Suddenly we find ourselves on a high spot, and
when we look down to one side, we stop in surprise. The mountain falls
in a sheer cliff down a 100-meter precipice, threatening the viewer.

We go farther. At last the summit. Below flows the Dunajec, wind-
ing in thousands of curves, with its bare, rocky banks glittering here and

there. The steep summit is surrounded by an iron railing. We rest and drink.

After a half-hour we go up to Sokolica. This mountain is similar to Czertezik, only steeper and wilder. We watch the other bank of the Dunajec, previously Czech.* We return home at dinnertime.

Thursday, July 6. Krościenko on the Dunajec.   A normal camp day. I practice reading English books. I keep having memories of home.

Friday, July 7. Krościenko on the Dunajec.   Our first long mountain trip. We get up at six, and after breakfast we set out toward Szczawnica. From there, downstream along the Dunajec, we enter the Pieniny gorge. The road is slippery. Its picturesque quality comes from powerful views of mountains magnificently covered with timber, of sheer gorges, and of the turns of the Dunajec. In some places the ledge is treacherous and rocky; there we have to resort to using "staples," iron hooks driven into the rock for us to grasp, so we won't fall into the water.

We come to a lovely Pieniny creek. Its water is crystal clear, unusually tasty and cool. We attack it and cannot slake our thirst. We climb for a long time through the forest and finally arrive at the slope of the Three Crowns [Polish, Trzy Korony], the goal of our hike. Here, in the heat of the sun, the real climbing begins.

Finally we arrive beneath the summit. An enterprising highlander maintains a small hut here and does an excellent business selling cool drinks. The boys rush for drinks, and then food.

After eating we climb the highest "Crown." The view of the Pieniny from this highest peak is truly unique. From one side, the Tatras seem to loom in clouds; from the other, mountains, some lower and some higher, crossed by rivers and flecked with villages. The combination appears powerful, wide and mighty, but each fragment of the view is delicate and small.

At five we finally return home, battered and weary.

Tuesday, July 11. Krościenko on the Dunajec.   Today we paid a visit to a camp of Jewish Scouts from Warsaw. We got acquainted with their way of life and learned from their leader about the origin of their organization. It was founded in Warsaw, Kraków, Lwów, Wilno [Vilnius], and

---

* On October 10, 1938, German forces took Czechoslovakia; Poland used the opportunity to annex a small area in the north.

lesser centers five years ago, on the initiative of a Polish activist in the ZHP [Polish, Związek Harcerstwa Polskiego; Polish Scouts' Association], A. Kamiński. The organization takes youths into its ranks from all segments of Jewish society, providing training in moral and physical health. The director said that this year the organization will also open a branch in Łódź.

Thursday, July 13. Krościenko on the Dunajec. We went on a very difficult and arduous excursion. Our aim was the Wysokie Skałki and Homole gorge.

We set out at seven in the morning, approach the gorge in good humor, but right from the beginning we have to climb up to the steep and difficult summit of Wylizana. The slope of the mountain is covered with dry and brittle grass, making climbing unusually difficult. We have to crawl up on all fours. I wear boots without hobnails, and their soles are getting terribly slippery. Every few steps I slide down. Sweat is literally pouring into my eyes; during breaks I wipe it off impatiently. On the summit we drop like sacks, wheezing horribly.

We can see truly lovely sights unfolding below: the powerful Tatras and, closer, the Pieniny with its dominating summits of the Three Crowns; here and there the sad summit of the Małe Pieniny range. Then the final effort. The Wysokie Skałki attained! We are on the highest summit in the area, 1,052 meters above sea level.

The descent is very difficult. We sit and slide down the steep rocks. On our way down we gaze into the unusually beautiful gorge, and the wonderfully clear water in the Grajcarek, which flows along the bottom.

Not unhappily, we finally say good-bye to this beautiful and mighty work of nature. We go home along a highway through beautiful Szczawnica. We come back at nine, raucous but tired.

Friday, July 14. Krościenko on the Dunajec. I realized only today how tired I am. I lie around all day and do nothing. We play a little Ping-Pong.

Saturday, July 15. Krościenko on the Dunajec. With the help of several friends, I prepared today's *Oneg Shabbas* [Hebrew; the snack shared after Sabbath worship]. The boys stayed in the dining room after the afternoon snack, and I, as master of ceremonies, began the program with two songs sung by Salek Rozenberg's camp choir. Next, Dr. Eck read *Pashat Harshavua* [Hebrew; the weekly Torah portion read in synagogues on the Sabbath]. More singing after that, interwoven with humorous sketches.

One of them was mine, written in biblical style, about a fight against fleas; another was Julek Wegmajster's, about some fourth-grade graphomaniac commonly called "flojzy." The singing was also excellent. Everything was a success, and I received hearty congratulations.

In the evening we went to the Scouts' campfire. They sang and we sang, but practically the whole camp suddenly got stomachaches. Back "home" there were long lines waiting for the toilets, while I sat with some more boys in the kitchen drinking tea, and holding a stove lid on my belly. We went to sleep at one in the morning.

Sunday, July 16. Krościenko on the Dunajec.   Our meal today is ten glasses of tea and a bread roll. Liver we ate was probably the cause of the pain.

Tuesday, July 18. Krościenko on the Dunajec.   Two horrible pieces of news. A Jewish student from Poznań drowned today in the Dunajec (They say he had a heart attack in the water, caused by exhaustion). Then a friend from the first grade of *gymnasium* received a shocking telephone call from home reporting his father's death. He left for Łódź immediately.

Wednesday, July 19. Krościenko on the Dunajec.   In the evening we took part in the student's funeral. A gruesome feeling.

Thursday, July 20. Krościenko on the Dunajec.   All day we have been getting ready for the campfire we invited Scouts to yesterday. I wrote another humorous sketch, this one about bellies, and a poem about Hakman. I was appointed master of ceremonies by the camp administrators, so I conducted the campfire program: songs—guests' and ours—my sketches written in biblical style, and Kahan's work. Everything went very well. Again I received hearty congratulations and thanks.

Friday, July 21. Krościenko on the Dunajec.   They informed me from home today that Nadzia* underwent a tooth operation. Poor, dear little sister. I'll see her next week. We must bear our troubles together.

---

* Natalia (Nadzia) Sierakowiak (August 12, 1927–1944 [?]) was three years younger than her brother, Dawid.

Sunday, July 23. Krościenko on the Dunajec. Principal Elenberg arrived, and then a group from the girls' *gymnasium* camp arrived in the evening.

Monday, July 24. Krościenko on the Dunajec. My last day at camp. Erev Tisha be-Av.* A serious campfire in the evening. I gave a speech in Hebrew about Tisha be-Av. Wegmajster spoke too, and finally the director.

Tuesday, July 25. Krościenko on the Dunajec. We pack quickly before dinner. At half past two we leave by bus to Nowy Targ. From there to Kraków by train. We transfer in Kraków, but have to wait for two and a half hours in the rain and wind. Finally, at half past eleven at night, the train to Łódź. Six of us have our own compartment. It's raining all the way to Łódź and in Łódź.

Wednesday, July 26. Łódź. We arrive after six in the morning. I take the luggage, and "under fire" from a terrible downpour, I go to a streetcar with my heavy bag. On the way I meet Mom. God, what joy! At home the same with Father and sister. I eat, go to bed, and sleep almost all day.

Thursday, July 27. Łódź. It's pouring again! In the afternoon I go downtown to see Brawerman's father. I feel terrific being at home.

Friday, July 28. Łódź. First greetings with friends: "Ah, so you're back already?" or sometimes: "You're already back, sir. So how was it there?"

Wednesday, August 2. Łódź. Politics are about to become hot again. The twenty-fifth anniversary of the outbreak of the World War . . . Meanwhile, the harvests are nearly completed.

Thursday, August 3. Łódź. The English Parliament is dispersing for vacation, and Lord Halifax announced that the situation remains serious. Tempers are running hotter and hotter . . . Meanwhile, the Germans are persecuting us in Gdańsk.

---

* The eve of the Jewish holiday Tisha be-Av, a day of mourning for the destruction of the First and Second Temples in Jerusalem. Four months after Dawid's campfire talk, the two monumental synagogues in his own home city would be burned to rubble by the Nazis.

Friday, August 4. Łódź. A ministry decree came out ordering the registration of all state citizens of both sexes between seventeen and sixty years old, showing their abilities and skills that might be useful in the state's defense. Good, it's about time.

Saturday, August 5. Łódź. In the whole country preparations are going on for the holiday of August 6.* Marshal Śmigły-Rydz† is supposed to give a speech at the legionnaires' celebration in Kraków tomorrow.

Sunday, August 6. Łódź. He spoke simply in a soldier's language. He clearly warned Hitler against any temptation regarding Gdańsk, since Poland will defend it to the last drop of blood. Poland has the same right to its territory as Germany. The speech did not last long, but it was greeted with extreme enthusiasm. Well, now let's wait and see . . .

Wednesday, August 9. Łódź. "Relaxation" again. There were incidents in Gdańsk, the Senate apologized, and Hitler kept silent. The little people bark. The German newspapers provoke and slander.

Thursday, August 10. Łódź. Calm, hot. I read and began to write a work I planned a long time ago about the imminent future of Jewry. *The Semite* covers a program of reconciliation and cooperation with the Arabs. In this work I predict a war that will put an end to German aspirations, and to Germany in general.

Friday, August 11. Łódź. Today's newspapers describe the present as the calm before a storm. We'll see.

Tuesday, August 15. Łódź. It's raining again. My cousin Jankuś called on me today. We talked for a really long time about socialism, its directions, and so on. He is in PPS [Polish, Polska Partia Socjalistyczna; Polish Socialist Party] and even spoke there about Zionism. I succeeded in

---

* On August 6, 1914, Marshal Józef Piłsudski's Polish Legion was instrumental in reuniting Poland and in gaining Polish independence by crossing from Kraków, which had been occupied by Austria-Hungary, into the area of Poland then occupied by Russia.

† At the outset of the war, Marshal Edward Śmigły-Rydz (1886–1943) escaped from Poland with its government and fled into exile in Romania; he was interned, but in 1941 escaped and secretly returned to Poland. He died in Warsaw. According to some accounts, he died of natural causes; others say he was killed by the Germans.

making him admit that socialist Zionism is a better direction for the Bund.*

Monday, August 21. Łódź. The political situation is beginning to worsen. The newspapers shriek that the final crisis will come in the next two weeks. The Germans are now demanding not only Gdańsk, but the Śląsk region as well.

Tuesday, August 22. Łódź. Terrible, interesting, strange news. The Germans are concluding a twenty-five-year nonaggression pact with the Soviets! What a turnabout! What a capitulation of Nazi ideology! The Soviets apparently do not want to interfere in European politics and want to protect their backsides for a fight against Japan. And what will Japan say about this pact? Germany will hardly be able to count on Japan's help anymore. In any case, it's quite a propaganda stunt on Germany's part. Who knows how the European situation will develop now? Chamberlain has summoned the English Parliament into special session.

Wednesday, August 23. Łódź. The situation is growing worse. The pact has come to be. The tension in the city is growing. Nobody talks about anything else but the European situation. Polish radio reports everything calmly, encouraging quiet and reason in the country.

Thursday, August 24. Łódź. Mobilization! A great many neighbors have been called. Although terrible scenes of farewell are taking place in the streets of the city, in our building there is heroic calm. The wives of men who have gone to the front shake their fists calmly but implacably at the Germans, and rush to register at the women's PW [Polish, Przeszkolenie Wojskowe; Military Training]. "Should have cut the Kraut's throat in the cradle" and "Don't wait, beat them now"—these are just about everyone's opinions today. There isn't the slightest sign of defeatism.

Our family is in trouble because we don't have any cash at all. No one knows what will happen. Just to have cash, and to kill as many Krauts as possible.

---

* Algemeyner Yidisher Arbeter Bund was the Yiddish name for the General Jewish Workers Bund, a socialist and anti-Zionist organization working in Poland with links to Socialist parties in the West.

Streetcars are overloaded with those called up. The boisterous sing-ing of drunken soldiers is heard frequently. In the afternoon a prohibi-tion was posted against the sale of alcohol.

At dinner Father brought 6 kilos of flour. In the afternoon Mrs. Heller was refused a purchase. Quite rightly. There is enough food in Poland. We aren't buying anymore, either, but those 6 kilos won't last long.

The radio says that the school vacation is supposed to be extended for a few more days. Not a bad idea at all. It's so hot (in both senses) that nobody feels like going to school.

The German–Soviet pact has been signed. So, the anti-Comintern pact has been dissolved. What a friendship! Ribbentrop* announced that the old German–Russian friendship has been revived, and that every time Russia and Germany went their separate ways it was bad for them, but when they came together they did well.

In the evening German radio said that the new head of the Free City of Gdańsk is Gauleiter Forster† (will he now wish to place himself under the protection of Germany?!). They threaten us constantly. Two German ground units and a plane crossed the Polish border today for the first time, but they were forced to withdraw.

The requisitioning of carts and horses continues. All schools have been assigned to the army. Men who have been drafted walk along the streets drunk (they say there is no vodka?!) and shout pathetically. The atmosphere of uncertainty is building. The OPLG headquarters [Polish, Obrona Przeciwlotnicza i Gazowa; Air and Gas Defense] has issued adequate orders. We sleep lightly and at the ready.

All over Europe the mobilization has begun. France has called up 700,000 people. In a special session of the English Parliament, Chamber-lain declared that God knows he has been doing everything to save the peace, but now the issue of restraining German aggression has become a matter of life and death for Europe. "And let those on whom the shed-ding of blood depends think what they're doing before they condemn millions of human beings to death." Meanwhile, Hitler answered Cham-berlain's letter, saying that eastern Europe should be under his domi-

---

* Joachim von Ribbentrop (1893–1946) was Hitler's foreign minister (1933–1945). He signed the Ribbentrop-Molotov Pact, which cleared the way for the German invasion of Poland on September 1, 1939.
† Albert Forster (1902–1948), a German politician and Nazi Party official, became Gauleiter of Danzig.

nance, that he will not give up his vital interests, and that he wants other countries to keep out of his affairs. England has mobilized its entire fleet.

Friday, August 25. Łódź.   When Mom went out shopping today, she couldn't even get rolls; they had been sold out. There is no end to the terrible run on the shops, and I can see now that we have to have cash to take care of ourselves because God only knows what will come later. Cash only.

The [political] situation reached a standstill, and there it remains. Belgian King Leopold, the pope, and Roosevelt strive for peace, but from Berlin come either haughty, provocative responses or silence. The German radio barks, provokes, and lies in the most insolent way, reducing itself to absurdity. They keep saying that England will not help, yet a Polish–English alliance is to be signed tomorrow.

Saturday, August 26. Łódź.   The alliance has been settled, and now the Germans must decide. But they are not in a hurry to do this. Hitler has put off a speech and an inspection tour in Tannenberg that were announced for tomorrow. So a new extension of the state of distress.

I read President Kwapiński's* appeal for volunteers to dig antiaircraft trenches. I immediately signed up at the police station, having received permission to do so at home before. Like all my friends, I'm going to work tomorrow morning. The lack of tools is no obstacle for the massive number of volunteers. All Jews (Hasids too), the old, the young, women, like all other citizens (except for the Germans), volunteer in droves. The bloody Kraut won't pass! At the border they record continual incidents of German aggression that are pure provocation.

Sunday, August 27. Łódź.   At six o'clock in the morning I went with Father to dig trenches using shovels provided by the municipal government. The work was difficult: dry, solid ground and, deeper, clay. Sweat was pouring into my eyes; it stung and smarted, and my hands began to burn. After an hour and a half I had to give away the spade, and from then on I worked on top. Before twelve I finished work and went home, where I changed clothes and drank, without exaggeration, well over ten glasses of various liquids. In the afternoon we visited my aunt, whose whole family worked too.

---

* Jan Kwapiński (1885–1964), a socialist, was the mayor of Łódź and president of the City Council in 1939.

Perhaps Nadzia will come home today. She went to Mrs. Grabiński's in Głowno last Saturday. She will share our worries. Although I miss her, I realize that this vacation was a splendid opportunity for her.

Henderson * left for London with Hitler's secret offers, and today or tomorrow he is supposed to deliver an answer back to Hitler.

Several shopkeepers—profiteers—have been put in jail in Bereza. Very well to feed oneself on someone else's misfortune!

Monday, August 28. Łódź.   Nothing is known yet, but certainty about Hitler's withdrawal is building. He has called off the Party Congress in Nuremberg! It's only today that my bones, like those of all the others, ache from yesterday's work. It doesn't matter! Fifty thousand people dug in Łódź yesterday!

As of today a night home-defense alert service was established. (We sleep in our clothes.) The evening radio bulletin solemnly denied all the German press and radio's lying reports and announced disturbing news about secret talks between Ambassador Henderson and Hitler, and a full mobilization in eastern Prussia. Could it be that Hitler is proceeding with his insanity?

Tuesday, August 29. Łódź.   Uncertainty, uncertainty, and even more uncertainty. The radio brings no news. Absolutely nothing is known. The English–German talks are kept secret.

Wednesday, August 30. Łódź.   General mobilization! All reservists up to the age of forty are called to the colors. Father, though he is forty-seven, has become very nervous, and so has Mother.

In the city it is much calmer than during Thursday's mobilization. The Air-raid Defense Headquarters for our block has been moved from Commander Marczewski's apartment to a cellar in the eleventh building. We brought a table and benches there.

At eleven at night, just after I've gone to bed, Bechler, the superintendent of the building, knocks and says that an air-raid warning has been announced. I put on my clothes with lightning speed and rush around to all the apartments with an order to put the lights out. Then I go to the headquarters; from there with some other messengers to the district offices for air-raid equipment. We bring axes, flashlights, small packs against mustard gas (do-it-yourself first aid for burns), and stretchers. We

---

* Sir Nevile Henderson (1882–1942) was the British ambassador in Berlin (1937–1939).

give it all to the superintendents, who distribute the equipment among servicemen. We cover the windows of the headquarters and wait.

Thursday, August 31. Łódź. At one o'clock an alarm was announced. It was canceled, however, after some time. At two we were ordered to go to bed. I slept for two hours in my clothes on a small couch, then took my chances, undressed and went to bed. There was no alarm. In the morning Mom brought thick paper with which we covered the vents and then blocked them with rags. For better or worse, it is some protection against gas.

The air-raid warning continues.

Friday, September 1. Łódź. Germany has begun the war!

This morning Chancellor Hitler made a declaration in the Reichstag in which he demanded Gdańsk, Pomerania, a number of new plebiscites, etc. At the same time, German forces began to cross the Polish border in a number of places. Simultaneously, air raids were made on such Polish cities as Kraków, Częstochowa, Katowice, Grodno, and so on. The world has caught fire. We are now waiting for England and France to join the war. Perhaps the United States will enter, too. Meanwhile, we fight off the German attacks valiantly. There were three air-raid alarms during which enemy warplanes were prevented from reaching the city.

I go to bed half-dressed.

Saturday, September 2. Łódź. An alarm at five in the morning. Fog, cold. I rush to the headquarters. Everyone gathers around. We talk; some jokes are told and we laugh. We wait for four hours. Shots and explosions can be heard in the distance. Finally, it's over.

I want to wash myself and take off my shirt, but there is a new alarm. This time we can see the airplanes and also little trails of smoke from the bullets shot at them. The explosions are getting closer. We go down to the shelter. There are several girls there, and the atmosphere turns gay. I even imitate Hitler's speech. Meanwhile, two German planes have been shot down, and a third is being chased by bullets.

After the alarm, people coming from the city say that a bomb horribly destroyed a house on Bandurskiego Street. Bombs were also dropped on the Kaliska railway station and the Julianów district.

I can finally wash myself. While I'm washing my legs there is a new alarm, but I don't care. I keep washing and dress calmly. After the raid I shave.

At night I sit on duty. A district liaison officer comes to us and says that some lights have been seen in one of the apartment buildings. We watch it closely, but don't see anything. The officer is as surprised as we are.

It is decided that Commander Marczewski will go upstairs and, on the pretext of having noticed a light from the street, will open a door from one room to the other so that those staying in the park will be able to tell if the light coming through the door is the one that was seen before by the police. To be certain that this is Marczewski, he is supposed to give a signal with his green flashlight. Commander Marczewski accomplished the task assigned to him, but it turned out that the light that came through the door was dim, while the one that had been seen before had been bright and had flashed clearly for the purpose of signaling. The problem was becoming more and more intriguing and disturbing. The police promised to keep an eye on the apartment and its owner, Mr. Ring (an interesting German name!).

Marek and I walk around the area until the end of our watch. Calm and quiet. At eleven I go to bed and sleep like a log.

Sunday, September 3. Łódź.   An alarm at half past twelve at night. I curse as much as I can. In the street it's cold, dark, nasty. In the shelter we want to amuse ourselves a little, but as usual the females raise an uproar, shrieking that it's no joke, this is war. We leave for the street. Bombs and cold are better than old women. This should always be kept in mind. Long live humor; down with hysteria!

Suddenly people rush in from the Pabianicka highway with a cry: "What are those lights there; who is signaling from the tower!?" It turns out that this is the third time that signals from the tower's fifth floor have been seen clearly. (There is a water reservoir in there.) We go to Pabianicka, and sure enough we can see bright signals. Several men go upstairs, but they find nothing. The light vanishes.

In the morning, unusually happy news. A radio bulletin informs us that England has declared war on Germany. We start crying out of happiness and rush to share the happy news with everyone. The radio is broadcasting "God Save the King," "Le Marseillaise," and "Jeszcze Polska" [Polish national anthem].

After dinner the first big air raid on Łódź. Twelve planes in triangles of three break through the defense lines and start bombing the city. We stand in front of the entry to our buildings' yard and watch the sky in spite of the danger. The squadron manages to get away from our antiaircraft artillery, and we can soon see clouds of smoke, surely from somewhere in the center of the city. Incendiary bombs!

Suddenly the planes turn in our direction, forcing us to fight our curiosity and hide in terror in the stairwell. We come out and hide again about twenty times in the course of several minutes. Three aircraft fly over us, and just when it seems that we will be bombed any moment, they leave us in peace to breathe a sigh of relief. The planes finally disappear, which we announce in the shelter to the terrified, nerve-racked, crying women, some holding small babies in their arms. Truly a moving sight.

All of a sudden a district liaison officer rushes in and announces that gas has been dropped in several parts of the city. The terror intensifies. The fortunate owners of gas masks put them on; others take out gauze pads. It gets cold and windy in the street. We ring the bell to declare a gas alarm. I rush to Bechler with word about the gas. Tumult, fear, commotion. Finally, everything calms down: the gas alarm turns out to be false.

In the evening comes news as happy as this morning's report. France and Australia have joined the war! Polish troops are holding on in Westerplatte* as if in the alcazar† [Arabic, al-qaṣr; castle or fortress]; they are not letting the Krauts move even an inch ahead, though they are in greater numbers. And the railway station in Zbąszyń has been taken back from the Germans! We disperse full of joy and go to sleep.

Monday, September 4. Łódź.   At night we had two alarms. It was terribly cold. We all gathered in the shelter, warming one another as we slept.

Nadzia has come from Głowno. The whole war story is beginning to leave me weary and bored. In the morning I sleep until ten.

After a cold night, the day begins nice and sunny. Once again, after about the third alarm, optimistic but outrageous news reached us about the Germans having torpedoed an English passenger ship carrying several hundred exceptionally rich and influential American citizens. Eight hundred people died! And even before receiving this information, Roosevelt had announced that the United States would not stay neutral! What will he say now!?

All alarms pass calmly today. I have nothing to do except go to headquarters to listen to the radio. We sit, talk, flirt . . . School on Monday at long last.

---

* The tiny Polish military base on a mile-long strip of land next to Gdańsk was attacked by the German cruiser *Schleswig Holstein* at 4:05 A.M. on September 1, 1939.
† In one of the most renowned battles of the Spanish Civil War, some three years before the diarist wrote this entry, 2,000 cadets and their officers defended the Alcazar, then being used as an infantry academy, against a seventy-day siege by Republican forces that had surrounded the fortress. Units led by Francisco Franco finally crushed the siege. He soon exploited the battle in a broad propaganda campaign.

Tuesday, September 5. Łódź.   The whole night passed without alarms. Interesting . . . Either they are saving Łódź for some reason, or England and France have got them so busy that they've given up here.

In the evening two German spies were spotted in Polish army uniforms. Because of that, I had to go on duty with Ignacy at the entrance to the park.

Wednesday, September 6. Łódź.   God, what's going on! Panic, mass exodus, defeatism. The city, deserted by the police and all other state institutions, is waiting in terror for the anticipated arrival of the German troops. What happened? People run from one place to another, finding no comfort; they move their worn bits of furniture around in terror and confusion, without any real purpose.

My duty ends at 1:00 at night. I go to wake up Rysiek Wójcikowski for his shift. He is in a pessimistic mood, and for the first time I hear something from his lips about a supposed plan to evacuate the city. He says that everything has been packed at the department where his father works, and they are leaving Łódź at any minute. I'm surprised. What? How? The Germans, I hear, are going to take Łódź at any moment.

At home I meet our neighbor Mr. Grabiński, who has come back from downtown and tells about the great panic and anxiety that has taken hold of the people there. Crowds of residents are leaving their homes and setting off on a danger-filled trek into an unknown future. In the streets crying, sobbing, wailing.

I go to sleep, but a loud conversation wakes me at five in the morning. A neighbor, Grodzeński, is sitting there with his crying wife, telling us to leave. Where? Go where? Why? Nobody knows. To flee, flee farther and farther, trek, wade, cry, forget, run away . . . just run away as far as possible from the danger. My mother, my dear, forever terribly sensitive mother, now shows an extraordinary amount of self-control. She comforts Mrs. Grodzeński and talks her out of making nonsensical plans. She gradually manages to calm the mass hysteria in the house— the psychosis of a crowd going to be slaughtered. Father loses his head; he doesn't know what to do. Other Jewish neighbors come for a meeting. They talk about the order commanding all persons capable of bearing arms to leave the city so the enemy won't be able to send them off to work camps. They don't know what to do. A moment of deliberation, and finally the decision: stay put. Whatever will be will be.

People keep leaving; lines of men to a gathering point in Brzeziny. All conscripts and reservists flee the city. After them, women with bundles on their backs—clothes, bedding, food. Even small children go. All the commanders have fled; jokingly, we appoint ourselves commanders and serve in the roles until noon.

Meanwhile, the situation is becoming more and more tense. With every new arrival there is a new bit of news. One man says that 150 English warplanes are standing by in Sieradz. Another says that the Germans have taken Zduńska Wola and are now marching on Łódź. The news becomes progressively strange and unreal.

At home there is crying; Aunt Estera has come with her children. Abek and Jankuś have escaped to Brzeziny. What to do; how to act? At five a bit of dinner is thrown together, consisting of only seasoned potato soup. Maybe others don't have even this.

Father rushes to my uncle, and my uncle back to Father, but each time the decision is the same: not to flee, to stay put. In the afternoon a citizens' guard is organized in our buildings. Father also registers.

In the evening, Rysiek Wójcikowski comes back unexpectedly with his father. The roads are terrible. They bought bicycles and are leaving again. Now they go to sleep, for the first time putting on all their night-clothes. There is no danger of an air-raid alarm; to possess something, one doesn't destroy it.

In the evening Polish army columns begin to arrive in the city. They pass calmly and in good order. It's not known whether they are retreating or going to rest. Later on, tanks begin to move out of the city. They are going to the front. Armor is needed in order to fight the German armor.

Józik Wolman took off for Brzeziny, and his mother despairs. What will tomorrow bring?

Thursday, September 7. Łódź.   Today hasn't brought anything new. In the morning I go outside. I don't do much, just like everyone else, but everybody is talking about what will happen. Will they come or not?

We trudge to the Pabianicka highway to watch the arriving Polish columns. It doesn't look like a retreating army. It looks like a regular army's troop movement. So a weak hope springs up: maybe the Germans will not come. Will the miracle on the Vistula [River] happen again? Will we live to see a second Marne now?* I sit with other boys

---

* In the Battle of Warsaw (1920), Polish forces defeated the Red Army against apparently overwhelming odds, breaking the Soviet front lines along the Vistula River. In the first Battle of the Marne (1914), the French successfully stalled a German attempt to encircle Paris.

and girls and try to get rid of the thoughts coming over us, but it doesn't work. What's going to happen?

A soldier on a horse comes up to our neighbor. It's her brother. He says that they are fighting off the Germans and holding on fiercely. In the afternoon the radio says that the French are moving forward into Germany and that the Poles are holding on. The militia is being organized. Father has registered. Maybe serving in it will reduce his anxiety and restore his sense of stability.

In the evening cannon fire can be heard and a fiery glow can be seen in the south. Is it really that close? Some fellow arrives and says that Łódź is surrounded and will be taken at any moment. I go home to sleep, not to see anything, not to hear anything. Whatever will be will be. Maybe a miracle will happen . . . Marne, oh, Marne, please happen again . . . , or maybe a miracle.

Friday, September 8. Łódź.   Łódź is occupied!

The beginning of the day was calm, too calm. In the afternoon I sit in the park and draw a sketch of a girlfriend. Then all of a sudden the terrifying news: Łódź has been surrendered! German patrols on Piotrkowska Street. Fear, surprise . . . Surrendered without a fight? Perhaps it's only some tactical maneuver. We'll see.

Meanwhile, all conversation stops; the streets grow deserted; faces and hearts are covered with gloom, cold severity, and hostility.

Mr. Grabiński comes back from downtown and tells how the local Germans greeted their countrymen. The Grand Hotel, where the General Staff is expected to stay, is bedecked with garlands of flowers; civilians— boys, girls—jump into the passing military cars with happy cries of *"Heil Hitler!"* Loud German conversation in the streets. Everything patriotically and nationalistically [German] that was hidden in the past now shows its true face.*

The streets are lit for the night. After all, there is no longer any danger of air raids.

Saturday, September 9. Łódź.   In the morning they posted an announcement in Polish and German (German first) calling on people to remain calm when the German troops march in. Signed: The Citizens' Committee of the City of Łódź.

---

* German nationals numbered about 60,000, or less than 20 percent of the Łódź population before the war.

I go to the Pabianicka highway to watch the arriving troops. A lot of cars. The soldiers are not so extraordinary; only their uniforms make them different from Polish soldiers—steel-green. Their faces tough, boisterous. They are the conquerors after all! A car full of high-ranking officers with grim faces passes at lightning speed. People on the street are quiet and look at the passing troops indifferently. Hush, hush!

We go back to our buildings and sit around on benches, talk, and make jokes. What the heck!

Sunday, September 10. Łódź.   The first signs of German occupation: they are seizing Jews to dig. A certain retired professor living in the eleventh building warned me against going downtown. A good old man—a Christian. And now what to do?

Tomorrow is the first day of school. Who knows how our dear school has been? My friends are going there tomorrow to find out what's cooking, while I have to stay home. I have to! My parents say that they are not going to lose me yet. Oh, my dear school! . . . Damn the times when I complained about getting up in the morning and about tests. If only I could have them back!

Monday, September 11. Łódź.   I get up in the morning and try one last time to get permission to go to school, but my parents won't let me. Too bad. I sit at home, read, review French, do something, and later go out and hear a story about people being seized for work.

My friends come back from their schools. Almost everywhere from the first moment on there were "normal" lessons. A few students in each class, but without books or notebooks. Only review for now. I gradually become depressed, since I don't know what's happening at our school. Our dear, lovely, new building! . . . Friends, teachers, are you working? . . . I resolve to go downtown on Saturday to find out everything, and to go over the material they did in school today and what they will do tomorrow. (On Wednesday it's Erev Rosh Hashanah [Hebrew; Eve of Rosh Hashanah], so there won't be school until Sunday.) I will do a bit of English, too. Language is of prime importance.

Tuesday, September 12. Łódź.   People are being seized again for forced labor; beatings and robbings. The store where my father works has also been robbed. The local Germans do whatever they wish. There are numerous stories of how they treat Jews at work; some Germans treat them very well, while others bully them sadistically. At one place, for example, the Jewish employees were ordered to stop work, undress, and face a wall. Then they were told that they would be shot. Indeed, they were aimed at with great precision. No one was hurt, but this procedure was repeated several times and it threw most of the Jews completely off balance—that's what Łódź Nazis can do.

Wednesday, September 13. Łódź.   Erev Rosh Hashanah. Again I don't go out anywhere! The holiday is sad and meager, no different from any other day. The same dry bread with a small bit of herring. (Only the herring makes the holiday different from any other day.)

According to an order announced today, the stores are to be open tomorrow. This is the worst blow to the Jews here in centuries. Rosh Hashanah! Open stores! At the same time, synagogues are to be closed. We have no chance to pray communally for mercy. All basic human freedoms are being destroyed.

Although I am not a traditionally pious man, and every year I have considered the avoidance of prayer as a liberation, I now experience every order pertaining to the Jews with great pain because I know what faith brings to its believers; they are at least partially at peace and happy. To take away from a man his only consolation, his faith, to forbid his beloved, life-affirming religion is the most horrendous crime. Jews won't let Hitler get away with it. Our revenge will be terrible.

Thursday, September 14. Łódź.   We prayed at home in the morning. Uncle Salomon and a neighbor, Mr. Kamusiewicz, were also present. Again, stories and rumors about who captured what city and who beat whom, but nobody knows anything for sure. The evening radio bulletins contradict one another. We are without mail, telephone, or any word from the outside. Those who fled now keep coming back. Their stories fill most of the days spent in boring captivity.

It rained a little before dinner. If it had been raining like this from the beginning of the war, the Germans wouldn't have been in Łódź yet. Tanks are helpless machines on Polish roads after it rains: mired and stuck.

In the afternoon it's nice again, and we see the German planes that have kept whirring overhead at ridiculously low altitudes since the occupation of Łódź. Why are they wasting gasoline, bloody things! We walk the streets, chat, and tell jokes, but become bored. If only I could go to school.

Friday, September 15. Łódź.   Today for the first time Mom went for bread but didn't get any. For a week she got up at five in the morning, stood in line until seven, when they opened the bakery and gave a kilo of bread to everyone. Today she went again, but there was no bread left. Maybe we should get up at 1:00 A.M. to get there, and wait.

Downtown, Nazi agents remove Jews from all food lines, so a poor Jew who doesn't have a servant is condemned to death by hunger. These are German humanitarian policies in the twentieth century.

The Rabinowiczes and their neighbors have come back from wandering around. They look terrible. Their two sons rode on another cart, and they didn't come back. Nobody knows where they are. The Rabinowiczes tell of shootings, searching for places to sleep, long marches, dangers, etc. It makes my flesh crawl. There are some humorous mo-

To take away from a man his only consolation, his faith, to forbid his beloved, life-affirming religion is the most horrendous crime. Jews won't let Hitler get away with it. Our revenge will be terrible.

ments, too. Evidently humor can be found everywhere. A laugh amid all
the unhappiness.

Saturday, September 16. Łódź.   The looting of shops continues. They
carry away everything they can. At the Epsztajns' store in Reymonta
Square, they stole the entire stock of jewelry and watches. The poor
Epsztajns barely managed to escape alive.

   In the afternoon I wanted to go downtown to find out about our
school, but my parents wouldn't let me. Tomorrow Mom will learn
what's what from a fellow who was supposedly in school on Monday.

Sunday, September 17. Łódź.   It turns out that our *gymnasium* has
been discontinued. The *gymnasium* No. 1 is now scheduled to join the
one for girls and ours.

   Despair overwhelms me. While I am walking with Jadzia in the afternoon, Marek Rabinowicz suddenly runs up to us with strange and terrifying news. Russia has broken the nonaggression pact with Poland and has
occupied its eastern areas! There aren't any detailed reports yet. At first I
cannot comprehend anything. Soon German, Soviet, English, and Polish
radio reports slowly explain the situation. The Soviet government has
mobilized its army because it feels endangered (what happened to the
nonaggression pact with Germany!?), and since there is no Polish government in Warsaw, Russia feels obliged to defend Byelorussia and Ukraine
from the Germans. The Polish High Command announced that it won't
fight against Russia (so this act, though aggression, may suit our purposes
in some way), and that it will direct all its forces against the Germans.
English radio has announced that the Russian army will apparently cooperate with the Poles. So what does this mean? Could it be that Russia
has remembered that its greatest enemy is Nazism after all!? We'll see.

   Meanwhile, German troops have surrounded Warsaw and sent an
ultimatum for the city to surrender. The command in Warsaw did not
give any answer that would satisfy the Germans. The German army
began further bombings of the city, vowing to turn it into rubble. The
Poles took 12,000 German POWs.

Monday, September 18. Łódź.   In the morning Mom went to my father's boss for money. (He didn't give her any, damn it. We will probably
die of hunger.) On her way, she stopped by the girls' *gymnasium* on
Piramowicza Street, where she found out that as of today our three
schools have been united into one coeducational *gymnasium*.

I am finally going to school tomorrow. Coeducational classes! There are great girls there, they say. Only let our education be normal. We are supposed to receive certificates of "immunity" so we won't be seized for work.

In the evening I listened to the news at Marek's. Russia has occupied Wilno, Kołomyja, Baranowicze, and Tarnopol. Voroshilov* announced that Russia is taking Byelorussians, Ukrainians, and Jews (!) under its protection since they are suffering a lot in German captivity, and so that they will not be released into the Nazis' hands. The Germans claim, however, that Russia is sharing Poland with them.

England broadcasts news on the radio in all major European languages about great victories by French troops who have moved 160 kilometers into the heart of Germany. The Germans have hurriedly formed a front outside Berlin. England also broadcasts an appeal from President Mościcki,† who took refuge with the government in Romania. English radio denied the report of Marshal Śmigły-Rydz's resignation, pointing out that he is personally commanding action at the front near Kutno, and that Polish troops won great victories both yesterday and today.

Meanwhile, a rumor is circulating in the city that red banners have appeared in Warsaw, and that a leftist government has been formed with former prime minister and PPS activist Barlicki‡ at its head, and the president of Łódź, Kwapiński, as a deputy premier. Well, quite a turn. Maybe we will now receive Russian help against the Germans. We'll see. Meanwhile, I'm going to school tomorrow. Long live school!

Tuesday, September 19. Łódź. I rode to school in a clean uniform (I came back on foot, however, and will go on foot every time now because there is no money to go by streetcar). At the gate I met two boys from our class (Lolek Łęczycki and Epsztajn) who took me to a classroom. There are fifteen girls and eighteen boys from the three *gymnasiums*. We had three lessons; mostly review. We haven't received any certificates of "immunity." There are only a few of our old teachers. It's not known yet whether we will have classes together with girls or separately (it's getting crowded).

At five I listened to Hitler's speech. After an enthusiastic greeting

---

* Kliment Efremovich Voroshilov (1881–1969) was a Soviet military and political leader. He eventually became chairman of the Presidium of the Supreme Soviet.
† Ignacy Mościcki (1867–1946) was the president of Poland (1926–1939).
‡ Norbert Barlicki (1880–1941), a leader of the Polish Socialist Party, died in Auschwitz.

and welcome he spoke from *Die befreite Stadt Danzig* [German; the liberated city of Gdańsk]. The speech, however, wasn't worthy of this otherwise great statesman. He raged, quibbled, got excited, insulted, begged, coaxed, and, above all, he lied and lied . . . He lied by saying that Poland started the war; he lied by speaking about the oppression of Germans in Poland (*"Barbaren!"*); he lied by speaking of his always good, peaceful intentions, and so on. After that he served up series of insults against Polish authorities, Churchill, Cooper (Duff),* and Eden.† He spoke about his desire for an accord with the English and French peoples, and he still talked about the injustice of the Versailles Treaty, at which point he announced that Poland will never exist within the borders established by this treaty(!). Finally, he announced that English efforts to overthrow the ruling regime in Germany will never succeed, which proves the existence and seriousness of such movements. At the end Hitler discussed his good relations with Russia (?) and the impossibility of a German–Russian conflict breaking out. After a few pathetic remarks about Gdańsk, he finished his speech.

Wednesday, September 20. Łódź.   I got up earlier today, and at 7:20 I set out on foot for school. A long and boring way, over 5 kilometers, but it is definitely worth the effort to go to school.

They told us that, as of tomorrow, separate classes for boys will be from 12:30 to 4:20, five classes each day, excluding Saturdays and Sundays. So there will be no classes on Saturdays.

The girls felt bitter when they heard that they were going to be separated from us. Too bad, they said, but that's that. Life is not romance! War is not peace.

The Germans have already issued regulations about currency. The German mark (2 Polish złotys for 1 mark) and the notes issued by the Citizens' Committee are in circulation on equal terms with the złoty. They haven't failed to issue several anti-Semitic regulations as well. A Jew is not allowed to have more than 1,000 marks (or 2,000 Polish złotys) at his home, and he can get only 250 marks a week from a bank account. The looting of stores and the "sales" have let up somewhat, but seizure "actions" for work continue.

---

* Alfred Duff Cooper (1890–1954) was a prominent British political leader and writer.
† Anthony Eden (1897–1977) reentered British Prime Minister Chamberlain's government as dominions secretary. He served as foreign secretary from 1940 to 1945. He became prime minister in 1955.

Thursday, September 21. Łódź. I went to school at the designated time in the afternoon. I felt somewhat odd. No wonder: for the first time in my life, I have classes in the afternoon. We had physics for the first time today. The topic was measurement; a very interesting subject.

After classes I went to [Lolek] Łęczycki's, where we did mathematics homework. I received an old student registration card with six valid tram tickets from him. They will serve me for six days of one-way travel to school! I'm trying to get a loan of several złotys from Łęczycki to buy notebooks. Otherwise, I can't buy them.

Friday, September 22. Łódź. No classes today. Erev Yom Kippur. The weather is ugly, so I stay home almost all day. A new newspaper came out in Polish today: *Gazeta Łódzka.* It seems to be a direct translation of the Nazi *Freie Presse.* They are damnably down on Jews! Except for those two rags there aren't any other newspapers in Łódź, not even any German ones.

Saturday, September 23. Łódź. We all fasted today. I felt all right, though. Since the German authorities closed all synagogues "forever," we prayed at home. After supper I went to listen to the radio. The most important news appeared to be the death of the German general von Fritsch.*

It is rumored that General Thomée or Langner, a Polish commander of the section of the Sieradz–Wieluń–Łódź front, has been executed for treason and for giving up those cities to the Germans without a fight. We know how bravely Warsaw is holding on. Józik Wolman has returned from there.

Sunday, September 24. Łódź. The streets of Łódź feel eerie. Although richly decorated with Nazi flags, they are gray and sad. Dozens of *Verordnungen* [German; regulations], *Bekanntmachungen* [German; public notices], and so on have been posted. An official price list for food products has been announced, but profiteering remains rampant. People voluntarily offer more money just to get the goods, so they won't have to chase around begging for necessities. A person has to wait in line for bread for five or six hours, only to go away empty-handed 50 percent of

---

* General Baron Werner von Fritsch (1880–1939) was killed in the German attack on Warsaw.

the time. They are still seizing people for forced labor. Nothing seems to go well.

Monday, September 25. Łódź.   I come back from school after five, do some of my homework, and go to the Grodzeńskis' to listen to the evening bulletin in Polish from London. It has become my daily routine. After the bulletin we discuss it, and our discussions always end with sighs.

The war is not going very rosily. Russia has already taken over 60 percent of Poland's land, and, in addition, it has extended its control to Estonia. Warsaw's in ruins, there is no water or food there; it will fall any day, while the French are still grinding on the Siegfried Line. Tomorrow Ribbentrop is going to Moscow on Stalin's invitation. Apparently, they will divide Poland between themselves.

I have borrowed 2 złotys from Łęczycki to buy notebooks. I will give them back to him when I can. The arrangement won't do him any harm, and it's a help for me. I am more and more attracted to Marx when I consider our present social relations, even those at school. This war will become a real liberator.

Tuesday, September 26. Łódź.   Ribbentrop and Molotov talked for five and a half hours at the Kremlin, but nothing specific is known. Meanwhile, things remain as is, and nobody knows anything for certain. School proceeds normally.

Wednesday, September 27. Łódź.   Warsaw has capitulated! They couldn't hold out any longer without support, especially because there was no food, water, or ammunition and because the city was badly destroyed. The terms of surrender have not yet been settled. Meanwhile, they continue to confer in Moscow.

Thursday, September 28. Łódź.   The Polish army has secured a safe departure from Warsaw, after which it is supposed to be disbanded. Each disarmed soldier is to go home. Officers were left their sabers. The French are waging massive battles against the Germans, but they are moving very slowly. Last Friday, Professor Sigmund Freud, the founder of psychoanalysis, died in London at the age of eighty-three. In Romania the murder last week of Premier Calinescu is being blamed on the Germans. The assassins were caught and hanged. They were Romanians, members of the dissolved pro-Nazi "Iron-Guard." Surely they must have been paid by the Germans to do the job.*

Friday, September 29. Łódź.   The pact has been signed in Moscow. The division of Poland between Germany and Russia has been settled. Two Jews, Lozovski† and Kaganovich,‡ attended the banquet given by Ribbentrop. Well, well, what an insult!

Without changing Estonia's state sovereignty in any way, Russia took it under its protection today just to borrow its Baltic ports. Romania is said to be concentrating its army in Bessarabia out of fear of a possible annexation attempt by Russia.

Saturday, September 30. Łódź.   It's a bit warmer again after a cold week. The sun is shining, and you can take a walk. We heard a radio bulletin in the evening at the Grodzeńskis' regarding changes in the Polish government [in exile] in Paris. Later we had a long discussion about Communism. A neighbor of ours, Mr. Dyraga, explained to other Christian neighbors who had adverse attitudes that as a matter of fact Christianity is also communism, but distorted by the church and the rich. Gradually everybody admitted that he was right, convinced of the substance of his words, which showed extensive reading and thought. I said the very same things to my friends, two girls who were there, and they admitted that I was right. I think that they will soon understand the principles of Marxism. Even Mr. Sobierajski, another neighbor who had never been a Communist, spoke out about the parasites of society who are so influential because of their money, but who are actually totally worthless people.

Perhaps it is only the brutal forms of revolution that have caused women to have doubts, but as Dyraga explained, making use of the Gospel, there is no other way, "The weed has to be torn out by the roots." Besides, hostility that has accumulated over the millennia must explode, and no one can stop the process. We talked away until late in the night.

---

* Armand Calinescu (1893–1939) became prime minister of Romania in March 1939. He hoped to inspire a "national rebirth" and attempted to forcibly suppress the fascist Iron Guard. Guardist terrorists assassinated him on September 23 in Bucharest.

† A. Lozovski (1878–1952) was the pseudonym of Solomon Abramovich Dridzo, the son of a poor rural Hebrew teacher who was the Soviet deputy minister of foreign affairs from 1939 to 1946. A staunch defender of Joseph Stalin, Lozovski survived every one of Stalin's purges but the last. He was executed at the age of seventy-four.

‡ Lazar Moiseyevich Kaganovich (1893–1991) was a Soviet Communist leader and supporter of Joseph Stalin.

Sunday, October 1. Łódź.   The composition of the new government [in exile] has been announced. General Sikorski,* who fled Poland last year because of his criticism of the government, was appointed prime minister, minister of military affairs, and commander of the Polish army in France. Meanwhile, Hitler proposes peace and wants to create a Polish "buffer-state," which would include Warsaw, Łódź, Kielce, Siedlce, and Lublin, with no access to the sea. What generosity! England has declared that it will fight until victorious. That may take a long time.

Monday, October 2. Łódź.   People who fled from Łódź to Warsaw are already coming back. Their stories leave a sad impression. Warsaw is literally in ruins, if one can imagine it. Entire streets have been wiped out. The Royal Castle, Belvedere, and thousands of other historical and beautiful buildings have all been destroyed. They say that the entire Jewish district has been destroyed. There is terrible hunger there. Thirty złotys for a loaf of bread! Dead bodies lie in the streets. Nobody cares about anything anymore. The city is in total ruins.

According to today's English bulletin, some sort of Anglo-Russian agreement has been reached. That's great if it's really so!

Tuesday, October 3. Łódź.   Slowly and painfully, people are getting used to the new conditions and are beginning to return to their businesses. Although that's possible for some clerks, workers, and shopkeepers, it's harder for the Jews. Jews: businessmen, shop owners and private factory owners, middlemen, merchants, etc. are all losing their livelihoods; because of forced seizures for labor, they are afraid to stick their heads out of their homes. Like most of our neighbors, they try to take up odd jobs like, say, door-to-door selling. They sell stockings, bread, sugar, knit goods, etc. Everybody has something to sell. Products go through dozens of middlemen, wholesalers, and merchants, but nothing can protect the Jewish masses from rapid impoverishment.

My father doesn't have a job and simply suffocates at home. We have no money. It's all shot! Disaster!

Wednesday, October 4. Łódź.   I didn't escape the sad fate of my countrymen who are being seized for work. As luck would have it, some older people talked me into going to school by way of Wólczańska

---

* As head of the Polish government in exile, General Władysław Sikorski (1881–1943) was forced to move from Paris to London as the war advanced. He was killed when his airplane went down over Gibraltar. The cause of the crash remains in dispute.

Street, a slightly shorter route. As I walked along there yesterday I could see almost nothing but swastikas on all the buildings along the street, as well as a lot of German cars and a great number of soldiers and Łódź Germans with swastikas on their arms. I somehow made it through, and today, thus emboldened, I went the same way. Then, near Andrzeja Street, some student from the German *gymnasium* ran up to me with a big stick in his hand and shouted: "Komm arbeiten! In die Schule darfst du nicht gehn!" [German; Come work! You can't go to school!] I did not resist because I knew that no papers could help me here. He took me to a square where over a dozen Jews were already at work picking up leaves! The sadistic youngster badly wanted to make me climb over a 2-meter-high fence, but seeing that I couldn't do it, he gave up and went away.

The work at the square was supervised by a single soldier, also with a big stick. Using rude words, he told me to fill puddles with sand. I have never been so humiliated in my life as when I looked through the gate to the square and saw the happy, smiling mugs of passersby laughing at our misfortune. Oh, you stupid, abysmally stupid, foolish blockheads! It's our oppressors who should be ashamed, not us. Humiliation inflicted by force does not humiliate. But anger and helpless rage tear a man apart when he is forced to do such stupid, shameful, abusive work. Only one response remains: revenge!

After about half an hour of work, the soldier called us up (some of the people had their hats turned around backward "for fun"), lined us up, and ordered one of us to take back all the spades and the rest of us to go home. A display of generosity. I came to school in the middle of the first class. It was the first time I've been late to *gymnasium*. The teachers can't do anything about it: "For reasons beyond the Jew's control."

On my way back I took the old way through Kilińskiego Street, and at home I aroused Mother's anxieties when I told her of the incident. Father also gave up the "shorter" way through Wólczańska. In the evening we learned that one of the Germans who lives on our street "keeps an eye" on Jews from our buildings, watching us closely. This made my poor, nervous parents completely upset. Meanwhile, they announced at school that students who don't pay a certain amount of money will be forbidden to attend. We'll see what'll happen to me!

Thursday, October 5. Łódź. In spite of today's Shemini Atseret holiday [Hebrew; Eighth Day of Assembly, conclusion of the nine-day harvest celebration of Succoth], we had two classes at school. I had to go both ways on foot because I had run out of student tram tickets.

*Oh, you stupid, abysmally
stupid, foolish blockheads!
It's our oppressors who
should be ashamed, not us.
Humiliation inflicted by
force does not humiliate.
But anger and helpless
rage tear a man apart. . . .
Only one response remains:
revenge!*

At school we organized elections for the student council of the combined third grades of the first and second *gymnasium*s. Five boys were elected to the council, two from our *gymnasium* and three from the other. Three assistants were also elected, one from ours and two from theirs. From our class, Rajchenberg and I were elected to the council, with Łęczycki as a deputy. After classes we had our first council meeting, during which a president and other members of the leadership were elected. I was elected president; Blumsztajn from the first *gymnasium*, secretary; and Grabowiecki from the first *gymnasium*, my assistant.

Friday, October 6. Łódź.   Hitler gave a speech at a meeting of the Reichstag, which was assembled today. In the first part of the speech he justly ridiculed the former Polish government. The second part contained his "final" offer of peace. The conditions were announced last week on the radio, but they are unacceptable. Hitler said that he is ready to settle the Jewish question, and at that point he ridiculed English rule in Palestine. In any case, the speech contributed nothing new.

Saturday, October 7. Łódź.   Real frost is coming. In the morning it was already only 1 degree above zero [Celsius] [32°F]. Bad news! It's cold at home, and there is no coal. Brr! What's going to happen?!

Sunday, October 8. Łódź.   In the city there is a persistent rumor about Russian–German conflicts and Soviet demands. There must be something to it. Many troops are leaving the city, heading in an unknown direction.

There are no food supplies in the city. Everything is increasing in price at a terrifying rate. There is no coal.

Women who come to Łódź from the villages of Ruda and Rzgów say that trenches are being dug around the city. Should we believe it? Meanwhile, the Germans are confiscating the nicest and most comfortable apartments.

The Jewish Community Council has posted an announcement saying that it will provide 700 Jews a day for work.* Will they now stop the seizures in the streets?

---

* As a member of the Jewish Community Council, Mordechai Chaim Rumkowski (1877–1944), the director of a Jewish orphanage, took the initiative to propose to the Germans that they notify the council how many Jewish workers were required; the council would then turn them out voluntarily. This readiness to deliver Jews on demand may have been a

Monday, October 9. Łódź. Principal Perelman has announced that the students who haven't paid [tuition] will have no reason to come to school tomorrow. He is an exceptionally severe and mean man. I tried to talk to him after classes to explain our dire food situation, but he pushed me back, saying: "I don't care, there are no exceptions." I cursed him in my soul with all my strength, and vowed to settle accounts with him some day "in another social system." I don't know what's going to happen to me.

Tuesday, October 10. Łódź. All classes passed calmly until the last one, when the principal again called us to his office and told us to go home. However, since the class period was nearing its end, he let us stay. After classes I asked Gurewicz for the address of Braude, the president of our society. It turned out that Rabbi Dr. [Markus] Braude lives at 46 Gdańska Street. I went there, but the rabbi had just been taken ill and I was received by his wife. After consulting several times with her husband, she said that they cannot help me. She expressed her sympathy and told me to wait for Principal Elenberg's arrival from Warsaw. Sure, if "Eluś" [Principal Elenberg] were here, I wouldn't be in any danger of being expelled from school.

From Braude's I went to see Lolek Łęczycki, who is sick, and brought him my notebooks. There I was offered unexpected help from his mother. After hearing about my troubles at school, she said she would talk to the principal tomorrow. But will it help?

Wednesday, October 11. Łódź. He expelled us, anyway! I don't know whether he always acts like this, but today he behaved really brutally. He entered the classroom at the end of the second lesson, read the names of about ten boys who hadn't paid the fees, and ordered them to "leave the classroom immediately. Immediately!" Pale and angry, I didn't go home, but rather to see Lipszyc, who was also expelled and whom I, at this opportunity, converted from a *bejterowiec* [Polish; member of the Zionist youth movement, Betar] to a leftist. At home they were saddened by the school news, and said quietly, "The damned war!"

significant factor in the Nazis' appointing Rumkowski "Eldest of the Jews" of the ghetto to be established in Łódź. He ruled the ghetto from its creation on February 8, 1940, until its final liquidation in August 1944, when, with nearly all surviving ghetto dwellers, he was deported to Auschwitz. Eyewitness accounts vary, but the consensus of surviving crematoria workers is that he was beaten to death in an anteroom to a gas chamber, by Jews he had deported from the ghetto.

Thursday, October 12. Łódź.   Early today I went to Łęczycki's to await the outcome of his mother's conversation with the principal. It turned out that nothing can be done for now, so I didn't go to school but went to see Goldblum, from whom I borrowed a book. Then I went to some old friends of my mother's, stayed at their store, and had dinner there. Since I was already downtown, I joined a line for butter, which I haven't eaten for months. I didn't get any, though. Feeling chilled, I went over to Łęczycki's again, and learned what they did in school and what the homework was. I also had a talk with his mother, who told me to go to school and to just refer to her.

Friday, October 13. Łódź.   I was at school today and wasn't expelled. The principal told me, however, that nothing has been settled yet and he would wait only until Monday. After classes I went to see Mrs. Walfisz, who told me they would try to solve the problem tomorrow. Maybe I will finally be able to go to school.

Saturday, October 14. Łódź.   The cost of living is rising higher and higher. The hunger begins. There is no coal in the entire city, and to get a loaf of bread people pay 3.50 złotys! It has been three days since Mom got any bread. We eat leftovers and potatoes.

In the morning Mother and Father got in line at the only working bakery in the Chojny district, but they didn't receive anything from the morning batch of bread. Like everyone else in line, they didn't give up, however, and waited for new bread until four in the evening. People reserved their places in the line with others and went home to eat breakfast. As soon as Nadzia came home from school, she went to the bakery to take Mom's place [in line], so Mom could take a rest at my aunt's nearby. When they finally arrived home with two loaves of bread, they had to go to bed immediately. Meanwhile, I prepared water for washing, cleaned the apartment, and even cooked dinner! I've got the job in hand!

English radio says there is going to be a famine here because the Germans are taking everything away to the Reich. Russia has given Polish Wilno back to Lithuania and ejected all Germans from the Baltic countries. It is pressuring Lithuania to demand Memel, fortifying the border with Germany, and gathering its troops on the Slovak border. I wonder if the Soviets will oppose or help the Germans, or perhaps remain neutral.

Sunday, October 15. Łódź. Suddenly it has become wonderfully warm. The sun is shining, and there is no wind. Well, so what when the spirit's down, hunger is staring us in the face, and there is no way to get bread?

Monday, October 16. Łódź. I was at school and wasn't expelled! Mrs. Walfisz and some other women paid the school office the damned money for me, Lipszyc, and Kahan, so we will be all right until December 1. In December there are holidays, so half a year will be completed. After that we will see what we can do. I have school now, but I don't have bread.

Announcements have been posted about a campaign against profiteers (*"jüdische,"* naturally). High time. They want 8 złotys for 1 kilogram of butter.

Thursday, October 17. Łódź. I met Mrs. Perec, whose son I tutored last year (1 złoty per lesson!). Perhaps I will tutor her son this year as well. I hope so! Then I could ride at least one way to school, have my shoes and coat repaired, etc., etc.

Wednesday, October 18. Łódź. Today I saw the German newspapers, directly from the Reich. A German police station has been set up in one of our buildings. They visit the apartments of Jews and take away radios, carpets, comforters, etc. They will probably evict us soon.

Thursday, October 19. Łódź. We don't have classes in Polish history anymore. Chapters regarding Poland are omitted. We will probably have German-language classes, which makes me very happy. Knowing one more language won't hurt.

Meanwhile, we are running out of coal at home, and it's impossible to get bread even if you wait in line. Mom intends to bake bread from rye flour by herself. It will cut down on our reserve of fuel, but it will save potatoes.

Friday, October 20. Łódź. The Germans are going into action. They have issued an order forbidding Jews to trade manufactured goods, leather, and textiles. Jews are forbidden to buy anything, and they can sell only to Christians. A shoemaker is allowed to buy leather only for soles and heels; he is forbidden to make new shoes. While this order may effectively fight profiteering on clothing, it forces thousands of Jewish families into ruin.

Saturday, October 21. Łódź.   Tired after running around all week, I sat home all day and read. It is beginning to rain heavily, and the holes in my slippers and shoes are becoming bigger.

Sunday, October 22. Łódź.   They knock at eleven in the morning. Mom opens the door, and a German army officer, two policemen, and the superintendent come in. The officer asks how many persons are in the apartment, looks at the beds, asks about bedbugs, and if we have a radio. He doesn't find anything worthy of taking and finally leaves disappointed. At the neighbors' (naturally they go only to Jews), he took away radios, mattresses, comforters, carpets, etc. They took away the Grabińskis' only down quilt.

I could see that Father was very frightened because he stood and prayed in *tallis* and *tefillin* [Hebrew; prayer shawl and phylacteries, the prayer boxes containing quotations from the Jewish scriptures that are attached with leather straps to head and arm]! But the officer didn't pay any attention to him. (Exceptional luck because they say that in similar cases they have rushed Jews out onto the street and made them run until *tallis* and *tefillin* fell.) Now it's almost 100 percent certain that they will throw us out of our building.

Monday, October 23. Łódź.   I went to Mrs. Perec to find out about the tutoring, but she wasn't home. The "lady" apparently forgot.

I have dug out an old pair of slippers that have better soles than the "new" ones I have on my feet. They will serve me for a while. Everyday I have to walk to school and back, 10 kilometers, in soaking-wet slippers; I don't eat any meat, or fat, or bread. Potatoes for breakfast, dinner, and supper. Naturally, in all different forms. That's the way we live now, and under threat of being thrown out of the apartment as well.

Tuesday, October 24. Łódź.   I went to Mrs. Perec's again. Stirring, buzzing, crowds. She is packing bedding and clothes in gigantic boxes because she is also supposed to be thrown out of her apartment. Naturally, her little son doesn't go to school, and I won't be giving him any lessons either.

Wednesday, October 25. Łódź.   It's pouring and pouring. From time to time there are snowflakes among the raindrops, but it's only water when it reaches the ground. The "miraculously" discovered slippers won't do any longer.

It's slow in the store where Father "works," so we have no income. Sometimes German officers bring trucks and load furniture, telling the owners to wait to be paid from heaven. At home all we have to eat are scraps. The potatoes are running out; there is no coal or wood. A truly wonderful life.

Thursday, October 26. Łódź.   We already have two tests scheduled in school for next week: English and Polish. Classes are proceeding normally, and the course of study is quite interesting. Only let it continue. But what will really happen?

There is no information from abroad. The Germans confiscate all radios, while the newspapers (both those published in Łódź and those brought from elsewhere) tell us nothing.

Friday, October 27. Łódź.   Classes now begin at one o'clock; we have six of them every day. Meanwhile, the situation in our buildings is worsening. Today they came over to Mrs. Heller in the eleventh building and ordered her to get out by four o'clock tomorrow, acting as though it were nothing out of the ordinary. The building administration gave her a vacant apartment, but only until she finds another apartment in the city. We are all in danger.

Saturday, October 28. Łódź.   What a nasty day. It's hard to imagine our terror and nervousness. It actually began yesterday. Father came back pale and depressed. What happened? They simply took all the furniture away from the store. Collapse, bankruptcy. They spent all day emptying out the store until nothing was left, and then threatened the owner that if he continues to trade privately they will shoot him.

At eleven, Herszkowicz and Rubinek came over unexpectedly, and we went for a walk as far as Ruda, to Lublinek station. On the way back Rysio Herszkowicz bought a head of cabbage for 15 groszes (in the city they pay 50 groszes for one head!).

After dinner (cabbage and potatoes), when I was reading a book, Mom went outside for a moment and immediately rushed back frightened: in building after building, German officers are dropping in on Jews looking for radios! (They use the opportunity to take away whatever they want.) As soon as Mom finishes telling us what she has seen, they knock on our door in a way befitting soldiers. Mom opens it; Father goes pale as a tall officer comes in with a boy my age and the superintendent's son. He looks around, asks about a radio, and finding out that today is my day off from school, says that he is taking me with him. After that he goes into the other room, opens a wardrobe, and takes two flashlights; he looks into Mom's purse; he also opens the drawer with my books, seems surprised, and asks Father what he does; finally he opens the third door of the wardrobe, notices the *tefillin*, and advises Father not to pray so much. Then he closes everything, gets up, and calls me to come with him. A cold shiver runs down my spine, but I get a coat and put it on. Father asks where I'm being taken. The officer answers that I will come back soon.

Next we go to Grabiński's. The young German would like to take everything, but for some reason the officer doesn't find anything worth taking. While we are going down the stairs, the superintendent tells the officer that it's not worth continuing the search because he won't get anything from the Jews here. The officer gives in and, with the other German and me, goes to the police station in the first building. He tells me to wait out on the street, consigning me ("Das ist ein Jude") to the guard's "care."

When the officer finally comes out with a friend of his, I can see Marek Rabinowicz behind them. Marek has also been taken from his apartment, and his mother was "jokingly" threatened by the officer that he would never come back. We go on as a pair ahead of the officers. Marek says that we are going to some store on Rzgowska Street for a lamp. After that we go to rich Jews on Reymonta Square. (On our way there, Jakubowicz spots us—a friend of Marek's. We don't stop, or say anything, and having noticed the officers, he takes off.) We wait alone in front of the store. The officers finally come out with two small packages. They hand them to us so we won't be without work. Over our shoulders we see that two others have joined our officers in the battle against the Jews, or rather against Jewish property. We visit two more houses on Reymonta Square, where they "fish out" a typewriter, a radio receiver at my father's boss's, a radio receiver, and a gigantic basket full of various things at some doctor's. I have to carry the basket, which is awfully heavy. I trip, weighed down, and realize I won't get far. Marek's officer sympathizes with me and says that we'll take a streetcar. We drag ourselves to the stop and clamber aboard. The conductor wants money, but the officers announce that Jews carrying things in the service of the "police" don't pay. We get off and begin the road to Calvary. I stop frequently, the basket is becoming heavier and heavier, my hand is burning, and my arm is straining; sweat is pouring off me. Eventually the officer called Marek, who gave me the typewriter; it was no lighter, but easier to carry. At last we reach the police station, where they let us go.

My father is waiting in front of our building for me, worried and nervous. Mom, weakened, is crying inside. All the neighbors stare at me. Julek Wegmajster is waiting for me at home. I am helping him with English. We talk and then I walk with him to the streetcar. I go to sleep, aching. Don't let this kind of day happen again.

Sunday, October 29. Łódź. I woke up tired and aching. All day I have felt as though I were just getting over some illness. We went to my aunt's for a while in the afternoon. In the evening Mr. Pomeranc came to our place. He said that tension is high in the city, and there's talk that some kind of change is imminent. It all seems like gossip to me. I don't believe anything anymore. We have deluded ourselves so many times for nothing.

Monday, October 30, Łódź.   Machine guns have been set up in front of the cathedral on Piotrkowska Street and at several other points in the city. They say that riots are expected on Wednesday, All Saints' Day.

At school, Szarogroder announced that we would have a mathematics test during the next class.

I have borrowed a first-year German *gymnasium* textbook from Lipszyc. It's awfully easy; I will get through it in a short time and then will know one more language. I'm also doing excellently in French.

Tuesday, October 31. Łódź.   Another search in the morning. The boy who always accompanies the officers (he lives in the second building) has apparently taken up harassing Jews, and brings new searchers every day. Today there were four of them, including our young lad: one SS officer, a Wehrmacht officer, and a Wehrmacht MP. They ransacked the wardrobe and took my shaver and two old razor blades; they wanted money and new underclothes. They can take all our "riches"! The Aryan lad who was giving the tour whispered to the disappointed officer that he should at least grab me for work, but the officer didn't respond. Mom was pale and trembled for a long time after they left. She made me something to eat and sent me off to school quickly; what if they changed their minds and gave me an "occupation"? Later on we learned that they took Marek for work and roughed him up. They took a few pairs of new socks from the Grabińskis, a shaver, and some handkerchiefs, and a cigarette case and a watch from Mrs. Abramowicz. Whatever can be taken, they take!

At school we couldn't figure out whether we would have classes tomorrow or not. Until the sixth period they kept saying that we would, but just before the last lesson Dr. Braude arrived; then Principal Perelman entered the classroom during the lesson to announce that there will be no classes tomorrow or the day after tomorrow, and that we mustn't go outside because "unpredictable events" might occur. Anyway it is better to stay at home. When I was leaving school a young, smart girl stayed with us. It turns out that I might teach her Hebrew.

In the evening Father came back from a German customer who told him that some kind of "action" is expected. What and how, nobody knows.

Wednesday, November 1. Łódź.   I had my first German lesson. I did five units from the textbook.

The news reached us today that Warsaw has been cut off from Łódź; there are no train connections. There are rumors about a formal change in the name of the occupied areas and allusions to a change in the territorial status of Warsaw and maybe of Łódź as well.

Thursday, November 2. Łódź.   Blissful, rainy calm. Goebbels, the minister of propaganda, is said to have visited Łódź today. The purpose of the visit is unknown. Meanwhile, there will be a test in mathematics tomorrow at school. I hope I'll pass it.

Friday, November 3. Łódź.   The test took place, but I don't think I did too well. A typical beginning for wartime!

In the city there is talk of various Russian demands, suspended conferences, etc. Russia is making demands of Finland, the world is indignant, and Finland is giving in. Russia is pushing further and further.

Saturday, November 4. Łódź.   My cousin Abe's wedding party was today (he picked an excellent time for the wedding!). It was celebrated at lightning speed, with no alcohol.

I'm reading Rolland's *Jean-Christophe*. A great work! So fine, wise, serious, and interesting.

Sunday, November 5. Łódź.   I have learned about yesterday's radio news from London. It is very interesting. It turns out that Goebbels and Hess were in Łódź to discuss the formation of a Polish "government." They decided to turn management of the government over to Prince Radziwiłł, but Prince Radziwiłł is in the area occupied by Russia, and the Russians have announced that they won't release him since his government would oppose Russia. According to London, the Soviets have added that they would like to have their troops in the former Congress Kingdom of Poland.* Meanwhile, Finland has given in to all the Russian demands. London also says that Berlin doesn't like Russian interference in German affairs and territory. What will come of it? Nobody knows.

In the evening my cousin's husband returned from Kowel, which is occupied by the Russians. He says that food is very expensive and no quarters are available there because of the excessive population. Nevertheless, the situation is much better than what he finds here. In Kowel there's no harassment, and order is kept fastidiously. Everyone likes the Russians because they are kind and helpful.

Monday, November 6. Łódź.   We received our tests back. In spite of my dismal expectations, I got an A!

A gloomy mood pervades the city. A rumor is circulating about the execution of more than a dozen Jews. Even names are mentioned.†

I went to Mrs. Perec's to see about the ill-fated tutoring. It is really doomsday there. On Thursday Mr. Perec was taken from his factory for forced labor, and he has still not come back! Naturally, I couldn't talk about the tutoring.

On Piotrkowska Street, Julek Wegmajster and I heard an announcement from a speaker mounted on an NSDAP [German, Nationalsozialistische Deutsche Arbeiterpartei; National Socialist German Workers'

---

* The Congress Kingdom of Poland was established at the Congress of Vienna in 1815 as part of the settlement of the Napoleonic Wars. The kingdom was bordered on the north and west by Prussian provinces, on the south by the Austrian province of Galicia, and on the east by Russia. The kingdom was ruled by the Russian czars until they lost the territory in World War I.

† The Nazis immediately proceeded to eliminate those significant local figures—heads of industry, politicians, clergy—they knew would oppose their rule. Robert Geyer, one of the dominant textile magnates in the city, was one of the first murdered by the Gestapo in the initial October actions. See the diary entry for December 24, 1939.

Party] propaganda truck about Gauleiter Greiser's* visit to Łódź, which is scheduled for tomorrow. They say that Greiser will annex Łódź to the Reich. What a prospect! Everyone is convinced that in such an event the Jews will definitely be forced to leave the city, of course following enforcement of a whole series of anti-Jewish decrees, harassment, and the like.

Tuesday, November 7. Łódź.   And the prophecy has become truth! There is an announcement in today's *Deutsche Lodzer Zeitung* about the annexation of Łódź to the Wartheland [Western Poland] and thus to the Greater Reich. Naturally, the "appropriate" orders have been issued, namely, that Jews are forbidden to be on Piotrkowska Street because it is the main street of the city; next, that Jews and Poles are obliged to give way to uniformed Germans everywhere and in every respect; and finally, it is forbidden to wear four-cornered caps,† uniforms, army coats, shiny buttons, or a uniform's striped trousers. Jewish bakeries are allowed to bake only bread, and all Jewish stores must post a "*jüdisches Geschäft*" [German; Jewish business] notice and a yellow "Magen David" [Hebrew; star of David] with the inscription "*Jude*" on it. It's a return to the "yellow armband" of the Middle Ages (the yellow armband is already being worn by Jews in Radomsko, for example).

Wednesday, November 8. Łódź.   I went to school in everyday clothes and without a school badge (the proud ornament of schoolboys).

Horrible things were taking place in the city today. Jews were being seized and ordered to report tomorrow morning with a shovel, food for two days, and 20 złotys. What kind of scheme is that? What sort of new torture?

Posters announcing the annexation of Łódź to the Reich have been put up at street corners. Nazi Party and Nazi Youth Party chapters have been formed in the city: marches, songs, processions. You want to stay home, not to go outside, not to see it all.

Tomorrow is some German holiday, an anniversary of the death of some prominent National Socialist activists or something. A conference between the "Jewish Elders of Łódź" [members of the Nazi-appointed Judenrat] and the German authorities has also been set for tomorrow.

---

* Artur Greiser (1897–1946), head of the Nazi Party in the territory and Gauleiter of the Warthegau, was hanged by Polish authorities after the war.
† Four-cornered caps were part of the traditional Polish army uniform.

We will see what happens. Anyway, school classes are to be held tomorrow as usual.

Thursday, November 9. Łódź.   Although we had been told to come to school, there were no classes today. The girls were let go at ten, and our classes didn't even begin. Yesterday the Germans came to the school and ordered that the Polish–Hebrew school sign be removed and the library put in order. Łęczycki and I worked a little, helping to rearrange the books in the library. I made use of the opportunity to borrow several books, and a *Berliner Illustrierte Zeitung* from Łęczycki. Very nice photographs.

At home I learned that the Jews who were seized and ordered to come to work with food and money have been let go after a day of work (their money taken from them). Passes for 5 złotys per person are issued for the Jews who live on Piotrkowska. Everything is apparently being done for money. Meanwhile, the members of the Jewish Community Council who are conferring with the authorities haven't returned to their homes yet.

Friday, November 10. Łódź.   We had only three classes. I learned from Łęczycki that all the members of the Jewish Community Council have been imprisoned. However, later on there were rumors in the city that they were released.*

At school we were advised not to go outside tomorrow (November 11, the former Polish national holiday!). Three criminals were hanged today at the Bałuty Market in order to frighten everyone. They say that two Poles were hanged for murder, and a Jew for profiteering. What a wonderful way of demonstrating a hard line! Order will be maintained! The Germans are apparently afraid of a provocation tomorrow. I am sure, however, that nothing will happen because no one will dare.

Saturday, November 11. Łódź.   It's calm in the city. In spite of the calmness, many teachers, old independence fighters, Piłsudski followers, policemen, etc. were arrested yesterday and today. *Gazeta Łódzka* has been suspended from publication. An order has been posted that all signs must be in flawless German. We are in the Reich after all!

All Poles and Jews have to turn in their radios by [November] 15.

---

* Twenty-two members of the newly appointed "Council of Elders" were rounded up and executed. Rumkowski, who pleaded for them, returned beaten. See Lucjan Dobroszycki, *The Chronicle of the Łódź Ghetto* (New Haven, Conn., 1984), p. xvi.

We won't know anything after that. The Germans do whatever they wish, terrorizing people on the streets and robbing at will.

Sunday, November 12. Łódź.   I stayed home all day, and just before evening I went to the Hamers'. Like everywhere else, various kinds of rumors are being discussed there: disagreements between Russia and Germany, or Russian demands for [a return to] the 1914 borders.

The Jewish primary schools that have become the property of the Jewish Community Council will teach German and Hebrew. Jews have been expelled from all Polish state and private *gymnasium*s. Two *gymnasium*s, Orzeszkowa (for girls) and the public one (for men), that have a great majority of Jewish students will become Jewish *gymnasium*s (all Christians will be expelled). What a paradox! In German times new Jewish *gymnasium*s are being created. But the fact is that they don't exist yet.

Monday, November 13. Łódź.   Classes at school are irregular again. There are frequent changes in the schedule, the number of classes has been reduced, and several teachers are absent. The changes are endless.

There are new rumors about a Russian ultimatum to Germany. It just seems like an excuse to console ourselves. The two powers will again come to an agreement and crush us.

My cousin Rózia's fiancé, Julek, left for Warsaw today. From there he intends to smuggle himself to Russia. Maybe he will succeed. He used to be a well-known leftist activist.*

Tuesday, November 14. Łódź.   Nothing new has happened. The rumors intensify. Classes are still irregular.

Wednesday, November 15. Łódź.   A synagogue has been burned. Barbarian methods of destroying the world are being activated. It is said that 25 million złotys have been demanded in return for stopping the terror. The Jewish Community Council did not have the money, so it was not given. Another synagogue on Wolborska Street is also reportedly on fire. There's something sick about the Germans. Yesterday they started horrible, chaotic looting. They were taking everything: furniture, clothes, underclothes, food. Poles and Jews are ordered to turn in all their shovels and pickaxes.

Mobilization has been ordered for the *Selbstschutz* [German; self-

---

* Many Polish Jews did, in fact, survive the war by fleeing to Russia.

defense] of Łódź Germans between the ages of eighteen and forty-five. The German army is leaving Łódź (nobody knows for where) so someone has to remain in the city. This will affect us negatively, first of all because it's worse to deal with the local Łódź Germans than with a whole regiment from the Reich. But perhaps they won't oppress us for long.

Thursday, November 16. Łódź.   We are returning to the Middle Ages. The yellow patch once again becomes a part of Jewish dress. Today an order was announced that all Jews, no matter what age or sex, have to wear a band of "Jewish-yellow," 10 centimeters wide, on their right arm, just below the armpit. In addition, Jews are forbidden to leave their apartments between five in the afternoon and eight in the morning. The armband becomes obligatory on Saturday, [November] 18, and the curfew is already in effect.

We had only four classes. I hurried home so fast I covered the distance in fifty minutes and was back at ten minutes to five. So, the Middle Ages? Yellow armbands and imprisonment, like in the ghetto. But it doesn't matter; we will live through this action to see a fine, shining future.

Friday, November 17. Łódź.   A gloomy mood pervades the city. It's hard to get accustomed to persecution. The banded Jews are afraid of acts of harassment. The field is wide open for ridicule and oppression. I wonder how the Poles will act. Will they conform to the German mob? Or perhaps they too have already grasped the real meaning of the Jewish sacrifice. Perhaps they will remember their priests, who yesterday had to break up the Kościuszko* monument on Liberty Square with sledge hammers until the Germans, seeing their ineffectiveness, blew it up with dynamite. We'll see.

At school we took a history test.

I have received two pieces of leather for shoe soles and heels from Lipszyc. At least I will have something to wear and won't get totally wet, which happened today. Lipszyc is no richer than I am, but he had a certain amount of leather and gave me part. At home the yellow armbands have been prepared.

* General Tadeusz Kościuszko (1746–1817), a Polish national hero, was the leader of the national uprising against Russia (1794); he also fought for the independence of the United States.

Saturday, November 18. Łódź.   I stayed at home for the entire day.
I've had my shoes repaired with new iron reinforcements and nails.

The Poles cast down their eyes at the sight of the Jews with their
armbands; friends assure us that "it won't be for long." The Germans act
completely indifferent now.

Curfew hours were changed for Poles and Germans today. They are
allowed to go out only after six o'clock in the morning (it was five in the
past), but in return for that they can stay out until half past eight in the
evening (it was eight before today).

Sunday, November 19. Łódź.   We learned from certain people that
London broadcast news yesterday about battles that had been going on
for seven hours near Lwów between the Russians and the Germans. In
addition, 2,000 English warplanes bombed Berlin yesterday, turning it
into a second Warsaw. Finally, it was announced that the English army is
in Belgium. Last week rumors were circulating about a declaration of
war by Belgium against the Germans, or the other way around. Nothing's certain, though. We can be glad about the other news. The yellow
patch will be revenged.

Monday, November 20. Łódź.   The rumors intensify, but the more
there are of them, the more I lose faith. I don't believe yesterday's news
anymore.

School is totally confused. There are no administrators; classes are
not conducted as they should be, not to mention the fact that there are
only four of them a day now because of the curfew.

Tuesday, November 21. Łódź.   The rumors diminish; everyone again
falls into a rut of boring, repugnant, bitter days. Seizures for forced labor
don't stop. They are almost always accompanied by beatings and sadistic
acts. A great many Jewish men are leaving the city. Trains to Warsaw are
terribly overloaded, with everyone heading to Warsaw and Russia!
Smuggling across the border is prospering. Father has also begun to
consider leaving. Every day is worse here. There are no jobs, decree
follows decree, and life becomes harder and harder. Among the neighbors in the building the "run-away" movement also begins to predomi-
nate. Grodzeński and his family and the Rabinowiczes are leaving.

Wednesday, November 22. Łódź.   When I got on the streetcar today, a
conductor told me that Jews are forbidden to ride in the first car. He

didn't throw me out though, a kindly man. I was scared the whole way, but nobody did anything to me.

At school I learned about a new decree: all Jewish warehouses and shops have to be sold to the "German Society for the De-Jewing of Trade and Industry in Łódź." A new wave of people is leaving the city.

Thursday, November 23. Łódź.   Mrs. Pines informed us that as of next week we will not learn English at school, but German. She advised us not to neglect the language and to work on it at home. It's fine with me. It seems I didn't need to start working on German by myself at home.

Friday, November 24. Łódź.   Father definitely wants to leave. The Grodzeńskis and the Rabinowiczes' two sons left for Warsaw today, the Grodzeńskis intending to reach Białystok, and the Rabinowiczes' sons to reach Lwów. The Kamusiewiczes are also considering leaving. Just like us, they are concerned only about the lack of money. You only wish you could cash in all your old furniture and flee this life of poverty and fear.

Saturday, November 25. Łódź.   The first accumulating snow has fallen.

I don't go out; I read and contemplate the prospects of leaving, and all the pros and cons. We can still wait. The Rabinowiczes are leaving together with Marek on Monday or Tuesday.

Sunday, November 26. Łódź.   Two friends of mine from Górny Rynek [section of Łódź] have returned from Russia to take their families back with them. They say that bread and meat are very cheap in Russia; on the other hand, sugar costs 12 złotys a kilo, and there is a terrible clothing shortage. But that does not discourage anyone. Russian soldiers pay incredibly high amounts for used clothes, underwear and shoes.

Monday, November 27. Łódź.   The situation is deteriorating. Father wants to go. He doesn't want to go alone, however, but there isn't enough money for all of us. We have no income, and they will surely throw us out of the apartment. School is almost useless, and there are rumors about closing it down. I don't know what will happen.

Tuesday, November 28. Łódź.   Mom's crying; Father despairs. We are still hesitating. Father wants to go alone now; on the one hand, he is scared to stay here, but on the other hand, he is scared to leave, not knowing what will happen to us. It's sad in the city. We want to sell everything, but somehow can't find a buyer.

Wednesday, November 29. Łódź.   School is falling apart like an old slipper. Yesterday two men from the Gestapo came to the school at four o'clock. They will be taking the building away from us.

Father wants to go with the Rabinowiczes, who are leaving on Saturday. He intends to go to Białystok.

Thursday, November 30. Łódź.   The school has been taken away. The students help the hired porters. They gave us until tomorrow evening to clear everything out. A deadly feeling; mass looting of the library. Uryson, the librarian, distributed several books to everyone who was present. I got a German history of the Jews, a few copies of German poets, and Latin texts, together with two English books.

At home I learned about a new edict: It's obligatory to pay rent immediately. Not paying is sabotage. A new misfortune. Father has already become completely unstrung.

Friday, December 1. Łódź.   The long-averted Finnish–Soviet war broke out today. But that affair does not concern us as much as the rent. All the neighbors gather for a meeting, but no one can come up with any solution. Father is nervous and cannot leave, not knowing what will happen to us here. If we don't pay all the overdue rent, the eviction will be carried out immediately, and all our things will be seized by the administration. We won't be allowed to take even a thread with us. Father is hastily looking for someone to buy our furniture so that we can pay the rent. Even though nothing can be taken out of the apartment, if we had a down payment from a purchaser, we could pay the rent and give him the furniture. In any case, Father will at least save our underwear. He will take it to Uncle Szlamko, who has paid his rent.

Again "political" rumors begin to circulate. Hamburg is "supposedly" occupied by English airborne troops; Berlin's in flames, the Rhineland in ruins, and Gdańsk on fire. Nice images, but how can they help us?

Saturday, December 2. Łódź.   The Rabinowiczes have left with Marek. Several times Father wanted to go with them at first, but then got hold of himself and stayed. In the afternoon we learned that nearby towns

(Tuszyn, for example) have been completely evacuated. Fortifications will be built there. In the evening, our neighbor Pomeranc hurried over to our place with the news that Gdańsk and Gdynia have been taken over by English army troops. Now, this kind of rumor seems a bit too optimistic. My pessimism, on the other hand, has already become heavy.

Sunday, December 3. Łódź.   The clothing has been taken to my uncle. Yesterday Father put on several shirts and several pairs of socks and long underwear, and took them off over there. Then packages were taken.

In the afternoon I went outside for a while and visited Ela Waldman. She had been chucked out of school, as they do to all the Jews. They also beat Jews terribly in the streets of the city. They usually come up to the Jews who walk by and slap them in the face, kick, spit, etc. Is this evidence that the end for the Germans will probably come soon?

Monday, December 4. Łódź.   Two young men who had left Łódź last week returned today. They brought some really comforting news. In Warsaw they learned about battles between German and . . . Polish (!?) troops near Przemyśl and Lwów. They also heard that the Soviets are mobilizing all the refugees from Poland for the Polish army. What and how? Nobody knows. One of these young men read a French weekly paper dated November 26 with an article by General Sikorski, who assures us that it won't be long until liberation. Very nice prospects, but they seem as fabricated as all the previous rumors and "news." We'll see! There is nothing we can do but wait.

Tuesday, December 5. Łódź.   Today I went downtown to find out what's happening about school. I went to see Epsztajn, from whom I learned that our school will now be located at 28 Południowa Street. We are supposed to come to school at twelve o'clock on Thursday. I also learned that Łęczycki's house has been taken over, and that he has left for his father's in Warsaw. Later on I went to Kahan's, where I exchanged a Hebrew book. I took *Goml Yesharim* by Smoleński. Since it was still early and I was afraid to go back home, I went to Julek Wegmajster's, where I had an opportunity to gulp down dinner with meat, the way a dinner's supposed to be. Holiday!

A new price list has been issued. Officially, bread now costs 1 złoty and 10 groszes (50 groszes in the past), while meat, as a rare commodity, is not listed at all. Evidently it's priceless!

Wednesday, December 6. Łódź.   We lit the first Chanukah "candle." Lacking real candles, Father lit a wick made of twisted cotton wool, stuck into a potato he had hollowed out. An original menorah! All our Jewish neighbors are awaiting a new Chanukah miracle. Maybe the heartfelt prayers of millions of Jews begging for liberation will succeed after all!*

We finally have a buyer for a wardrobe and sofa. He is giving us 130 złotys for both pieces of furniture! (They cost about 350 złotys.) He is a German, but a very decent man, known for his kindness toward Jews. Father is now soliciting the administration for a sales permit, and I wrote an application for "Permission to Sell Furniture in Order to Settle the Rent." They should allow this.

Thursday, December 7. Łódź.   There were no classes today, but those arriving at our new school location were being registered. The rooms are quite nice here, but they are not really suitable for school use. After registering I went to Herszkowicz's. Blausztajn was there as well, and we talked until almost four o'clock.

At home I learned that the Social Security Administration approved the sale of the wardrobe and sofa. Father is constantly upset, however, and instantly gets nervous. I would like to have it done already.

Everybody is surprised that nothing has been heard about Hitler lately. They say that he either is dead or has been removed from power, etc. News about major German air and sea defeats is reaching us. Everybody would like to have reliable information at last. An old Jewish saying: "I need *rachemim*" [Hebrew; mercy].

Friday, December 8. Łódź.   The wardrobe has been taken away at last, and the rent has been settled until December 31. If Jews are allowed to continue living in the buildings here, we can sleep peacefully.

Again, dozens of rumors circulate throughout the city, good and bad. Gossip in any case.

Saturday, December 9. Łódź.   We have learned about a big beating of Jews yesterday on Reymonta Square. In Nowo-Zarzewska Street even three-year-old children were being kicked.

---

* Chanukah, the Jewish "Festival of Lights," celebrates the Jews' victorious fight under the leadership of Judas Maccabeus in 165/164 B.C.E. for liberation from the Syrian-Greeks. The "Chanukah miracle" refers to the one-day portion of lamp oil that burned for eight days in the recaptured and rededicated Temple in Jerusalem. It is commemorated by the daily lighting of candles during the holiday.

The Jews have reached the stage of Messianic prophecies.* A rabbi from Góra Kalwarii supposedly announced that a liberation miracle will happen on the sixth day of Chanukah. My uncle says that very few soldiers and Germans can be seen in the streets. This tendency to take comfort from nothing irritates me. It's better not to say anything.

In the evening a rumor spread about an armistice. England is supposedly demanding from Germany only the return of Austrian, Polish, and Czech lands, with retribution payment for Poland's restoration, in exchange for which England would leave the present government in Germany.

Jews (and Poles) are forbidden to travel by train until February 11. Why? Nobody knows.

Sunday, December 10. Łódź.   A great many buildings in the central district of the city have been "cleansed" of Jews. There are rumors about sending many Jews from Łódź into the Protectorate.† Not a very pleasant prospect.

We received a message from our cousins who left for Białystok. They are in good health there, but they don't have any jobs yet.

Monday, December 11. Łódź.   School is deteriorating. There are no teachers or classes. Everything is vanishing before our eyes.

In the evening we went through hours of fear and anxiety, which turned out to be unnecessary. Father went to a neighbor, Mr. Hamer, and came back in a hurry with news that at six o'clock deportation of the Jews from Łódź would begin. All the neighbors were packing their backpacks, bags, etc. We followed their example, and soon were more or less ready. I said that it was only a rumor and went to sleep. Everyone soon calmed down somewhat and followed my example.

Tuesday, December 12. Łódź.   A horrible day. (At school there are fewer and fewer teachers. I don't even want to attend these substitute readings and shortened classes anymore.) On my way home I suddenly saw a horrible scene near Kilińskiego Street. A German dressed like a

---

* Talmudic writings prophesized a period of terrible chaos and destruction, called "The End of Days," which would precede the coming of the Messiah. Some pious Jews indeed interpreted the onslaught of the Holocaust as the realization of this prophesy, and so as part of their Jewish fate. See Helen Sendyk, *The End of Days* (New York, 1992).

† After the partitioning of Czechoslovakia in March 1939, the Germans referred to the territories of Bohemia and Moravia as the Protectorate.

wagon driver was following a Jew, hitting him on his back with a huge stick so hard that the Jew (who was trying not to turn around, not to be hit in the face) kept bending lower and lower, while the German reeled in his effort. I shuddered and as soon as possible turned onto Cegielni-ana Street. I went to see Frydrych, a friend from the first *gymnasium*, and stayed there until the final hour before curfew, when the chances of being caught are minimal. At Frydrych's I read an order changing the Jewish yellow armbands to yellow 10-centimeter "Stars of David" (*Da-vidstern*) that must be worn on the right chest, and on the back of the right shoulder. The barbarity proceeds. They will soon order us to smear tar on our noses and wear shorts. The ingeniousness of sadism has no limit. New work in the evening: ripping off the armbands and sewing on the new decorations.

Wednesday, December 13. Łódź.   I was not allowed out to school today. Before dinner we had new reason to be fearful and anxious. An hour after Nadzia went to school, Dadek Hamer came to say that the Jews from Nowo-Zarzewska and Rzgowska Streets were being packed into market halls (which were emptied yesterday) and will be sent to Lubelszczyzna [the Lublin area]. Father naturally assumed that they had seized Nadzia (whose school is on Nowo-Zarzewska). Fortunately every-thing turned out to be a rumor, and Nadzia came back safely.

In the evening, however, horrible but real information came. There was a panic in the city because the Jewish Community Council an-nounced that Jews are required to leave Łódź. They say that everyone may go wherever they want (as long as it's not within the boundaries of the Reich) in the next four days. After that a mass deportation will begin. The administration will provide 50 złotys to the poor for the trip, and will start evacuating them today. Everyone's panicking. Backpacks, bags, and suitcases are being stuffed.

Thursday, December 14. Łódź.   It's been three days since the mass arrests began. Thousands of teachers, doctors, and engineers, Jews and Poles, have been taken from their homes, together with their families (infants have not been spared), and hurried to the market halls, and from there to various German jails. All old activists, former legionnaires, even simply rich people share the same fate. Groups of more prominent people are often dispatched immediately into the next world. The repair-man who came to fix the faucet said that his wife and some engineers have been arrested. They could not touch the engineer because he's sick (the last phase of tuberculosis.) So the Germans sealed the apartment with him and his servant inside. They were, for all practical purposes, condemned to death from hunger. His merciful neighbors lowered a string with bread (challah) so the servant could catch it through the window.

In the evening Mrs. Pomeranc came for a visit. She had been to the Jewish Community Council and learned what's really going on. It's true that Łódź is to be cleared of Jews. All the poor who register at the Jewish Community Council receive 50 złotys per person and are literally thrown out of the city: they are taken to Koluszki by train, and are let loose into the world from there.* Mrs. Pomeranc was advised at the Jewish administration to wait. We, too, considered various plans for departure, but in the end nothing came of them, and we have to wait. Either they will throw us out, or they will not . . . In any case, the Hitlerjugendpartei [German; Hitler Youth Party] leader gave a huge speech, and what he said could be summed up in one sentence: "We will exterminate the Jews because there is no place for them in the Reich!"

Friday, December 15. Łódź.   Worse and worse. Last evening Jews were thrown out of several places in the Bałuty district and were deported to the Reich. Nobody knows what happened to them or exactly where they are. Everyone everywhere has their backpacks ready, packed with underclothes and essential clothing and domestic equipment. Everyone is extremely nervous.

Saturday, December 16. Łódź.   My uncle has everything packed, and in the coming days he will leave by cart with his son-in-law and his brothers.

Thousands of carts full of people, bedding, and clothing are continually moving from the city to the Protectorate. There is virtually no room in any car, and a space in any one of them costs thousands of złotys. Half a hundred people are often packed onto a single truck for the trip to Warsaw, for example, and everyone pays up to 10,000 złotys. All this just for us!

In the evening the news came that the deportation will be stopped, and talks on the subject are being conducted.

* See Oskar Rosenfeld, "The First Mass Deportations of Jews from Łódź," in *Łódź Ghetto: Inside a Community Under Siege,* edited by Alan Adelson and Robert Lapides (New York, 1989), p. 27. The Nazis had determined that there were too many Jews in the city to be concentrated in the ghetto to be established in the northern sector.

Sunday, December 17. Łódź.   Yesterday's information appears to be true. Jews may stay in Łódź until March 1. After that, departure!

Eighty infants, all frozen to death, were supposedly brought to Łódź from Koluszki today. They were the children of deported Jews.

Monday, December 18. Łódź.   I wanted to go downtown to find out about school, but Mom wouldn't let me. I'm not sure whether I should do my schoolwork at home by myself or wait until after the break. The frost is intensifying.

Tuesday, December 19. Łódź.   I've been downtown. There are lots of soldiers in the streets going home for the holidays. The school was closed, so I dropped in on a friend who lives on our courtyard.* I learned from him that many teachers were arrested; many others, as well as many students, managed to escape. The upper grades were merged into one class, and everyone was sent home with a certificate that they were students of this or that grade as of such a date. The other friend I visited was not at school either. Everyone in the city is packed.

I came back home in a sour mood, still not knowing what to do. Tomorrow the winter vacation begins.

Wednesday, December 20. Łódź.   Citizen registration cards requiring information about food, and food coupons, have been handed out in our buildings. They are supposed to be filled out by the superintendents, but it's not always done that way, and I myself had to fill out these cards in German. It was the first time I made use of my knowledge of German, but I used the Latin alphabet.

Thursday, December 21. Łódź.   I'm still bored at home. I go over to my friends', but it doesn't help. I study languages before dinner, and I read in the evening. I am not sure whether to start my schoolwork on my own, or to wait for the beginning of school.

Friday, December 22. Łódź.   I scrubbed the floor today. I did not want Mom to tire herself out because of her arthritis, and besides, I got 15 pf [German; pfennig] for my job! Everybody is amazed at the thoroughness of my work.

---

* An architectural feature characteristic of Łódź clustered numerous buildings around single courtyards.

Saturday, December 23. Łódź.   Reichminister Goebbels gave a speech yesterday. I think that he is slowly preparing his nation for defeat by saying that "either we will be destroyed, or we'll win."

The Christmas holidays are sad and humble this year. All our Christian neighbors complain that they don't have any food for the holidays. The prices of meat and lard are becoming more and more unreal. Butter: 12 złotys a kilo; goose meat: 9 złotys a kilo; beef: 6 złotys a kilo; and so on. Everything is three to four times more expensive than before the war. It does not matter to us anyway, since we would not have enough money for these products even if they cost their regular prewar price.

Sunday, December 24. Łódź.   Only now are the murders of more prominent people among the Łódź Germans being brought to light. Obituaries have been posted about the deaths of Robert Geyer* and Guido John, well-known Łódź factory owners. They "died" on December 12! They are said to have been murdered in a cruel and elaborate way.

Monday, December 25. Łódź.   A Soviet delegation has arrived in Łódź, charged with exchanging the German population from the Polish areas taken over by the Soviets for the Ukrainians and Byelorussians who live here. There is hope that the Jews who were born in those districts will also be exchanged, but I think they won't because there would be too many candidates.

Tuesday, December 26. Łódź.   They don't accept Jews. Our weak hopes, arising because of Mom's origin,† have fallen through.

A very hard frost has come. Naturally, not as hard as in Finland, where the fighting has stopped because of the −38 degree [−36°F] frost. It's only −12 degrees [1°F] here. The vacation time weighs heavily on me.

Wednesday, December 27. Łódź.   The conviction that Hitler has died or has been removed from power is growing more certain. Everybody won-

---

* Robert Geyer (1880–1939), a wealthy textile manufacturer who opposed the Nazis, may have been put to death months earlier. See Dobroszycki, *Chronicle of the Łódź Ghetto*, p. xxiv.
† Records found by journalist Konrad Turowski in the Polish National Archive in Łódź indicate that Dawid's mother, whose maiden name was Sura Churgel, was born in Rubieżowice, near Pinsk. The region had passed from Polish into Russian rule, and was then integrated into Poland in 1918 when the country regained its independence. Dawid's father, Majłech Sierakowiak, was born in Łódź.

ders why he hasn't been heard from. He hasn't uttered a single word since fall. There are also rumors about fighting on the western front and on the North Sea, where England is desperately attempting to land. The remnants of the Polish army are supposedly trying to severely damage the Germans in the Carpathian Mountains and are carrying on a relentless guerrilla war.*

Thursday, December 28. Łódź.   Void, boredom, nothing specific is known. For practice, I read a German newspaper from cover to cover. The most interesting things are the short stories, essays, and advertisements. Except for these, there's nothing to it.

Friday, December 29. Łódź.   The frost is intensifying. The temperature reached 17 degrees below zero today. Fear seizes me at the mere thought of being thrown out into such cold. Brr . . .

Saturday, December 30. Łódź.   The newspaper says today that if someone wants Jews for work assignments, he has to go to the Jewish Community Council, and they will deliver the workforce on demand.† It appears, however, that nobody will heed it and they will still seize people for work.

Sunday, December 31. Łódź.   The last day of the year 1939, a year that began in tension and ended in war. All that's left for us is the sincere wish that the new year, beginning a new decade, will be better and brighter. It appears, however, that the new year certainly won't be any better than the old one, and it will probably be even worse. The war will take time, as will the German occupation. Who knows what's ahead of us and what will happen or change in the world? *Shana tova* [Hebrew; Good Year, Happy New Year].

* The rumors Dawid reports of fierce guerrilla fighting by units of the former Polish army could well have been based on truth, though subject to exaggeration. While the Polish army broke up in late 1939, many of its soldiers found their way into various Partisan units that continued to fight and harass the Germans through the course of the war. Jewish fugitives hiding in the same heavily forested areas and swamp lands where the Partisans were encamped never knew if a particular brigade would lend them assistance or behave as murderously as the Nazis. See Shalom Yoran, *The Defiant* (New York, 1996), and Miriam Kuperhand and Saul Kuperhand, *In the Shadow of Treblinka: Long Days, Dark Nights* (Urbana: University of Illinois Press, forthcoming).
† See note with diary entry of October 8, 1939.

Never-ending hunger

Sunday, April 6. Łódź.   I'm beginning a new notebook of my diary, and thus dare to express the wish that it will become the start of a new, brighter, and better period in my life than the one I covered in the preceding notebook. That seems just another pipe dream, though. In spite of a gorgeous (and expensive) holiday food ration, the situation remains as tragic as before.* There's no hope for improvement.

Monday, April 7. Łódź.   We know now how much matzoth will cost. 2.5 kilos (a portion for one person for the eight days of Passover) will be as much as 3 RM [German, Reichsmark], 25 pf. And that's only rye flour, after all. For religious and sentimental reasons, mother would prefer to have matzoth, but can't afford it, so we'll obviously have to eat bread during Passover. Anyway, we are selling bread to buy our food allowance. Our holiday starvation will be identical to what we experience every other day of the week.

Tuesday, April 8. Łódź.   Something is finally beginning to happen in international affairs. Germany has declared war on Yugoslavia and Greece for having let in English troops. There is also heavy fighting in Africa. The Jews are hoping that the Balkans will bring us liberation, but I don't share this feeling at all, and simply wonder how much time the Germans will need to capture Yugoslavia and Greece.

Wednesday, April 9. Łódź.   The weather is still nasty. It's cold, and raining almost incessantly; absolutely no sign of the sun. It looks like there won't be any spring this year. I just hope that such weather won't have a tragic effect on the harvests.

This week I wrote an article about the plight of school youths for a newspaper organized by the textile workers' association (Communists). I handed it in today, but it seems to me that before anything comes of it (there are enormous technical problems), the article will be out of date.

Thursday, April 10. Łódź.   Rysiek Podlaski sent his brother to me with a note urging me to go immediately to the tailor workshop where his father is the manager. I will be able to earn a few marks there. I went right

---

* No notebook covering the first four months of 1941 has been recovered. During that time, the Sierakowiak family, along with all the Jews remaining in Łòdź, were forced into the area designated by the Germans as the Litzmannstadt Ghetto.

away, and, indeed, I got a job from Podlaski for a few days as a 2-mark laborer apportioning and weighing vegetables for workshop workers. My job is to deliver and distribute rutabagas and carrots in equal allotments. Every day I will get an additional dinner (for 20 pf).

Friday, April 11. Łódź.   I worked from eight in the morning until six in the evening. We portioned out over 3,000 kilos of rutabagas. The work is hard, but not overly strenuous. The only thing that irritates me is the system of connections employed by people doing the weighing to favor clerks and other parasites in workshops. An enormous line of tailors must wait their turn, but when a young lady from an administrative office arrives, she receives her portion without waiting. On top of that, her portion is "of the right weight" and the best quality. I have also noticed that a policeman who supervises weighing, or clerks, commissioners (of the police), or other parasites, have several coupons each. And when the policeman's maid (I know her, but pretend to have no idea who she is) comes with a single coupon for rutabagas, the policeman pretends that he doesn't know her and cleverly orders that she be given two portions for two coupons, while sticking only one coupon on the spindle. Well, what can you do? This is the rotten, bourgeois-bureaucratic basis on which the ghetto exists, and on which it will perish.

Saturday, April 12. Łódź.   The first day of Passover. Although there is no official holiday as a result of the German occupation, we don't work today. The holiday hardly exists in reality, though: the same food as previously, and hunger's everywhere. It also continues to be cold.

Just as I expected, the Germans have broken through the front line in the Balkans, and gained enormous victories in Yugoslavia, Greece, and Africa. In the near future they will become the overlords of all of Europe, excluding, of course, the Soviets.

Sunday, April 13. Łódź.   I worked all day long again. Since we do not cook at home anymore, we went for dinner to the restaurant where we have registered with our food coupons. Dinners there are poor, so after

The weather is still nasty. It's cold, and raining almost incessantly; absolutely no sign of the sun. It looks like there won't be any spring this year.

Passover we will register with the community kitchen. They have better dinners (bigger and richer), and they're cheaper (15 pf). Dinners in the workshop (here, just like everywhere else, "dinner" means a single portion of soup) are usually good and rich, but these days they are "holiday specials," which means they contain no barley, negatively affecting their thickness.

Monday, April 14. Łódź.   We finished the distribution of rutabagas in the afternoon, and then there was no more work. I am already acquainted with everybody and everything in the workshop. They try to please me in every way in order to receive a better grade of rutabagas or carrots. Podlaski has promised me that I will receive a coupon for rutabagas. In addition, almost every day after a full day of "marketing," I manage to secure a rutabaga from the policeman.

Tuesday, April 15. Łódź.   Two carts with carrots arrived in the ghetto today. I went with the policeman to the vegetable market for them. We won't apportion the load until tomorrow.

Continuous clouds, rain, and cold wind; summer will pass this year in a single day.

Wednesday, April 16. Łódź.   On Friday an announcement was posted for the voluntary registration of men, eighteen to forty-five, and women, twenty to thirty, for labor in Germany. On Saturday all those who ever registered for labor but have not yet left began receiving notifications to report immediately for departure. Several thousand persons have left. They are probably lucky beggars with better chances to survive the war than we in the ghetto. All the letters that arrive from those sent out for labor assure us about satiety there ("We can eat, eat, and eat again"), something that's no longer experienced in the ghetto.*

---

* The Nazis regularly claimed that deportations from the ghetto were to provide labor for camps in Germany and elsewhere. In most cases, the actual destination was Chełmno, in Poland's Koło County, where the deportees from Łódź were held in a small church in town, and then driven in vans that asphyxiated them on the way to a field in a nearby forest where the bodies were dumped and burned. The Nazis sought to avoid future resistance by compelling some deportees to write fictitious letters and postcards back to the ghetto before putting the Jews to death—a fate that many by then had realized they would be facing, if only by reading the words that others had scratched into the woodwork and altar of the church. Using Yiddish words, some deportees cleverly concealed warnings in their postcards to those still in the ghetto (for example, "Send our regards to Uncle Death"). For a discussion of how the Germans confused the ghetto dwellers further by mixing cards from Chełmno with others written by those actually sent to labor in Germany or in one of the conquered territories, see Lucjan Dobroszycki, *The Chronicle of the Łódź Ghetto* (New Haven, Conn., 1984), p. xix.

Thursday, April 17. Łódź.   We distributed carrots yesterday. I was free today because a new load did not arrive.

Since a lot of matzoth was left, Rumkowski decided to give an extra treat to workers and clerks in the administration. He gave each worker a package of matzoth for the nominal price of 3 RM, 25 pf. Father received one package at his workplace, and I received one in mine. We sold one of the packages for 11 RM! This is the kind of *Geschäft* [German; trade] that can be made in the ghetto! The matzoth is hard and darker than the wheat one, but considering our hunger, it's simply wonderful.

Friday, April 18. Łódź.   There are no more carrots in the ghetto at all. Those people who haven't yet received carrots for their food coupons will now get rutabagas instead.

School is going to be reopened next week. Only a part of it though, for those boys and girls who live on our side of the bridge.* For the time being, only the upper grades will be taught in a small building in Marysin. They say that extra nutrition will be given in the school, but nothing certain is known yet.

Saturday, April 19. Łódź.   The last day of the "holidays." There is no work, only rain. I'm wandering around, idling all day long. Together with a group of friends, Communists, we've started to learn Esperanto.† The language is awfully easy, simple, and logically constructed. The vocabulary is absolutely clear to me because it comes from languages that I already know or that I'm learning. And as for grammar, it's just fun. I prepare lessons and give them to our circle.

Monday, April 21. Łódź.   It's still cold, and we can't get out of our winter garb. It's raining and drizzling incessantly. Meanwhile, the Germans move farther and farther on. They have captured almost all of Yugoslavia and Greece, and gain enormous victories in Africa. They also bomb England heavily, but—as the Jews say by way of consolation—they get bombed, too. It's a poor consolation, though. It looks like the war will drag on for many more years.

Tuesday, April 22. Łódź.   Rumkowski has come up with a splendid idea to prevent the workers in the bread cooperatives from eating on the

---

* The ghetto consisted of sections connected by bridges over the restricted-access "Aryan" thoroughfares.
† Invented by Polish philologist Ludwig L. Zamenhof in 1887, the language was intended to give all cultures a common means of communicating.

job. Starting tomorrow a 2-kilo loaf of bread will be given to each person as a ration for five days. This way, weighing, slicing, and eating bread will be avoided in the cooperatives. Furthermore, the private sale of wood (which usually comes from the theft of fence parts, latrines, and all other wooden structures in the ghetto that have not yet been torn down by the ghetto administration) will be prohibited. Wood now costs 80 pf a kilo. (It's been months since the last allocation of coal was issued, and the last time Rumkowski gave wood was in the beginning of February.) So we will again have to satisfy ourselves with a single soup a day from the community kitchen because even though our supplementary allocations include potatoes, barley, and vegetables, we will have nothing to cook them with. If they don't beat us with a stick, they'll beat us with a club. The inevitability of death by starvation grows more evident.

School is going to be reopened next week. Only a part of it though, for those boys and girls who live on our side of the bridge. . . . They say that extra nutrition will be given in the school, but nothing certain is known yet.

Also tomorrow the administration is instituting an action to clean up the ghetto to protect us from epidemics. It is about time.

I have registered at the school secretariat at Dworska Street. On Sunday, the third and fourth levels will be reopened for the students living on our side of the bridge. The *gymnasium* is located at 6 Smugowa Street. There will be additional nutrition in school, but details won't be known until Friday. So I'll go to school again (of course, only if I don't have some other job to do). There will finally be an end to the anarchy in my daily activities and, I hope, an end to too much philosophizing and depression.

Wednesday, April 23. Łódź.   It's constantly cold and rainy. I don't think there was one single sunny day during this unfortunate year. I still don't have any work to do because the rutabagas haven't arrived yet. It certainly makes the people furious because they've been waiting for two weeks. Although I did not have any work to do, I ran to the workshop almost every hour to learn whether the rutabagas arrived, whether they needed me. It took me almost the whole day, and of course they will not pay me for it.

Thursday, April 24. Łódź.   Rutabagas have finally arrived, and I worked all day. I received my coupon and was able to take my portion before the "finishing off" of the load.

Friday, April 25. Łódź.   We've finally finished distributing the rutabagas, but it means that my job has ended. I have just found out that we will not be paid for the number of days we worked, but for the total amount of rutabagas we distributed. Thus I can't count on more than 10 to 12 RM for those two full weeks of running around.

Saturday, April 26. Łódź.   School starts at nine o'clock tomorrow. We'll have five months to cover the fourth grade at best, and it's a whole lot of material. I only hope that no new obstacles will get in our way.

Sunday, April 27. Łódź.   The first day of school. The trip to Marysin is quite long, but the worst thing about it is the awful mud from the incessant rain. I must cross all kinds of fields, and my shoes are in terrible shape. They are beginning to "go," but any repair is out of the question. I suppose I'll soon have to rush to school barefoot.

The school is located in a tiny building that can hardly hold our benches. There are no other supplies (not even a blackboard). Nor is there a cloakroom, and we sit in the classroom wearing our coats. We had six classes today. During the last class, Rumkowski himself arrived for a visit accompanied by Praszkier,* Karo† (the "minister" of educa-tion), and a number of other ghetto "dignitaries." Rumkowski toured the kitchen, tasted the soup (which was simply delicious, probably for his sake), and addressed the students. He spoke about the difficulties connected with opening the school, and said he will try to get more for us; he demanded that we work diligently, keep clean, and behave well.

After Rumkowski's speech (incidentally, he has grown fat and looks incredibly younger) I went up to Praszkier, director of the Kitchen De-partment, to find out about my application, which he was supposed to submit to the president‡ for me. He informed me that I won't get the job because my role is to study (!), and that Mom will be the one who will receive a job from him. I wonder if he will keep his word this time. I have not been paying for the soup for several months because I was officially allowed to register for subsidy. But we are not eligible anymore, since Father's earnings exceed the allowed amount. So now again, study, study, study.

Monday, April 28. Łódź.   The Germans win one victory after another. The fighting in Yugoslavia and Greece is coming to an end, and the last English troops are leaving in a hurry; in Africa, where Germans are arriving through France (using French ships to reach French Tunis), the English are beginning to take heavy losses. Although they talk again about tensions in German–Soviet relations, these are naturally only consoling rumors. The Devil has taken too much of a hold over us, and nothing good can happen very soon in the world. We will certainly suffer much more here.

---

* Boruch Praszkier was Rumkowski's "special assignments" chief. His initial assignment of establishing and overseeing the ghetto's network of soup kitchens was later extended, ironically, to the administration of the ghetto's cemetery, which, as Dawid describes, was also much in demand.

† Presumably Mojżesz Karo, who shared responsibility for overseeing the ghetto's elemen-tary, trade, and middle schools, educating between 7,000 and 15,000 pupils.

‡ As the titular head of the ghetto's "Council of Elders" (a body that barely functioned since the Nazis required only one administrator), Rumkowski was often referred to as the president or the chairman.

Tuesday, April 29. Łódź.   Classes at school have been good from the outset. Every day we have six solid lessons, even though the conditions in which the classes are held are still very uncomfortable.

This is the second month of incessant rain and extreme cold. Even the oldest people in the ghetto can't remember such a bad spring, but if the days were hot, on the other hand, who knows how many epidemics there might be in the ghetto. In this respect spring is passing relatively calmly, even though fears are enormous . . .

Wednesday, April 30. Łódź.   After a long period of inactivity, we had a meeting of the Politburo to discuss an immediate return to regular work in our union. We've decided to call the first meeting of male units for Friday, and to aggressively wipe out laziness, tardiness, and passivity toward work. During the winter period, despite the hiatus in our activities, we've become a committed element of the political movement in the ghetto; we participate now in all youth and adult groups. Niutek Radzyner, as our representative, is now connected with the leftist movement in the ghetto, and we maintain close contact with everyone through him. We've also made real progress in our theoretical education. May we live to have the chance to make good use of our knowledge.

Thursday, May 1. Łódź.   Churchill spoke this week. He acknowledged the defeats England has suffered, but in discussing the war's future prospects, he concluded that the final victory will be England's. The impression his speech gave is, however, that the war will take many more years, if it ever ends at all.

Even wood sold secretly costs only 50 to 60 pf. If the situation remains like this, we will survive the remaining weeks until the new harvest.

The situation in the ghetto has improved recently in certain respects. The food allocations are substantial, and if you just have a job and money to buy your rations, you can eat more than during the winter. The products sold on the streets have also gotten cheaper: a loaf of bread is now only (!) 2.20 RM, a kilo of potatoes is 60 pf, and a kilo of barley, 4 RM. Too bad that we don't have cash to buy it all.

Friday, May 2. Łódź.   We had a meeting of male units in our organization. It was very successful, promising fruitful cooperation. Niutek

Radzyner* discussed the May 1 holiday, I discussed organizational matters, and toward the end of the meeting Niutek gave a lecture on youths in the proletariat revolutionary movement. A very lively discussion followed, from which everyone benefited greatly.

We continue to receive whole loaves of bread for our food rations, but now they check the weight carefully and, if needed, deduct or add the amount that the loaf's short. In any case, the loaf distribution system is no good. The portion of bread I receive won't feed me for more than two or three days; after that my stomach's empty, and all I can think of is the next loaf of bread.

Saturday, May 3. Łódź.   It has snowed all day. Enormous transports of workers are leaving again for work in Germany. Everyone between eighteen and forty-five who had not registered yet received departure notices. I wonder whether another registration will occur.

We had a meeting with one of the women's groups to discuss the necessity of dictatorship and a centralized proletariat government. We managed to defend the Soviet-government line successfully.

Sunday, May 4. Łódź.   It's damned cold. Even though the snow we had yesterday disappeared as quickly as it fell, the cold continues, and it rained again. Most agricultural work in Marysin and on all garden plots has come to a standstill. Nearly all the fields in the ghetto are already plowed, planted, or parceled out by the administration. Quite a wise idea. The grounds around our school are supposed to be cultivated by the students. We have to work for our education . . . I don't mind the work, though, because I'll get to know the soil a little better. Everything may yet prove useful . . .

Monday, May 5. Łódź.   For all my work with those vegetables in the workshop, I finally received only 12 RM. Well, even that will help. The most important thing is that Praszkier has kept his word, and Mom has received a job as a peeler in a communal kitchen. She works fourteen to

---

* Nataniel Radzyner (b. 1925), was one of the leading organizers of the underground Communist youth in the ghetto. Lucjan Dobroszycki describes Radzyner as an "Auschwitz prisoner" in *Dziennik. Dawid Sierakowiak* (Warsaw, 1960), p. 25. But he survived and lived out his life in Vienna, Austria. The date of his death is unavailable.

*The grounds around our school are supposed to be cultivated by the
students. We have to work for our education . . . I don't mind the
work, though, because I'll get to know the soil a little better.
Everything may yet prove useful . . .*

fifteen hours a day, and her salary is supposed to be 20 to 25 RM a
month. The main advantage is that she will receive the workers' two
substantial soups a day for free. So at least Mom won't starve; at home
we will also be better off.

Tuesday, May 6. Łódź.   It keeps raining, and it's still bitter cold. This is
the third month that we've had such awful weather. There is no hope for
spring, which is almost over anyway.

   At school our studying proceeds at a rapid pace. The soup they cook
for us here, though not too rich or thick because of the general lack of
potatoes in the ghetto, provides an excellent shot of energy during
classes. After all, the long trip to Marysin wears us down terribly.

Wednesday, May 7. Łódź.   If a loaf happens to fall short of 2 kilos, you can get the rest in the head bakery office. Lines are enormous there because no one will give up a single dekagram these days. You starve enough even with a full bread portion of 40 dekagrams, so you won't sacrifice even a bit.

Thursday, May 8. Łódź.   Extremely interesting news: Molotov has resigned as premier and commissar of the Foreign Office, and both posts have been taken by Stalin! Molotov is now a deputy premier. I wonder if this arrangement will bring any political change. In any case, Germany is getting ready to invade either Spain or Russia. But it seems to me that, as Churchill put it, "the first snowstorm on the Russian steppes will be the beginning of Hitler's end."

We had a Politburo meeting at which four of our members were elected to the all-youth unit of lecturers: Niutek Radzyner, Jerzyk Rapaport,* Szyjo Sonnabend,† and I. First we'll discuss Lenin's famous work, *State and Revolution,* and then we'll lecture on it to all other active youth units in the ghetto.

Friday, May 9. Łódź.   I have started studying Mehring's *Karl Marx;* extremely interesting. I also work intensively on economics.

I met one of my former students. He wants to review the first grade of the *gymnasium* curriculum, but the pay his family offers is awful. All they would give me is 1.50 RM for six lessons a week. I want a minimum of 40 pf an hour, and I'm not going to give up even a single pfennig. I still value the little remaining energy that I have. I will get their answer on Sunday morning.

Saturday, May 10. Łódź.   Before noon I went to the May 1 celebration (which was in fact a bit overdue). Comrade Ziula Krengiel‡ gave a speech, and in her splendid lecture she discussed the meaning of the May 1 holiday; she also discussed the observance of the holiday in the

---

* Jerzy Rapaport (b. 1925) survived deportation to Auschwitz. According to Dobroszycki in *Dziennik. Dawid Sierakowiak,* Rapaport died "tragically" in 1947, but the cause of death is not given.
† Szyjo Sonnabend (1924–1942) died in the ghetto of tuberculosis.
‡ Rachela Krengiel-Pacanowska (1904–1942), a teacher in the ghetto *gymnasium,* was a central figure in organizing a Communist organization in the ghetto. She was deported in 1942 to Chełmno, very possibly a direct victim of Rumkowski's policy of using the Nazis' deportation quotas to eliminate what he commonly called the "troublemakers" in the ghetto. She was put to death in an asphyxiation van. In 1958, Polish Communist officials honored her posthumously with a ceremony and a medal.

Soviet Union, and finally pointed to the need to hold out and survive the ghetto. She spoke of being ready to act and fight.

In the afternoon we had a meeting with girls, during which our most active members (Niutek, Jerzyk, and I) had a difficult time explaining the concept of surplus value. We have eventually been totally successful, though, and generally our work is proceeding very well.

Sunday, May 11. Łódź.   It's raining constantly, and it absolutely won't get warm this year. I feel awful and look worse and worse. I hear that it's hard to recognize me.

I haven't yet accepted the tutoring, and am waiting for an answer. It will probably be positive because, although I obstinately want 40 pf, the price is in fact low, and I don't think anyone would be willing to review the *gymnasium* curriculum for less.

Monday, May 12. Łódź.   What sensational news! Rudolf Hess, Hitler's deputy, escaped to England in his plane. The Germans say that he went crazy, and it seems to be the most logical explanation. But is this really so? No one is able to provide a definite answer. The English and Germans don't give any more detailed explanations either. In any case, it's produced a great furor.

Tuesday, May 13. Łódź.   Hess is in a hospital for POWs in England. The Germans proclaimed him a traitor and a madman, while the English don't say anything in particular. In Germany, arrests of persons who were close to Hess have begun, even reaching down to the party's lowest levels. Naturally, the Jews in the ghetto are full of hope.

Rumkowski is leaving for Warsaw to bring doctors,* and is reorganizing the food-distribution system in the ghetto. The number of food cooperatives is increasing; separate vegetable units are being created, while the bread and other food units are being combined. Creation of new squares, lawns, and even cobblestone and construction works completes the "Spring Program" in the ghetto, marching in "glory on the road of ascent and highest achievement."

---

* "My ghetto is like a small kingdom," Rumkowski said in a speech given in the Warsaw Ghetto. "Many things can be achieved . . . Work is the best blessing . . . Through dictatorship I earned the Germans' respect" ("Dictatorship Is Not a Dirty Word," in *Łódź Ghetto: Inside a Community Under Siege,* edited by Alan Adelson and Robert Lapides [New York, 1989], pp. 145–47). For a rebuttal by Dr. Israel Milejkowski, see "The Evil of the Ghetto," p. 147.

A student from the same grade as ours died from hunger and exhaustion yesterday. As a result of his terrible appearance, he was allowed to eat as much soup in school as he wanted, but it didn't help him much; he's the third victim in the class.

Wednesday, May 14. Łódź. On the teachers' council's initiative, a meeting of delegates from all classes was called today to organize the student board (all members of the teachers' council were also present). Niutek Radzyner and I have been elected from our class.

This was the first meeting in my life when I had to be an outspoken, stormy oppositionist and scrap with higher authority, namely, with the student board's superintendent, Prentka* (our German-language teacher). A proposal was put forward to consider the problem of additional nutrition (double portions of soup for those particularly weakened by hunger). Prentka, however, ordered us to reject discussion of these endeavors, and to consider the more important (!?) matter of students' responsibilities! I protested and declared that additional nutrition for students before their death seems to be a worthwhile cause to me, and that immediate resolution of the issue is our most urgent problem. It went on like this until the principal adjourned the meeting because of the late hour. I protested once again and declared that I considered the meeting void because its agenda and course had been imposed. Prentka got furious, and other teachers wrangled with me, but tomorrow I hope to push my proposal through.

Thursday, May 15. Łódź. I won! Despite Prentka's fury, the nutrition problem was discussed at the outset. The newly formed seven-member committee, under my leadership, is supposed to deal with the problem immediately. The student board has decided to file an application immediately to the Kitchen Department asking for additional soup portions for us. Furthermore, the board established a student militia, and considered the problem of hygiene and the collection of money for self-help purposes.

The weather is nice at last, though it's not quite warm yet. Winter coats still hang on our backs. And the story with Hess, like all other sensations of recent months, has somehow been quickly forgotten. As if to spite us, nothing will happen! . . .

---

* Maria Prentka was deported to Auschwitz in the final liquidation of the ghetto in 1944. Her fate is not known.

I protested and declared that additional nutrition for students before their death seems to be a worthwhile cause to me, and that immediate resolution of the issue is our most urgent problem.

Friday, May 16. Łódź. I have been examined by a doctor at school. She was terrified at how thin I am. She immediately gave me a referral for X rays. Perhaps I will now be able to get a double portion of soup in school. In fact, five such soups would be even better, but the two will do me some good, too. In any case, one soup is nothing.

The checkup has left me frightened and worried. Lung disease is the latest hit in ghetto fashion; it sweeps people away as much as dysentery and typhus. As for the food, it's worse and worse everywhere; it's been a week since there were any potatoes.

Niutek Radzyner has turned to me with an original suggestion. Together with Jerzyk Rapaport, Sonnabend, and Fredek Taub (they are the best members of our organization), he has formed a close group, nearly a commune, in which (in addition to their general work in the organization) they discuss many theories (Marx's *Capital*, Lenin's works). Niutek wants me to join them. It would lead to very close personal contact, which I am not used to. I agreed, but I wonder what will come of it. In any case, it's an interesting undertaking, and I'm sure I will profit a lot.

Saturday, May 17. Łódź.   They sent for me to accept the tutoring we talked about last week. I will probably receive 1.50 RM to 1.60 RM for four lessons a week. It will come in handy. I just hope that I will be able to manage my entire schedule: Marysin, tutoring, organization work, political theory, languages, books. The main thing is to have the strength to survive. But that won't come from 40 dkg [dekagrams] of bread a day.

In the afternoon I attended the next part of Comrade Garnfinkiel's* lecture on world literature. He discussed decadence and positivism.

In politics there's nothing special, unless you consider the rumor about arrests in Germany, etc. Hess has given the English General Staff the secrets he brought with him.

The sun shines for barely half a day, and after that it pours again. What a cursed time, in every respect! . . .

Sunday, May 18. Łódź.   Niutek's Communist composition on Radek† from *Sysyphean Labors* became a hit in our class and gave us the idea to publish a class newspaper. We also want to publish a newspaper for all the Communist youths in the ghetto. I wonder which of these projects will come off.

I've had the first lesson with my student. There is an awful lot of work to do. Blausztajn has promised to arrange the X ray for me quickly, something that is very hard to do in the ghetto. If I can just be healthy, then everything will be all right.

Monday, May 19. Łódź.   I've received 10 RM through someone from Łęczycki in Warsaw. It's a godsend. I'll spend some of the money to have my shoes repaired, and the rest, together with Father's and Mom's wages, will buy our food rations. As of today I receive two soups in school. It does make me feel better.

---

* Feliks Garnfinkiel was a poet. He, too, was deported to Auschwitz in the final liquidation in August 1944. His fate is unknown.
† Radek is a character in the novel mentioned, the first to be published (in 1897) by prominent Polish novelist Stefan Żeromski (1864–1925).

We had a Politburo meeting in the evening. I have been delegated to attend an all-youth sociology course, and we've settled a number of local matters. The most important things are schoolwork and studying Marxist theory.

Tuesday, May 20. Łódź. Before noon we had a meeting of male groups, during which I gave my short lecture on Comrade Wolf's* paper about materialism in the eighteenth century. Then in the evening we had the first meeting of the youth lecturers' unit. (We, the *gymnasium* students, compose the majority; the meeting was run by Comrade Gienia).† We discussed the question of the essence of the state, and its class structure—the issues examined in the first chapter of Lenin's *State and Revolution,* which we studied individually earlier.

Wednesday, May 21. Łódź. Rumkowski has returned from Warsaw. He brought twelve physicians back with him, and announced that antiaircraft equipment will be readied and antiaircraft defenses will be organized.

There are no new food allocations at all, and the soup in the communal kitchens is becoming thinner and thinner. There is no barley or potatoes at all, and we are already running out of vegetables in the ghetto.

We've had another meeting of a unit of lecturers. We discussed the difference between a proletariat revolution and a bourgeois-democratic one.

Thursday, May 22. Łódź. I had an awful day. Just before leaving for school I tried to cut a piece of bread, and literally cut off a piece of my finger. So much blood was gushing that I had to rush to an emergency room, where I had my finger dressed. It was already so late by then that I decided not to go to school. I lost a lot of blood and also the two soups I receive in school, "thanks" to my awful look. I really feel dreadful.

In the emergency room I witnessed the arrival of a Jew who had been shot in his side. Two Germans were parading in the streets of the ghetto, battering and shooting. They killed one Jew and wounded another. What luck!

Friday, May 23. Łódź. My finger is not too well. I think it's beginning to fester. I hope it will heal soon.

---

* Wolf Goldberg, a leader in the underground organization, was deported to Auschwitz in August 1944.
† Gienia Szlak (1908–1944), a worker in the ghetto, was deported to Auschwitz in the final deportations from the ghetto in August 1944.

It's nice and warm. Winter's gone, but unfortunately the war remains. We got our first mathematics tests back. I got an A-minus. Niutek Radzyner's project cannot be realized now because I am too weak and too busy. I finally have the lessons: four times a week for 1.50 RM.

Saturday, May 24. Łódź.   I've been catching up with classes all day today. I'm damnably hungry because there isn't even a trace left of the small loaf of bread that was supposed to feed me through Tuesday. I console myself that I'm not the only one in such a dire situation. When I receive my ration of bread, I can hardly control myself and sometimes suffer so much from exhaustion that I have to eat whatever food I have, and then my small loaf of bread disappears before the next ration is issued, and my torture grows. But what can I do? There's no help. Our grave will apparently be here.

Sunday, May 25. Łódź.   It's really like May now. Even though the emaciated, famished people (like me) can't yet afford to fully "summerize" their garb, winter coats have finally been put away. It's already dry everywhere, and the smell of spring in Marysin makes your heart break with the memory of prewar times. In normal times we would now be three weeks away from the *gymnasium* pregraduation exams, and the longed-for vacation. There would certainly be an excursion and after that a camping trip or a visit to the country. Damn it! You feel like crying when you remember those things. Blast it!

Monday, May 26. Łódź.   At school everything proceeds normally. We're working on Cicero's often-praised speech against Cataline, and will start metrics next week; in mathematics we're doing exponential equations, and before long we'll start on the measurement of volumes. We are falling behind in other subjects, though not in German. Dinners in school are relatively substantial, and my extra portion of soup comes in awfully handy. Even five such portions would not be too much. A school paper is being organized. I've submitted a caricature for it, and perhaps one of my articles in Yiddish will be accepted as well. (All the others I wrote turned out to be unacceptable to the censors. The ghetto has its own precisely formulated bourgeois ideology.)

Even though Mom has a job, things are not too well at home. She leaves at seven and comes back at nine in the evening. Father works from eight to eight. So all our housekeeping falls on Nadzia's shoulders; she takes care of all the food lines, cleaning, etc., and she performs all these efforts, having only one soup and 30 dkg of bread a day. (Just like

When I receive my ration of bread, I can hardly control myself and sometimes I suffer so much from exhaustion that I have to eat whatever food I have, and then my small loaf of bread disappears before the next ration is issued, and my torture grows.

Mom, she gives away 10 dkg of her bread to Father. He doesn't know, however, how to appreciate it, and his attitude toward them is bad and reveals unmitigated egotism, just as it does toward me.)*

We don't cook at home anymore because we have nothing to cook. We can't get any potatoes because they are not available in the ghetto. Any increase in the daily portion of bread is beyond hope.

Tuesday, May 27. Łódź.   Everybody is anxiously awaiting Roosevelt's speech, which was scheduled for today. People are saying that it was on May 27 that the United States declared war on Germany in 1917. Unfor-

---

* Majłech Sierakowiak's relationship with his son, Dawid, appears to have been showing some signs of strain before the family was forced into the ghetto as well. Cecylia Felisiak, a former neighbor of the Sierakowiak family, told journalist Konrad Turowski: "I remember Sierakowiak teaching his son to ice-skate about a year before the war. 'Hey, bungler! Bungler!' he'd shout each time the boy fell."

tunately, I don't have a textbook to check this fact, but even if it is true, it doesn't seem to be a reason for the United States to join the war today.* I hope I'm proven wrong, though. Otherwise, everyone is ready to tyrannize me endlessly for my relentless pessimism. Too bad they always have to admit I've been right. That's what's killing me . . .

Wednesday, May 28. Łódź.   According to Roosevelt, we must wait, wait, and wait. Listening to this disgusting blabber drives you crazy. The statistics show an unbelievable increase in the number of children and young people sick from tuberculosis here, and the hearse is as busy as ever. Meanwhile, over there they wait. Damn them!

Thursday, May 29. Łódź.   Rumkowski once again presented us with a real treat as he was issuing a tiny portion of food for the holidays [Shavuot†]. Namely, he announced that the next allocation of bread will be given for only four days instead of five days, which means 50 dkg a day. If the larger portions of bread remain for longer it will be really something. But now people will just encourage their stomachs, and later it will be even worse. All the excitement is about a single common, dry piece of bread. It's horrible. All this weighing of portions, the squabbling "about weight," grabbing for crumbs—will it ever end?

Friday, May 30. Łódź.   *Gettocajtung‡* has published an article by Rumkowski in which he writes that since there is nothing to be cooked, instead of supplementary soup, workers will receive 20 dkg of bread, 5 dkg of sausage, and a cup of ersatz coffee with saccharine for 25 pf a day.

In school I managed to finagle a third soup. After everybody had their soup and after several quite brutal refusals, I persuaded the kitchen manager with my begging to give me an extra portion. But even with the weight of the soup I lapped up in my stomach, I was as hungry as before. I don't think I'll ever be able to satiate my hunger.

Saturday, May 31. Łódź.   What a wonderful treat! An announcement has been issued that the loaf of bread that was issued for four days will have to feed us for only three days before we receive the next ration. I

---

* The declaration of war was actually made on April 6, 1917.
† Shavuot, the Feast of Weeks, or Feast of First Fruits, is an early harvest festival that also celebrates God's revelation on Mount Sinai of the Law to the Jews.
‡ Eighteen issues of the official newspaper of the ghetto's Jewish Administration were published between March 7, 1941, and September 21, 1941, in the ghetto's own printing plant.

guess it's an increase for the holiday. Because of Shavuot, we now have three days off (today, tomorrow, and Monday), but it doesn't make me happy because I lose two soups each day.

We had a meeting of our organization in the afternoon. I have received a note from Blausztajn for the X ray on Wednesday. Connections are connections! It's usually over a month's wait for an exam.

Sunday, June 1. Łódź.   In spite of the holiday I had a lesson with my student. I also did all my homework.

We had a meeting again in the afternoon; we read and discussed Radek's articles.*

There was a dreadful incident today. On Limanowskiego Street, which is excluded from the ghetto area, a ten-year-old boy playfully threw a stone across the wire fences, aiming at the sidewalk on the other side. He hit a passing streetcar and broke a windowpane. Jews were immediately forbidden to walk along the fenced streets, and the boy was taken by the Jewish police; Rumkowski was raving like a madman. I just hope that nothing bad will come from this. In any case, we're living in fear.

The interesting thing is that an enormous number of infantry troops and vehicles are continually passing through Zgierska Street. Never in my life have I seen such machines as they have. At such times the Jews are forbidden to cross the bridges. Where are they trucking to in such numbers? Nobody knows.†

Monday, June 2. Łódź.   I will have one more lesson, with my student's cousin. I will teach her Yiddish and Hebrew, which will mean an additional 60 pf for four lessons a week for me. Ten pf a day will go for soup, and the rest of the money will go for other school expenses and sometimes for "supplemental nutrition."

Lolek Dudelczyk‡ and I had an "editorial meeting" of our school newspaper in the afternoon. We composed an introductory article that I immediately translated into Yiddish. My own Yiddish article and the caricature will also appear in the first issue. Initially I wrote quite

---

* Dawid's political study group was analyzing the work of Karl Radek (1885–1939), possibly his "Portraits and Pamphlets" (1935). Radek rose to become one of the foremost Soviet ideologues. He served as chairman of the Communist International, but eventually was attacked for his views and killed in one of Stalin's purges.
† In three weeks, Hitler would shock the world by declaring war on Russia.
‡ Some of the poems written on ghetto subjects by Dawid's schoolmate Lolek Dudelczyk were found with Dawid's diary and are in the collection of the Jewish Historical Institute in Warsaw.

sharply, but later I had to change the tone (because it wouldn't have been accepted otherwise) and only mildly reiterated the obligation to provide additional nutrition. The time for sharper articles will come in following issues. We are very limited by language; we need articles in German, Yiddish, and Hebrew, not in Polish, but the articles arrive in the reverse linguistic order. We'll manage somehow.

Tuesday, June 3. Łódź. It's really warm now. Folks already feel it's summer. Kuba Blausztajn told me to take off from school before twelve and go to the hospital at 34 Łagiewnicka for an X ray. I went to the hospital after the third lesson, but wasn't X-rayed until three in the afternoon. The conditions in the hospital are not too hygienic or healthy. They let a group of men in, and when they undress, they are forced by lack of space to put all their clothes in a single pile.

My X ray has shown no change in my lungs, but there are some problems with my heart. Everybody comforts me, saying that what's most important is that the lungs are all right. I will now give the X-ray results to the school doctor for her opinion. Perhaps she will prescribe a coupon for additional food for me.

My friends brought me my soup from school. They actually smuggled it out because it's forbidden to take anything out of Marysin. The most important thing is that I didn't lose the dinner.

Wednesday, June 4. Łódź. There seems to be no end to the German victories. They have been able to take Crete, an island they could reach only by air. They used paratroopers to capture it. Is this what will happen to the British Isles?

Thursday, June 5. Łódź. Rumkowski has issued a notice that because of gunshots that were allegedly fired from the ghetto last week, no one will be allowed to take even a single step out of their home on Saturday under threat of the most severe penalty. He also claims that the ghetto population was in great danger because of those gunshots fired by an unknown criminal, but that thanks to his intervention this punishment has been reduced to Saturday's house arrest. No one believes his story, yet no one is able to provide any explanation for Saturday's punishment.*

Friday, June 6. Łódź. I have finally received a letter from Lolek Łęczycki in Warsaw. It was sealed and registered, and a really very

---

* Reichsführer Heinrich Himmler was scheduled to tour the ghetto.

encouraging and important communication for me. It's basically an answer to my postcard, in which I informed him that I had received his 10 RM. He writes that he'll continue helping me (how? I don't know) and that he will even send me underclothes next month. Then he informs me that Rumkowski, who visited their ghetto two weeks ago, took with him to Łódź his friend Heniek Lantenberg, who is supposed to become

My X ray has shown no change in my lungs, but there are some problems with my heart. Everybody comforts me, saying that what's most important is that the lungs are all right.

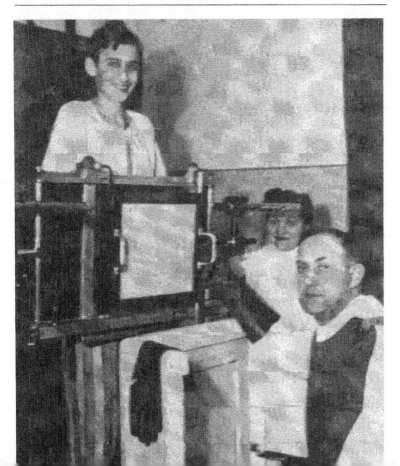

Rumkowski's secretary here (which means major influence). And so Lolek tells me to see his friend immediately. I'll do it tomorrow or on Sunday. (Tomorrow we can leave home only between eight and nine in the evening.) Finally, Lolek tells me that he has Jochanan Tartakower's* address in Japan! . . . he will try to send me the address. As for himself, Lolek writes that he works half a day, and for the other half he goes to school. He says the situation there is awful. He doesn't appear to be in the worst condition, though.

Saturday, June 7. Łódź. I threw up terribly last night, and stayed in bed all day today, weaker than ever before. I haven't done any of the written homework I scheduled for today, and could barely do any reading. There is almost nothing to fill up this greedy stomach, and now I have thrown the food up without having made use of it. What a waste! May it just pass and not turn out to be something worse.

Sunday, June 8. Łódź. I could hardly move today, but I dragged myself to school. And I was right to do so because there was a test in German. Besides, the wonderful air in Marysin and the two little soups left me remarkably refreshed.

In the afternoon, right after classes, I went to 28 Żydowska Street† to see that Heniek Lantenberg. He is a short (and bloated) lad my age. He told me that Lolek had already written to him about me and that as soon as his position is secured, he will do everything that he can for me. Then he did what all powerful people in the ghetto do: took down my name and address and told me to come again in a week. I also managed to glean a bit of information about Lolek and about conditions in the Warsaw ghetto in general. I guess it's enough to say that a 2-kilo loaf of bread is 60 złotys (30 RM) there!

Monday, June 9. Łódź. It's already hot—stifling. But in Marysin it's lovely. Unfortunately, we're allowed to stay there for only half a day, and only in the school. Then we're supposed to leave the area immediately.‡

Itonejnu [*Our Newspaper*] has come out at last. For the first time an

---

* Jochanan Tartakower was their friend from before the war.
† This address was an annex to the main Jewish Administration offices nearby on Plac Kościelny.
‡ In Marysin, on the outskirts of the ghetto, a resort area was established for ghetto dignitaries and those connected to them. Oskar Rosenfeld, the ghetto chronicler and journal author, was one of those who benefited from a rest period there. His notebooks are in the Yad Vashem archive.

article I've written has appeared in public. Although very few people read the article because it is in Yiddish. The caricature has become a hit. I've also been officially appointed the head of the Judaic department (Yiddish, Hebrew) on the newspaper, and we are already thinking about the next issue.

In politics more interesting things are going on. Turkey, feeling that it's in danger, has committed itself to United States protection; Germany has concluded a trade treaty with the Soviets (Ukrainian grain for German machines); England has captured Syria because, in its opinion, France let the Germans in there; the United States has captured the French islands of Martinique and Guadeloupe, taking the French treasure; France is on the verge of war with the United States and England; the Japanese are taking a terrible beating in China. In a word: a wonderful mishmash. Only the Devil knows what will come of all this, and when.

Tuesday, June 10. Łódź. Now our organization will study Lenin's *What Is to Be Done.* Our work is in full swing. We've gained several new members, while the old ones have made real progress.

The ghetto administration is beginning to prepare antiaircraft [civilian] defense. This is done by appointing commanders, messengers, etc. Naturally, they will not bother to prepare shelters (which, unfortunately, are impossible to arrange in the [crowded] ghetto anyway), but will simply use the opportunity to acquire new titles and honors.

Wednesday, June 11. Łódź. We took the first test in Latin since the second grade. She gave us an extremely easy text of Caesar to translate into Polish.

In the evening we held a meeting of our unit of lecturers, and discussed a bourgeois republic. One more meeting, and we will finish up the first chapter of *State and Revolution.*

Thursday, June 12. Łódź. Potatoes arrived in the ghetto this week after a fairly long "absence." Although we should receive 25 kilos for our coupons, we got only 5 kilos. After two months, something was finally cooked at home. Meanwhile, letters from Warsaw say that conditions have become stabilized there. It must be only us, here, who are so cursed.

Friday, June 13. Łódź. I will have a new student from Mrs. Szeps.* He is a first-grade student, somewhat retarded and a stutterer. I got an A

* Guta Szeps was a teacher in the *gymnasium.* She died in the ghetto in 1942.

on my geometry test, and I was the only student in the class who got an A on the German test. There will be a test in Hebrew on Sunday.

Saturday, June 14. Łódź.   I attended a great lecture by Comrade Ziula Krengiel on dialectics. An excellent scientific formulation and explanation. Also today I had the first lesson with my student, a total blockhead. There was an alarm in Łódź last night. As usual it was only an alarm, with no air raid. Everybody in the ghetto could have sweet dreams (provided they had supper); somehow, no one fears "enemy" air raids.

Sunday, June 15. Łódź.   The sadist-moron Rumkowski is doing horrible things. He fired two teachers, Communists, from their jobs (our preceptress, Majerowicz,* and Mrs. Laks†) The overt reason: they organized resistance among teachers against the installation as commissioner—Superior Principal—of Mrs. Weichselfisz. The probable reason: alleged Communist activities in the school. Various events are expected in school. We are laying low, and, following the leadership's advice, we will not organize any meetings for a week or two. There is danger of a purge among the students, and possibly of a shutdown of the school. The Party leadership in the ghetto has not yet taken any stand on the issue—a wait-and-see state.

Monday, June 16. Łódź.   We had an inspection during religion class. They've apparently decided to take "better care" of the school. There was no class in physics (it used to be run by Majerowicz). We are told that her mother is sick and that's why she is absent from work, but half the school knows what it's really all about. The state of dissent continues.

I went to that Lantenberg again. Nothing for now; if anything comes up, he will let me know. In other words: don't be a nuisance; get out and don't come back.

Tuesday, June 17. Łódź.   There was an alarm at noon. There was commotion at school, but not much more than that. Somehow nobody seems to believe in a real air raid. Apparently, it's too soon for our liberation. The Devil hasn't choked us enough yet in this ghetto.

* Estera Majerowicz (b. 1905) taught physics in the ghetto *gymnasium*. She remained in the ghetto until the final deportation to Auschwitz in August 1944.
† Rykla Laks was deported to Auschwitz in August 1944.

The sadist-moron Rumkowski is doing horrible things. He fired two teachers, Communists, from their jobs. . . . We are laying low, and, following the leadership's advice, we will not organize any meetings for a week or two.

Wednesday, June 18. Łódź.   The threat of a German–Soviet conflict continues. They say that the Soviets are ready to make concessions, but the German demands are too excessive (they want Baku, Ukraine, and military support.) Egoist that I am, I want this war because I hope that with it I will be liberated.

The anti-Communist campaign has been reintensified in the ghetto. We constantly receive warnings from well-intending people. Our work is being interrupted every other moment because Majerowicz's case is not closed yet, and we are in danger of various consequences at school.

I have submitted my first Yiddish poem, "Der umet" ["Sadness"], for the school newspaper. It was reviewed by Wolman, a literary man, now a teacher of Yiddish in the school.* He decided that the poem shows talent, though it is "obscured by graphomania." It will appear together

---

* Mojżesz Wolman was deported to Auschwitz in the final liquidation of August 1944.

with my Yiddish editorial note in the second issue of our school newspaper, which is posted on a wall.

Thursday, June 19. Łódź.   Germany has concluded a friendship pact with Turkey.* Is this supposed to be their provision for the war against the Soviets? In any case, bread is now also rationed outside the ghetto, so we expect our bread rations to be reduced (as though it were not enough that people eat their 2-kilo loaves of rye–chestnut bread in two days and go hungry for the other three). Nevertheless, an additional portion of meat is said to be coming to the school kitchen tomorrow (I wonder what kind of holiday this is). It was the only thing they talked about in school today.

Friday, June 20. Łódź.   A new notion and plan from Rumkowski. In today's *Getto Zeitung* he orders a new system for earning a living. Welfare for children up to age fourteen will be increased . . . All men and women between seventeen and fifty who are getting welfare are obliged to work ten to fourteen days per month without pay, getting only soup . . . Thousands of people will lose their jobs . . . Mr. Chaim Rumkowski works in a very sophisticated way.

And as for the Communists in the ghetto, our little Chaim is going after them fiercely again. We've been warned by the leadership that special notice has been taken of us. We must really watch ourselves.

In school there was real meat today. It was very good, but then . . . You know what's next! Were it not for the war, I would have received a *gymnasium* certificate today.

Saturday, June 21. Łódź.   This afternoon, together with youths from tailor and metal workshops, we discussed the difference between bourgeois and socialist upbringings.

The Gestapo is coming down hard on the Jews in the ghetto. All "newsmen" have been arrested (that is, those who listened to the radio and were the source of political information in the ghetto). More than forty persons have already been locked up. The Gestapo and Kripo [German, Kriminalpolizei; Criminal Police] are said to have recently hired a great number of new Jewish informers. We must really beware of them.

* Dawid's information was absolutely up to date. The German–Turkish friendship pact was concluded the previous day.

Sunday, June 22. Łódź.   Incredible, wonderful news! May it not turn out to be only a false rumor. Germany is said to have declared war against the Soviets! The entire ghetto has been electrified by this message. So they have managed engage the Soviets in war. May it not be a pact concluded between the Germans and the English. May the united world bourgeoisie not strike against the free, beloved, great Soviets. Hitler reportedly said that until now he was concealing from the Germans who their true enemy was, but now he has to announce it; he points to the cooperation (?) of Russian Communism and English–Jewish capitalism, mentions all the previous Soviet demands, and finally calls on God for help and hurries into battle. If the information appears in the newspaper tomorrow, it's true, but if it doesn't, it's a rumor like all the others.

Monday, June 23. Łódź.   It's all true! Today's newspaper brings an official declaration of war against the Soviets by Finland, Italy, Germany Romania, and Yugoslavia. There is also Hitler's speech and a warning against the Soviet paratroopers, whom he orders killed. The entire ghetto is buzzing like one big beehive. Everybody feels that a chance for liberation is finally possible.

Meanwhile, nothing very significant is happening in the ghetto. Arrests for political activity are reportedly being made. In the afternoon Rumkowski announced an obligatory registration of all male welfare recipients born between 1911 and 1917. Apparently, on the Germans' demand, they will be deported for forced labor (to dig trenches, ditches, or something of the sort). The antiaircraft defense is also being treated more seriously now. I'm trying to wriggle out of any involvement in *Luftschutz* [German; air-raid (defense)]. Even though it seems childish, I want to have a clear conscience that I didn't participate in the defense of the Germans against the Soviets.

Tuesday, June 24. Łódź.   The newspaper says that there will be no war *Berichte* [German; reports] on the Soviet front; they write only that the German offensive going on there is the greatest in history. They also claim that the Soviets will not be able to afford a counteroffensive. Even so, the Jews in the ghetto wag their tongues and blab all kinds of rumors. One says that the Germans have captured Lwów, while others say that the Soviets have captured Lublin and Kraków. In a word, it's all rubbish. I'd like to know something certain. Oh, if only we could be liberated! I can't stand the ghetto any longer! . . .

Wednesday, June 25. Łódź.   Quiet, hot, sultry; there are real heat waves now. I finally feel that I'm "in my own element." At school we have classes outdoors. The Soviets are on everyone's mind.

There is nothing new from the front, and everyone lives under awful stress. The Soviets are rumored to be attacking, while the Germans are reportedly taking a lot of goods out of the city. We hear this, that, and something else, but I would finally like to hear something certain and good.

Meanwhile, in the ghetto arrests of politically active Jews grow in number.* The Gestapo and Kripo work full strength. We have to be very cautious, even though our tongues itch to speak.

Thursday, June 26. Łódź.   At four in the morning the whole ghetto listened happily to the firing of antiaircraft guns, and watched flares soar quite close by. There must have been an air raid over some strategic target.

I received a letter from Lolek Łęczycki in Warsaw. He writes that he has sent me underclothes, and that Dr. Mazur brings me personal regards from Warsaw. Dr. Mazur must also be the person who has underclothes for me. I will have to find him and get the package.

Friday, June 27. Łódź.   A rumor has spread through the city that Warsaw has been captured by the Soviet army. All over the ghetto, all kinds of supposition and speculation are swarming. It reminds me of the mood last year before the rumored arrival of the Soviets. People are now much more cautious and pessimistic, however. Yet, everybody hopes: maybe this time . . .

The Germans supposedly want the barbed wire on the thoroughfares taken down so that people riding streetcars could hide in the doorways during air raids. Rumkowski is said to oppose the idea, telling the Jews that he is afraid of a pogrom (while telling the Germans that he will not be responsible for Jews escaping from the ghetto).

The food situation is deteriorating in the ghetto. Reserves are running out, and new transports don't arrive. Only the Devil knows why this war has been going on for two years! . . .

Saturday, June 28. Łódź.   Calm and quiet, but the air is full of electricity. Rumkowski has issued another notice about an additional registra-

---

* A period of intensive dissent was developing in the ghetto, marked by large, militant demonstrations and strikes in the major workshops. Rumkowski eliminated the leaders by putting them on early deportation lists.

tion of male workers. All men between seventeen and forty are going now. I wonder whether it also affects my older school friends. Several train cars that arrived in the ghetto with food have supposedly been backed out.

Dr. Mazur gave me the parcel with underclothes from Lolek Łęczycki. The kind boy has sent me a shirt, a gym shirt, long underwear, and socks; they are enormously useful.

Today I faced a very serious and difficult issue that made me very tense and excited. Niutek Radzyner told me that because all political party work in the ghetto has been suspended, a Party cadre is being established to operate in great secrecy. It is supposed to consist of people devoted body and soul to the cause, for whom nothing else will matter. They are supposed to be at the Party's disposal at all times for any kind of action. Five such persons are expected to come from among school youths who, of course, will be selected after very thorough consideration. I was included in the list of candidates, and Niutek, being completely open about the whole thing, asked me what I thought of it. I was so bewildered and nervous I couldn't give him my answer, and put it off until tomorrow. At home, after giving a lot of thought to the matter, I arrived at the following conclusions: although I am totally certain of my convictions and ideals, my life's goal is by no means to be a professional revolutionary, ready for extreme actions, and I don't think I would be able to take part in something like a "suicide squad." As for my final answer to the proposal, I've decided to say that in case of a specific action, I am ready to take an active part at a crucial moment. However, a constant, so to speak, professional commitment excluding all other goals and interests under the threat of the most dire consequences is out of the question.

Sunday, June 29. Łódź.   I have communicated my decision to Niutek. Although he feels differently, he understood my position and promised to give me an answer tomorrow about whether my cooperation on limited terms with the central cadre is possible.

In the afternoon a rumor spread that the Germans supposedly broke the Russian front and captured Brześć on the Bug [River] and Kovno (even Białystok and Lwów are mentioned). What a story! In any case, the information is not certain.

Today there was a funeral for a student from our school, a girl who was killed by a thunderbolt on Thursday. There's no way to feel safe in the ghetto. They are talking about taking Marysin and building trenches there. Only the Devil knows what may happen to us!

Monday, June 30. Łódź.   Yesterday's news turns out to be unfortunately true. According to today's newspaper, the Germans have captured Kovno, Dyneburg, Wilno, Grodno, Białystok, and Brześć on the Bug. They have supposedly seized several thousand tanks and shot down 4,000 Soviet airplanes, losing 150 of their own. The numbers are amazing. On the other hand, the Soviets supposedly announced that they shot down 4,500 German airplanes, losing 800 of their own. Stalin is also reported to have said that Hitler is not going to be in Moscow in two weeks, but that Stalin will, rather, be in Berlin in that time because all 5 million soldiers in the German army are Communists. May it be so because after a week's revival, I have been like a corpse again since yesterday.

Tuesday, July 1. Łódź.   Rumkowski's order regarding the restructuring of the welfare and income systems has gone into force. It already has taken its toll on us: Father has lost his job and from now on is working for free while getting welfare; Mom may lose her job at any moment. What will we do now without Father's weekly wage? We truly don't know. Damn all these things! What we need here more than ever before are the Soviets. However, the situation is growing worse and worse on the front: the Germans have captured Lwów and Lipawa and are said to have taken several hundred thousand Soviet POWs. I have completely lost my head since yesterday. Can there be no end to the constant German victories? The myth simply has to burst some day! It has to!

Wednesday, July 2. Łódź.   The Germans keep moving ahead, pushing on as though nothing can stop them. There were rumors about the Soviets marching to Warsaw, but unfortunately they are only rumors. In the meanwhile, they [the Germans] are really going ahead as though there is nothing that can stop them.

Niutek told me that they haven't decided about me yet. I may be accepted into the Party cadre despite my Sunday declaration. Today I got another student, my classmate Engel. I will be teaching him German for 10 pf an hour. I don't know how many hours a week it will be.

The food situation is still bad, even though an allocation of 8 dkg of butter and one egg has been issued (Sensation! There have been no eggs in the ghetto since last year). There are almost no potatoes, no vegetables—nothing essential to eat.

Thursday, July 3. Łódź.   Niutek has informed me that I have been accepted into the highly disciplined Party cadre. A group of four other students from our school and I have been selected from our entire organization (Jerzyk, Fredek, Fela, Szyjo, and I). We will have an organizational meeting tomorrow. We are supposed to keep all members of our organization under our review and to prepare ourselves emotionally for the sacrifice that is to come. It will not be very soon because the Germans' situation becomes better while the Soviets' worsens. Obviously, we cannot believe every idiotic rumor we hear.

Friday, July 4. Łódź.   Today we had an organizational meeting of our unit of five. It was run by Niutek, the member of the highest-level unit of five. He briefed us on the general political situation, and discussed the problem of centralization of the Party, our goals, character, etc. In the end we distributed members of the organization among us to keep them, though unaware, in constant contact. Those who have fallen to my lot are Engel, Bryt, and Abramant.

The Germans write that the Soviets are retreating all along the front line. Only the Devil knows what will finally come of it! . . .

Saturday, July 5. Łódź.   After the whole week of toiling, I took a good rest today. But, of course, I am even hungrier.

In politics there's nothing new. The Jews console themselves that at least the Germans haven't gained more victories.

It's become cold. It's not like July at all. Everyone's in a coat, and the sun can be seen only once every three or four days. Let the Devil take this kind of life! I nearly fainted at school yesterday.

Sunday, July 6. Łódź.   Give them a single quiet day, and the Jews immediately produce rumors. Although today's newspaper says that the Germans have captured Kołomyja and Stanisławów, the Jews claim that the Soviets broke the German front and are rushing toward Warsaw. Oh, this everlasting stupidity, and the naïveté of everyone who believes everything so willingly.

Monday, July 7. Łódź.   There's nothing new from the front. The newspaper only reports all kinds of cretinisms and fabrications about the Soviets, their army, police, terror, etc., etc.

Meanwhile, the weather's quite cold for July. The food situation is worsening. Even though products such as margarine, butter, and sugar appear in our rations once in a while, there are no potatoes, barley, or vegetables at all. The [communal] kitchens arrange the dinners extremely skillfully, but their nutritional value is weaker every day. The *Beirat* [segment of the ghetto population designated for additional privileges] receives compensation in the form of fresh vegetables and fruits, but the "gray crowd" continues to die of hunger. And this is supposed to be the blessed summer.

Tuesday, July 8. Łódź.   It's worse and worse at home. It's the eighth day that Father has been working as a welfare recipient for nothing, because no welfare has been issued so far. Mom has less and less work in the kitchen, which has naturally taken its toll on her income. Thus my lessons again become the mainstay of our budget. I hope this situation will not last long, that it will take a radical turn.

Wednesday, July 9. Łódź.   America has captured Iceland to forestall a German invasion there. There's nothing new on the eastern front. The Germans are apparently not rolling so smoothly anymore. The tightening of English–American–Soviet relations is mentioned more and more often, and the bilateral agreements are supposed to be evidence of that. I wonder how the situation will develop after the Germans have been crushed. But—this tiny "but"—the crushing of the Germans still seems completely out of reach.

Thursday, July 10. Łódź.   Litvinov has been appointed minister of the Foreign Office again, and Molotov, minister of military affairs. Damn it! They're getting closer to the so-called democracies after all, at least for a while. A big offensive against Germany would be of greater use than the continual idle talk. I'm already steamed up by all this.

Friday, July 11. Łódź.   The Germans are said to have had successes near Białystok and Mińsk. It's as hot as Africa, and in school it's also humid as hell. The only thing that picks me up is soup. They will also give us imitation coffee soon; but something to eat would be more useful.

On Tuesday we had the first reporting from our unit of five. We discussed the political situation, and after that each of us gave a briefing on his conversations and thoughts about the members of our organization who had been appointed to him. We are slowly getting back to work in the ghetto. Mostly we are engaged in the struggle for workers' rights.

I went to see Majerowicz today. We visited her with Niutek a few weeks ago. She, too, has other expectations, and appears to be completely ours. She hopes to come back to school in the next few days.

Saturday, July 12. Łódź. There's nothing important in the newspaper. The Germans keep complaining about the savagery of the Russians; they say that the Russians have made the war the bloodiest in the history of the world. The number killed on both sides supposedly totals 2.5 million people. What slaughter! The best part of humanity is being killed there. Damn it! You really can't tell what else can happen in this world, if this war is not over quickly.

Sunday, July 13. Łódź. Rumkowski has given another treat to the starving ghetto population. Because he received a little wheat flour, he had 40 dkg strudels baked, and they are now given out as a special allocation together with 5 dkg of artificial honey. Folks are as happy as can be because it's the first white bread in the ghetto since last summer. The bad news, however, is that dinners in the kitchens have become awful because there are no potatoes, vegetables, or barley in the ghetto at all. There's only a small quantity of peas, a little wheat flour, and barley flakes of some sort. These are the ingredients that the "soup" is fixed from. A liter of water and 7 dkg of "solids." You may also spot sauerkraut from time to time. The only consolation is that the fields are blooming and the crops are supposed to be excellent this year.

Monday, July 14. Łódź. The Germans have captured Vitebsk. Although their march is very slow, they keep moving on. A wintry chill comes over me again when I remember that the war still drags on. Damn it! Everything's running out here already; most of all, my health. I have a feeling that next winter the ghetto won't see me.

Tuesday, July 15. Łódź. After quite a long break, the *Gettocajtung* has been published. Rumkowski writes that we should turn in long coats and capes, which he will have remade into winter jackets. From what's left, new coats will be made for the poor. So he is serious about one more winter here, and it seems to me that he is right.

Father has a job again, this time as a painter's assistant. Say what you will, you can't reproach him for laziness. He would be happy to do anything to provide bread for us. But what can he do? He has no luck. Meanwhile, Mom also has a job, and perhaps she will manage to keep it. The main thing is not to be cast aside, not to be finished off.

Wednesday, July 16. Łódź. It's been several days without German victories. Good cheer slowly creeps back into the hearts of the ghetto dwellers, and together with a tiny bit of fantasy, the boldest suppositions and rumors are being born. The United States is now almost totally ready for war with Germany; England is bombing, and there have been no new German conquests on the front. So perhaps the Germans are really in bad shape. But all this seems only wishful thinking. No one really knows what's going on.

Thursday, July 17. Łódź. Majerowicz was back in school today. Yesterday the "king" [Rumkowski] visited Marysin, and when he was *gut gelaunt* [German; in a good mood] they managed to extract from him his consent to allow the fired teachers to come back to school. We bought Majerowicz a bouquet, which moved her very much. It's easy to see how very moved and happy she is to be allowed back. We will finally start physics, which we have neglected badly. Meanwhile, the Germans keep moving on!

Friday, July 18. Łódź. A victory again! The Germans have captured Kishinev. They are also writing that the Russians are on their last legs. Apparently, they're the ones who are in such bad shape. Supposedly, the number of victims is simply unbelievable.

Niutek called me for an interview today and analyzed my coolness toward our work. For the second time I explained to him that Party work is not my main goal or obligation, and that I'm not working prominently now because there is no job to do; I don't think it is my task to create the circumstances for something to happen. We didn't finish our conversation. We will finish it on Sunday.

Saturday, July 19. Łódź. All day long I had nothing to eat but water (soup) in the kitchen. It's more and more difficult for me to go on starving. In the past I was able to not eat all day and still hold on somehow, but now I'm an empty pot. I was so weakened by the lack of soup at school that I thought I would collapse.

Meanwhile, the Germans have captured Smolensk. They're also apparently holding back something for tomorrow, so they can write about a new conquest. Tomorrow is Sunday, and on Sunday there are always victories. Ptui! I'm becoming superstitious again. They are really marching on, damn it! . . .

Sunday, July 20. Łódź. We will now have only 2 kilos of bread for an entire week, but we will also have two 40-dkg pieces of strudel (which means altogether about 40 dkg of baked goods a day). And strudel is strudel, except that it's very expensive: as much as 40 pf. But what else can you get in private trade for 40 pf these days? Eight toffee pieces, that's all.

In politics there is nothing new. If only those Krauts did not lumber any farther, you could say it would not be so bad. But so far the bloody beasts keep moving on. All of the Devils' power must be helping them.

Today we had a meeting of our unit of five and discussed the general political situation.

Monday, July 21. Łódź. It's still cold. It may be better for our health, but I would prefer hot days.

Even though everything seems to be in full swing in school, we are making little progress.

Meanwhile, the summer is approaching its end. If it's like last year, August will turn Marysin into one big pool of mud, and school, studies, and, most important, soup will become only a dream again.

Tuesday, July 22. Łódź. I've recently begun translating poems. I'm translating Ovid's *Deadal and Icar* into Polish, and Czernichowski's poem "Baruch mi 'Magenca" from Hebrew into Yiddish.* They say I do it well. I have an awful lot to do because of my tutoring. I can hardly manage to learn languages. Things are meager at home: Mom has no income, while Father's is very low. Everyone keeps waiting for these few marks of mine.

---

* Dawid chose to translate literature's most glorious and tragic story of escape, the Daedalus and Icarus myth from Ovid's *The Metamorphoses* (VIII, 183–235). Daedalus built wings to enable him and his son, Icarus, to fly out of the Labyrinth. The great tale could not have failed to resonate bitterly for Dawid, captive in the ghetto with his own father.

Jewish intellectuals in the Nazi ghettos summoned up centuries of literature on Jewish martyrdom as they interpreted their own experience of the most extreme occurrence of genocide in human history. Saul Tschernichowsky's poem "Baruch of Magenca" (1902) is a harrowing rendering of anti-Semitic genocide as it occurred in the Middle Ages. The Polish-Jewish poet (1875–1943) regarded Jewish martyrdom as a sacrifice that would lead to eventual dignity for his people. He wrote the following summary of Jewish persecution in the poem Dawid translated:

> Alas, my God, Thou has delivered
> Thy sheep, like things abhorred,
> Into the hands of strangers, who abuse them.

From Eisig Silberschlag, *Saul Tschernichowsky, Poet of Revolt* (Ithaca, N.Y., 1968), p. 117.

Wednesday, July 23. Łódź.   Today our class had the compulsory bath at Bazarna Street. What a marvelous thing! A wonderful hot and cold shower. What a pleasure! At least for a moment you can remember the good old days.

Today our class had the compulsory bath at Bazarna Street. What a marvelous thing! A wonderful hot and cold shower. What a pleasure! At least for a moment you can remember the good old days.

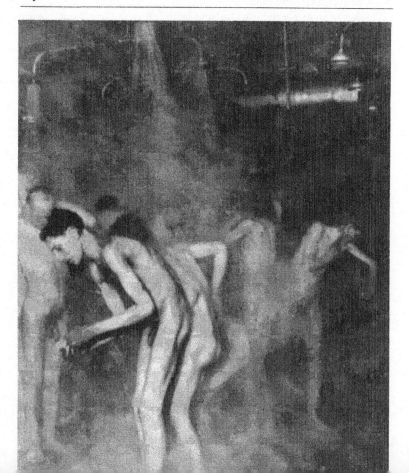

The Germans have reportedly been stopped and are being held back. Stories are also circulating about attempts to set up another front in the west. That would really be a great help!

Thursday, July 24. Łódź.   I get truly fired up hearing "nothing new" again. We barely stay alive here, but over there the Allies somehow still can't accomplish anything. It's obvious that the situation there is not all that easy, but I can't stand it. Oh, may it just end once and for all, damn it!

Friday, July 25. Łódź.   I have such a toothache I think I'll go crazy. Half of my face is terribly swollen.

I've accepted a new student. She is a girl who wants to review the third grade of *gymnasium*. I will get 10 RM a month for four lessons a week. Altogether I will now have about 32 or 33 RM a month. I just don't know how I will manage everything (naturally, I will have no more time to learn languages or write poems). I just hope that at least I will be able to do my homework. However, cash is cash, and the main thing is to have something to eat and to survive. Just to survive! . . .

Saturday, July 26. Łódź.   I went to the dental clinic with a note from my school doctor. It turns out that the tooth I had filled last winter was not fully treated, and now infection has returned. Supposedly it is quite dangerous.

I had the first lesson with my new student. She is quite sharp and very nice. However, she fell very far behind in the material.

In politics the most important thing is that the Germans have been stalled. Perhaps the era of their endless victories is finally over. Let it be so . . .

Sunday, July 27. Łódź.   Still nothing new. No victory was prepared, even for Sunday, and the newspaper is empty as usual. We had one hell of a delight in school, where we had no classes today because all the children in Marysin had to parade before Rumkowski. What's most important, we received an additional afternoon snack: a piece of bread with a slice of sausage. A truly lordly gesture by our ruler! We could not be spared a speech, naturally. The old man said that he gives us all he can, and in return he demands that we study, study and study well. A great number of dignitaries came with Rumkowski: guests, and the entire resort Rumkowski opened in Marysin for "deserving personnel of

We had one hell of a delight in school, where we had no classes today because all the children in Marysin had to parade before Rumkowski. . . . We could not be spared a speech, naturally. The old man said that he gives us all he can, and in return he demands that we study, study and study well.

the community administration." (Life in the resort is said to be better than the one most people had before the war.) The tenants of this paradise are doctors and members of the *Beirat*. Even wines are bought for the resort. The resort is such a horrible abscess, such a disgraceful blotch on the carcass of the administration that I don't think it can ever be forgiven! . . .

Monday, July 28. Łódź.   My time is packed so densely because of tutoring that I can barely manage to do my homework. I have no time to study languages. I keep receiving offers to take new students, but unfortunately I can't accept anyone anymore. In the winter, when we had no school, I wasn't able to get even a single student, and now, when school consumes so much of my time, they come as though out of a horn of plenty.

Tuesday, July 29. Łódź.   Simultaneously with the increase in welfare, all administration prices went way up in the ghetto. Rumkowski is very skillful at taking away the welfare increase; all he cares about is increasing productivity, while starvation can remain the same. In fact, starvation becomes ever more prevalent: the soup in the kitchens is awful, and we receive nothing to cook [at home] in our additional rations; meat appears only once in three or four weeks (10 dkg a person, plus 8 or 10 dkg of margarine a person). Once in a while a bit of greenery appears in the vegetable cooperatives (where it's distributed by the so-called free-market system): a scene resembling the attack of vultures on carrion takes place. And that's how weeks are passing . . .

Wednesday, July 30. Łódź.   There is nothing new from the front (at least we know nothing). Again, folks begin to speculate about the oncoming winter and what's ahead for us. But you better not think about the future if you want to have a moment of peace. (Peace with an empty stomach, naturally.) Oh, I want to satisfy my hunger so badly! . . .

Thursday, July 31. Łódź.   I have received a letter from Lolek Łęczycki in Warsaw. He sends me the address of Dr. Tartakower in New York and writes that he received a letter from Jochanan in Honolulu, where he is on his way to his father. Jochanan spent nearly two years in the Soviet Union and finally received papers to leave for the United States. I don't think I will use his address because it's hard to tell whether the letter would get to America. In any case, Lolek writes that he wrote to Jochanan about me. I wonder if Lolek's letter will produce any results.

Friday, August 1. Łódź. It's August already, and still we have not received our welfare. Critically, Father was called today to work for his August welfare. He got nervous and did not go. Only men up to forty-seven years old (there was a registration of men between forty and forty-seven) are working now, and Father is already forty-nine. I referred this matter to Frydrych, who assured me that we will receive the welfare. Who the hell can make sense of such chaos?

Saturday, August 2, Łódź. I'm finishing my treatment at the dentist. I'd prefer another kind of treatment now, namely, nourishment. But I can't get much without money. Vegetables and even potatoes are supposed to arrive this week, but even if they do arrive, I have no idea where to get cash for them.

Sunday, August 3. Łódź. It burns me up when I realize that summer is almost over and there's still no solution of the situation here. The Germans don't publish any war bulletins. I think the war will drag on through the winter.

Monday, August 4. Łódź. Vegetables have appeared in the cooperatives. There are a whole lot of cabbages, radishes, cucumbers, and other vegetables, but the prices are extremely high.

Tuesday, August 5. Łódź. A rumor has spread that a high court capable of imposing capital punishment for so-called political crimes (listening to the radio, spreading "false news," and supposedly even for political beliefs) will be established in the ghetto. The ghetto has become completely silent, and there are no political rumors at all. What a wonderful remedy for any problems in the ghetto: announce a high court. The Germans couldn't find a better man than Rumkowski.

Wednesday, August 6. Łódź. All kinds of leaves that seemed inedible before the war (like beet greens, outer cabbage leaves, pigweed, and a number of others) have become very popular food in the ghetto. All this grass and leaves, however, cannot even minimally satisfy our hunger.

Thursday, August 7. Łódź. Cherries arrived in the ghetto today! An incredible sensation! In the vegetable cooperatives they distribute the allocations, but the price is 2 RM a kilo! These prices must be to exploit and confuse the population. Naturally, we don't buy this luxury because we can't even afford the regular rations. Good fortune for the *Beirat.*

In Marysin students keep making constant expeditions for apples. Endless seizures by the police, lock-ups, expulsions from school all have little effect. The forbidden fruit tastes too good! . . . Especially when you are very hungry!

Friday, August 8. Łódź.   I have one more student as of today. He is a fifth-grade student at an elementary school. Because I have almost no time, I'll tutor him in the evening on my way home from school. Now I'll have up to 40 RM a month. I have never earned so much. In spite of these strokes of *Glück* [German; luck], however, there is nothing to eat at home, and all the time, all the hopeless time, I go hungry. Oh, may this torture finally end, once and for all!

Saturday, August 9. Łódź.   I'm utterly ill and simply can't move. I practically blacked out during the lesson with my student. Oh, this hunger!

Sunday, August 10. Łódź.   In biology class we had a lecture on tuberculosis. Our biology teacher, who also works as a *Hilfsarzt* [German; assistant doctor], told us that according to the ghetto doctors' latest estimations, 99 to 100 percent of the population is infected with tuberculosis. Wonderful prospects for us! The ghetto has become a wonderful scientific experiment. What a pity that our doctors can't present their scientific data to the entire world!

Monday, August 11. Łódź.   The nasty weather is continuing for a third week. It's cold and rainy. The summer definitely seems to be over. This is the second year that the summer has been so short.

The potatoes that arrived in the ghetto have been distributed among hospitals, the *Beirat*, "better" kitchens, and schools. Tomorrow our soup in school will be served with potatoes, so don't despair, keep smiling!

Tuesday, August 12. Łódź.   In politics it's so quiet, it's simply a pleasure. The newspaper doesn't bring any news, and people don't say anything either—under penalty of the gallows! (They will supposedly go into operation soon.) Brr . . . indeed, the devilish German idea: the ghetto Jews will sentence and hang other Jews! Germans are Germans! . . .

Wednesday, August 13. Łódź.   It was raining so terribly today that I came to school drenched through to my shirt, to say nothing of my socks. Autumn has already taken a strong hold; winter's at hand.

Thursday, August 14. Łódź. Even though Father has a job as a painter's assistant, our situation is tragic. Rysiek Podlaski's father is now the manager of the saddlery workshop, and promised me that he would try to find a job for my father. Perhaps something will come of it.

Friday, August 15. Łódź. I have received the first payment from my newest student. The work is very pleasant, but all the money for the tutoring goes extremely quickly, so that all my work seems to have been done for nothing. Even so, may I just not lose these lessons.

Saturday, August 16. Łódź. Today I ate my fill of soup in school because one of the kitchen workers turned out to be a neighbor of mine, and now he gives me the so-called connection soups. However, the water had no sooner run down to my stomach than I was as hungry as before.

Podlaski sent for my father today. He has a job for him in the saddlery workshop at some machine that is to arrive in the ghetto any day. Father will be able to earn up to 18 RM a week. We will finally have a regular income! I would just like this job to be an accomplished fact. If only Mom could also get back to work, then it would really be a paradise!

Sunday, August 17. Łódź. There was an informational conference for parents in school today, so we had only two classes, and dinner after them. No one from my family could come for the conference, but I will know my grades for the last semester tomorrow, anyway; I think they are not bad.

Monday, August 18. Łódź. Our grades were read to us. I got the best grades in the class: all As and Bs. But what good are they when I'm still hungry and keep feeling so terribly exhausted? It's already been several weeks since I stopped studying foreign languages altogether because I have absolutely no time for that. And even if I do catch a moment of free time, I don't feel like doing anything. I can guarantee that the war will not end this year.

Tuesday, August 19. Łódź. The rumors have fallen silent for good. The newspaper reports that the Germans move farther and farther into Russia: they have already captured Homel and Nikolayev and now threaten Leningrad. Damn it, the war will drag on for years! Meanwhile, we're on our last legs here. I think we will be pickled in this ghetto . . .

Wednesday, August 20. Łódź. Our class went on an "excursion" to the hospital at Łagiewnicka Street to see the X-ray machine and X-ray examinations that are made there. We witnessed an X-ray examination of elementary-school children who are sent there by the antituberculosis dispensary. Almost all of them have signs of tuberculosis.

Several dozen people arrived from Warsaw this week. They tell us incredible horror stories about the situation there, but none of them has the dreadful sallow skin we all have in our ghetto. (The cadavers walking along our streets have given the entire ghetto a pale, musty, tubercular look.)

Thursday, August 21. Łódź. Father has begun his work for Podlaski in the saddlery workshop. Oh, if only Mom could also return to work, then perhaps we wouldn't be in this horrible, starving state anymore; then my lessons would just be a good financial supplement, perhaps allowing me to have some additional soup in school from time to time.

Friday, August 22. Łódź. Mom got hold of Praszkier, the absolute ruler of the Kitchen Department, and through him she wrested a note from the department to allow her to be admitted back to work. However, the manager of the kitchen where Mom was assigned said that she would work there for only two days. I wonder what kind of new trick this is. A mistake in filling in the assignment form, or someone's mischief?

Saturday, August 23. Łódź. It's already totally autumnlike. Cold and clouds make me shudder. I was staggered today when I heard about the death of our former neighbor in the building, Mr. Kamusiewicz. I think his is the first death in the ghetto that has left me so deeply depressed. This man, an absolute athlete before the war, died of hunger here. His iron body did not suffer from any disease; it just grew thinner and thinner every day, and finally he fell asleep, not to wake again. Olek Kamusiewicz also looks like a cadaver. All this is a horrible act of destruction wrought by the war, and the end of this misery is still not in sight.

Sunday, August 24. Łódź. The ghetto is developing more and more gloriously. A large number of new workshops and factories are being established. Together with those already existing, they form what's called in jest the "Jewish Industrial District." In addition to schools, camps, sanitariums, Marysin—now a separate quarter—has a whole lot

Marysin—now a separate quarter—has a whole lot of new factories and employment departments (for example, a plant producing carpets from rags).

of new factories and employment departments (for example, a plant producing carpets from rags, a preserves factory, a candy factory, shoe-makers, decorative workshops, and many others). Everything is the "state property" of "Der Älteste der Juden" [German; the Eldest of the Jews]. Many new workshops have also been organized in the main area of the ghetto (for example, the saddlery shop where my father has a job, leather and embroidery shops, and even the one where army furs are cleaned). Furthermore, a metal workshop keeps receiving larger orders from the Germans. Hundreds of people are now finding employment, and everything appears to be going for the better, if it weren't for the high death rate and hunger, the never-ending hunger that will not abate at all. We are constantly short of money, and even if there are vegetable allocations, we are almost never able to buy them.

Monday, August 25. Łódź.   The Germans reportedly keep moving farther ahead. Meanwhile, their opponents confer, make plans for after the war, and keep retreating. Damn it! Apparently, we will spend not only this one winter in the ghetto, but many more. Our prospects for surviving the war grow ever weaker.

Tuesday, August 26. Łódź.   In school we are already talking about the end of the school year, about the break, choosing a *lyceum,* etc. I don't think I will alter my previous intention to enter grammar *lyceum.* As for the fourth-grade *gymnasium* material, we are way behind, finishing very few subjects. Meanwhile, the end of the school year is tentatively scheduled for the end of September. People are growing older! . . .

Wednesday, August 27. Łódź.   I went to Mrs. Kamusiewicz's. I didn't recognize her: an old, terribly hollow-cheeked woman with gray hair, crying all the time. Two days after the death of his father, [her son] Olek got a job as a laborer outside the ghetto. Every morning he leaves the ghetto with his group, and comes back at four. Perhaps they will do a little better now. It's high time for that.

Thursday, August 28, Łódź.   Mom's cousin came to see us today. She managed to get through to us from Warsaw. She tells all kinds of things from which you can draw the following conclusions: on the average, it's much worse in Warsaw than here; however, as a result of private trade, smuggling, and fewer restrictions, a unique wartime atmosphere was created there, and a shrewd and clever person can earn thousands and live like a king.* In Warsaw, for example, my father would be able to secure a fair life for us, but at the same time thousands of people are dying on the streets there, and they aren't even buried (which has already been organized perfectly in our ghetto!).

Friday, August 29. Łódź.   We were examined by a school doctor. Everybody is generally fairly clean, though a few boys had terribly dirty chests and armpits. A bit more of such dirt, and typhus would be at

---

* For a short period, the Nazis allowed Jews to pay to be moved between the Warsaw and Łódź ghettos. Large sewer pipes greatly facilitated the smuggling of goods and arms into the Warsaw Ghetto, but smuggling was almost impossible in the Łódź Ghetto, which totally lacked a sewage system. Fecal workers there pushed excrement tank wagons to the outer perimeter of the ghetto, which prevented the outbreak of a full-scale typhus epidemic in the ghetto, but meant almost certain death for those assigned the duty.

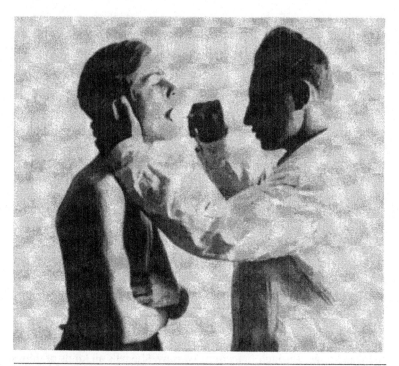

We were examined by a school doctor. Everybody is generally fairly clean, though a few boys had terribly dirty chests and armpits. A bit more of such dirt, and typhus would be at hand.

hand. Let's just hope it won't come to that. Frequent baths for students and workers and the disinfection of streets, houses, and community rooms help the situation in the ghetto somewhat, though dysentery is quite "popular." If there were more food, it wouldn't be bad. Such an insignificant thing, food!

Saturday, August 30. Łódź.   It keeps raining all the time. Mom has a regular job in the kitchen at 3 Wawelska Street. Perhaps our situation will now become a bit more bearable, but we still have nothing to eat because none of us has yet been paid.

Rumkowski gave a truly "Führer-like" speech in the afternoon. He announced that the welfare payment would again be only 10 marks, whereas people who work will receive an additional 2 marks and one soup a day. Rumkowski also announced that he has received a tremendous supply of potatoes (which, indeed, are arriving in the ghetto in great transports every day), but he failed to say where we can get the cash to buy them.

I have accepted a new student. He will come to my place every day, and I will get 50 pf an hour.

Sunday, August 31. Łódź.   We took a test in mathematics, and I had the first lesson with my new student. He is quite a bright boy, but absentminded. It's a true pleasure when a student comes to my apartment and I don't have to rush a great distance! It's a bit awkward, though, because we don't have a table at home, and everything has to be

Rumkowski gave a truly "Führer-like" speech in the afternoon.

done on the windowsill. My foreign languages and reading have completely perished, so to speak. School, lessons, and homework—so goes my whole day; not one free second, unless I sit until late at night. But I have no more strength for that.

Monday, September 1. Łódź.   The first day of the third year of the war. When I realize that this horrible state of things has been going on for two years, I simply can't believe it. So much has changed around the world during this time! How many more such anniversaries will we observe? If many more, we won't live to the final one. The ghetto will finish us off, even though potatoes are arriving, and even though there is more and more demand for our work.

Tuesday, September 2. Łódź.   Still more potatoes arrive in the ghetto, but we haven't been able to buy even a single kilo out of our 5-kilo ration. All week long our drudgery continues to find a few dozen marks for dinner and vegetable allocations (not to mention the so-called sugar allocations: sugar, salt, artificial honey, caustic soda, soap, vinegar, and other such products). The situation is awful. Mom will probably not receive her first pay until next week.

Wednesday, September 3. Łódź.   I've had an interesting and serious conversation with Niutek Radzyner. He told me about a complete change in his party's attitude toward me (allegedly provoked by my attitude toward their work), that is, identifying me as a so-called harmful individual. Niutek talked about me with Ziula, Gienia, and many other persons, and all of them advised him to simply exclude me from the work. Of course, he wouldn't let it happen completely, and as a result I've become something of a loose member who doesn't participate in the theoretical work (which has started again) because of technical matters (my tutoring), or in the organizational work because of matters of principle. I didn't say anything and agreed to everything; I only wonder when they will change their opinion again.

Thursday, September 4. Łódź.   Rye flour has arrived in the ghetto, so bread will be baked again with rye and chestnut flour, without an addition of wheat. I wonder about price. Cooking remains a problem, however, because few individuals can afford wood or coal. All kinds of electric and gas kitchens where you can cook "by the hour" have devel-
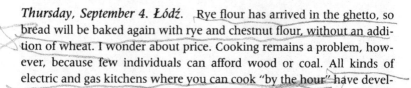

oped. An hour on gas costs 15 to 20 pf, on electricity 40 to 50 pf, while a kilo of wood is 1.20 RM. The only remedy is to have cash.

Friday, September 5. Łódź.   Our classes in school were cut short because of the Sabbath. Again, the wind is "pulling" in the morning, and the days are becoming shorter. It rains almost every day. Father finally received his pay, and we have bought our first potato allocation. We had a long wait, but this evening we had a potato treat. We still have a long way to feeling satiated, but potatoes are potatoes! The main thing is to have cash. (Fortunately, I will have a few marks tomorrow. Were it not for them, we wouldn't have money for dinner on Sunday, or for bread after that.)

Saturday, September 6. Łódź.   Potatoes for supper again (after all, we've received 20 kilos of them!). This year's harvest must have been incredibly plentiful in Germany and in the occupied lands because otherwise they wouldn't have sent "so much" to us.

Graduation exams have begun in school. They are our second graduation exams in the ghetto. Just like last year, Rumkowski has already arranged posts for the graduates. I wish we had a university. It's a scandal that a state like our ghetto doesn't have its own university. I should suggest the idea to Rumkowski. I'm joking, but meanwhile I am really hungry again—even after those potatoes.

Sunday, September 7. Łódź.   I got an A on the mathematics test. Many more tests await us in almost every subject before the end of the school year comes and classification [for higher education] begins. *Lyceum* soon! I never thought I would attend *lyceum* during the war.

Monday, September 8. Łódź.   Potatoes, potatoes, lots of potatoes everywhere. In the workshops they are giving half a bushel to everyone. In the kitchens they make *cholents** for Saturdays, and the soups contain more potatoes than we have ever seen in the ghetto. But I still need cash, cash! Things are very meager when it comes to that because our income is so minimal. Perhaps it will improve soon, but my main hope is that it doesn't get any worse!

---

* A popular Polish-Jewish dish, *cholent* is a baked casserole usually consisting of potatoes, vegetables, meat, and animal fat.

for deportation

Tuesday, September 9. Łódź. The ghetto is being motorized! A street-car has reportedly been set up to transport goods and food from Marysin to the main area.* So much is arriving in the ghetto that horse carts aren't adequate anymore. The ghetto, which is slowly becoming the Jewish work center of the Reich, has to be motorized! That's our latest slogan! No one ever expected this, damn it! I get enraged when I realize that the war will probably drag on for a long time, even with potatoes and a streetcar!

Wednesday, September 10. Łódź. We took a test in Latin and Hebrew, and will take tests in Polish and German, and possibly mathematics one more time. I have received the first pay from my newest student, son of "the chief of police" in Marysin. He's a big show-off, but not a bad man.† Just to endure! Lesson after lesson. I get up in the morning, then tutor my first student, second student, third student, go to school, tutor again, do homework, sleep, and get up in the morning again; on and on like this, each and every day. Sometimes I read a few pages of a book; sometimes a lesson is canceled, and time, in spite of the monotony, slips away so fast that before I notice, it's already Saturday, then Saturday again and a month is gone, summer is gone, and autumn is coming . . . Meanwhile, the war goes on.

Thursday, September 11. Łódź. In Marysin a big highway has been paved with cobblestones. I can take it all the way to school without drowning in Marysin mud. The highway is supposed to serve as a short-cut from the railway tracks in Marysin to the main area of the ghetto,‡ but we too will make use of it. It's raining buckets.

---

* In fact, these streetcars would soon be used by the Nazis to facilitate deportation.
† In all likelihood, Dawid's employer was the notorious Salomon Hercberg, who was appointed chief of the Order Service (police) precinct in Marysin and began to rule the district as its "lord and master." He directed the ghetto's Central Prison, and was given the special assignment by Rumkowski of rounding up all the community's "undesirable elements." Ironically, he was himself broken by the ghetto's overseers. On March 12, 1942, he was arrested by the German Criminal Police (Kripo). Searches of his three apartments turned out a tremendous store of food, jewelery, fur coats, and some 2,955 in Reichsmarks. He and his family were summarily deported, presumably to be put to death at Chełmno with the thousand others on their transport. See Dobroszycki, *Chronicle of the Łódź Ghetto,* pp. 136–38, and the Kripo report on the confiscation of Hercberg's loot, at the Jewish Historical Institute in Warsaw or at YIVO in New York.
‡ This was another public-works project engineered by the Nazis to move the Jews toward their deaths. By one report, the cobblestones were in fact gravestones that had been removed from the Jewish cemetery in Marysin and broken up for the road.

Friday, September 12. Łódź.   Father has received 45 kilos of potatoes from the workshop. (With our incredibly "frivolous" lifestyle, the previous 20 kilos had already run out the day before yesterday.) We will now have something to cook for another twelve days or so. And perhaps Mom will also get her half-bushel. If so, the coming New Year's holidays will be nearly "so-so." A fine "sugar" allocation is also rumored to be coming for the holidays. Rumkowski is boasting: "Ich hob geshafn arbet und esn" [Yiddish; I have created work and food]. A sly fox, this old man!

Saturday, September 13. Łódź.   I visited old Frydrych to discuss our welfare. He promised to do what he can. If we could just get this welfare payment, we'd be able to start breathing again. But I don't think it will happen. We should not have it too easy in the ghetto. May it finally end.

Sunday, September 14. Łódź.   We took a test in German today, and tomorrow we will have to do an exercise in Polish. September 29 has been designated for the end of the school year. It seems it's time for this because for thirteen months we've been in the fourth grade. The same dates have begun repeating in our notebooks. However, we are not doing at all well on the material. We are barely finishing in Latin, biology, algebra, and a few Judaic subjects. The status of other subjects is very meager. Physics is the worst, geometry after that. In German we are almost at the level of an advanced group; in Yiddish, too, we've done a lot; Polish and Hebrew are very bad; the history of the Jews and Bible studies are also in poor shape. In a word: a badly bungled school year.

Monday, September 15. Łódź.   We blew through the Polish test. There are no more tests in sight this year. The graduation exams are in full swing. The only thing with any value in the school now is soup. Potatoes keep arriving in the ghetto, and there is also a lot of work in the workshops. But we're still short of cash . . .

Tuesday, September 16. Łódź.   I saw the streetcar that goes along Brzezińska and Łagiewnicka Streets. It is a gray, open freight car with three small cars attached to it. A Jewish motorman, a German, and several other Jews were standing on the front platform. They are apparently learning to drive. The motorman comes from the Fire Department, as do the drivers who drive the trucks with goods and food. "The ghetto is becoming fully motorized."

Wednesday, September 17. Łódź.   Bread is made from various mixtures and is black as hell. A loaf will now be issued for six days (which means 33.3 dkg a day!). They must be afraid that we are eating too many potatoes. The main thing is the cash for "cooking" because an hour of cooking on electricity already has gone up to 60 pf, while a kilo of wood costs 1.20 to 1.50 RM. In a word, the same old story: the main thing is cash!

Thursday, September 18. Łódź.   Battles are going on at Leningrad and Kiev. I wonder when the Germans will conquer these cities. I have totally given up the hope that there is any place they might not conquer. They must be helped by some miracle from Heaven! They keep moving ahead like a ram smashing everything in its way. Will nothing ever stop them?

Friday, September 19. Łódź.   I got "almost very good" in the German test. We'll now have four days off: Saturday, Sunday (Erev Rosh Hashanah), then Monday and Tuesday (Rosh Hashanah). When I remember what these four days meant three years ago, I just get furious. In school we'll now have soup regularly, and on Sunday each of us will receive 5 dkg of candies. Rumkowski is also sending small parcels by mail to all the children (from two to seven years old), with 5 dkg of candies for each and coupons for two suppers during the holidays. A new era in the ghetto. . . .

Saturday, September 20. Łódź.   The Germans have surrounded four Soviet armies, and captured Kiev and Poltava! They are moving toward Kharkov, and will probably finish off Leningrad too. Apparently the war will not end in even five years. Wonderful news for the holidays.

The weather is unexpectedly nice today. Even though it's still cold, at least it's sunny and dry (a situation we haven't had for five or six weeks).

Sunday, September 21. Łódź.   We have no school today: Erev Rosh Hashanah. Tomorrow and the day after tomorrow are holidays. The main thing is that we'll receive soup and candies in school during the holidays.

I asked Niutek if there are any meetings scheduled that I could attend during the holidays. My offer was accepted favorably, and today I attended a meeting of one of the groups that has begun doing theoretical work again. Of course, I am considered a stranger somewhat. It amuses me greatly because I remember my role in creating the school youth organization last year. *"Tempora mutantur . . . "* [Latin; Times change].

Monday, September 22. Łódź. Since many boys don't come to school for their soup during the holidays, I can buy more [food] coupons and take Nadzia to school with me for dinner. Let her have a little something to eat during the holidays. It's enough to say that she gets only 25 dkg of bread a day.

The weather is unexpectedly nice during the holidays, and it's truly pleasant in Marysin. However, I don't have too much time to enjoy the weather because I have almost a full load of tutoring again. Today I also had a sociological meeting, after which we discussed the subjects "Why am I a Communist? And to what extent?" We also talked about the incident that occurred a few weeks ago in school. It was about signatures under the greetings for Rumkowski.* When a teacher came up to me with the card, I signed it. Niutek and others "made a demonstration" and didn't sign. It made an impression and "sent tongues flapping." I think it was idiocy, especially because they couldn't be consistent, and when, after several days, we were asked who hadn't signed, none of them answered. Anyway, they were ready to kill me after that incident. Now they don't want to talk about it at all, so our discussion fell silent in a moment today. There are no new meetings in sight for me.

Tuesday, September 23. Łódź. The last day of the incredible "holidays": nothing festive to eat; Mom's working, and I tutor, so there's no time for reading.

New stories are reported. Rumkowski said at the prayer in his concert hall today that new *gezeyres* [Hebrew; grave troubles] await us. What is it about? No one knows yet. Brr, something will begin again. Apparently we have been too well off.

Wednesday, September 24. Łódź. We already know what it's about. They are supposed to send more than 12,000 Jews into the ghetto from

---

* Rumkowski encouraged the practice of having elaborate tributes sent to him on holidays by the ghetto's schoolchildren. Many of these poignant tributes can be found at the Jewish Historical Institute in Warsaw and at YIVO in New York.

nearby small towns. The first transport will arrive from Włocławek. An emergency medical service has been established because it's expected that among the deportees will be victims of all kinds of pogroms on the way. Meanwhile, food prices in the ghetto have gone up twice. Suppos-

The weather is unexpectedly nice during the holidays, and it's truly pleasant in Marysin.

edly there will be less bread and potatoes. In the cooperatives they are already giving out rations of only 6 kilos of potatoes a family, while the previous allocation of 10 kilos a person has been canceled. So total starvation is to begin again?!

Thursday, September 25. Łódź. Marysin is being taken for the deportees. They are supposed to arrive tomorrow evening, and the school year has been cut short because of this. Tomorrow is the last day of school. The new school year is scheduled to begin on October 16, but no one knows where the school will be. I don't think it will be in Marysin anymore.

Friday, September 26. Łódź. The last day of school. My last day in *gymnasium,* and the end of a particular period in my life. How strange it is to remember that just a moment ago I was a *gymnasium* student and that I will never be one again! "Melancholy" comes over me again! Damn it, the world is going through so much now, and here I am moved by such a trifle. But yes, it moves me because it's about me, and a new epoch in my life begins. Whether the epoch of being a *lyceum* student, I don't know. But that's the way it appears, and I hope it will be so!

Saturday, September 27. Łódź. When I was on my way to school for dinner (we will continue to receive soup there daily, even on Saturdays) I saw several transports of women from Włocławek being taken to a bath. They look better than our women despite their rags and poverty. I've heard that not all of them liked our soup, and many didn't even touch the horse meat. They were accustomed to much better things! I don't think that the experience of recent days has taught them much. Anyway, nobody can be jealous of their fate. They came here without anything. Nobody knows what will become of them.

Sunday, September 28. Łódź. I lost the lesson with my idiot from the first grade. I tutored him for the whole summer. He was probably forced to repeat the same grade, so his mother has resigned from educating him further. As an influential ghetto dweller, she gave him to the Metal Department. She owes me a few marks, but I'm afraid I'll have difficulty getting the money. She asked me to come on Friday, but I'm afraid she won't pay me then.

Monday, September 29. Łódź.   I study English and French again, read, and slowly arrive at the conclusion that school will not begin that soon, if it will ever begin again in the ghetto. Several boys from our class have already started working, and others are about to start. Some will do their apprenticeship in various workshops and departments, while all the rest speak about such a necessity. In Marysin our small [school] buildings will be taken any moment because a new transport of deportees is arriving and an order to empty the school was sent today. The prospects for *lyceum* are becoming fainter.

[S]chool will not begin that soon, if it will ever begin again in the ghetto. Several boys from our class have already started working, and others are about to start.

Tuesday, September 30. Łódź.   Erev Yom Kippur.

A transport of deportees from Lubraniec near Włocławek and from Brześć Kujawski arrived at our former school building. They look great, have luggage, and say that they used to live well. What's interesting is that they know practically nothing about the conditions in this place, and show a considerable degree of optimism. They are in good humor and even make jokes. They are mostly women of various ages. All their men in their prime or boys are in work camps. Lubraniec residents wear a triangle patch on their backs, while others big Magen Davids on their left breasts. You can see that we have been marked in various ways. They say they brought a lot of food with them, but the Jewish police stole it from them (several policemen are said to have already been locked up). In any case, they're treated like cattle. Of course, the sick, children, and old people have been driven to hospitals, orphanages, and homes for the aged, but the rest are lying in empty houses on straw mats provided by the administration or on their own bedding. They complain about food and drink, yet if everybody in the ghetto had meals like the ones they've been given to eat, there wouldn't be so many fresh graves in the cemetery and such horrible-looking people. I talked to them for over an hour and came to the conclusion that these people have won two years of the war and haven't experienced the worst yet.

Wednesday, October 1. Łódź.   Yom Kippur.

Answering a fervent though silent wish of my mother, I fasted today. I stayed at home all day long and read the Jewish literature. The fast didn't affect me in any particular way, but in the evening after supper I felt badly and had to go to bed immediately.

Thursday, October 2. Łódź.   People are saying that the Germans are attacking Turkey. The news seems to be only a rumor, though. In fact, the ghetto has become almost completely silent. The only subjects now are food, work, workshops, rations, and potatoes. There are already several cargo streetcars in service in the ghetto. A great number of peasant carts have also arrived. Men and the oxen are harnessed to them. The ghetto is progressing . . .

Friday, October 3. Łódź.   I got the picture that we took of ourselves on the last day of school. It's very pretty. I came out excellently in it. A dark rumor has started circulating in the ghetto. They say that all schools and

*I got the picture that we took of ourselves on the last day of school.
It's very pretty. I came out excellently in it.*

libraries will be closed. I don't know where the rumor comes from, but it
seems to be true.

Hitler is reported to have given a speech in which he said that he has
begun a gigantic offensive in the east. I wonder how it will develop. It
looks like this one will be as victorious as all the previous ones.

Saturday, October 4. Łódź.   Rumkowski's conference with all the
ghetto teachers took place. He announced that because of the expected
arrival in the ghetto of 20,000 Jews from all over the Reich, he is moving

the school break that was scheduled for the winter to now, and in the winter we'll see what happens . . . Furthermore, he warned against teaching the Talmud under threat of the worst kind of punishment. Additional nutrition for children will be continued, and some of the teachers will be employed to assist the deportees. It seems to be the end of education in the ghetto. I will not be a *lyceum* student, at least not in the ghetto, if I'm a student ever again (I've been lucky enough to snatch the *gymnasium* graduation). We are supposed to get real printed certificates.

Again a run on work begins. A large number of youths will be employed by the workshops, and several friends of mine will start working as apprentices in Podlaski's saddlery shop. I will talk to [his son] Rysiek about the same thing tomorrow. After only a few days of practice, I could start making an income. This seems to be a better option than taking some stupid messenger's job because I'd have a secure trade should something happen. The main things are not to be idle, not to grow sluggish, not to go crazy, and not to fall into depression. Action, work, change—these are the goals, and a route to productivity.

Sunday, October 5. Łódź.   I talked to Rysiek about the workshop. He told me that the list of apprentices already has been submitted to the School Department, but he will ask his father what else could be done. The tutoring has been giving me very little income lately, and I'm becoming worried and anxious again. Just to get a job.

A man was shot to death near the wires in Marysin today (I saw him being carried on a cart to the cemetery). Did he want to escape the ghetto?* Only the Devil knows. The situation looks pretty bad in the ghetto, *oy*, pretty bad! . . .

Monday, October 6. Łódź.   Despite the Succoth holiday, all workshops and stores are open. The Germans have apparently taken tough action against the Jews, whom they want to reduce to mere work robots without any other needs or rights. Meanwhile, only vegetables arrive. The golden potato period seems to be over already. "Vegetable" rutabaga–carrot soup begins to dominate our nutrition again. I have a new student as of today: my classmate Bryt, whom I will teach Hebrew. I will have three lessons a week, 40 pf each. Just not to be idle.

---

* A few attempts to escape the ghetto were made—nearly all of them disastrously. But more often, ghetto dwellers despondent with their miseries would commit suicide simply by approaching the barbed-wire fence within sight of a German guardpost, quickly drawing a bullet. The practice came to be called "going to the wire."

Tuesday, October 7. Łódź.   Rumkowski gave a speech in the afternoon. He said that he will have enough food and that it's only "temporary" that they are not sending in potatoes. He complained about the profiteers who now want a mark or more for a kilo of potatoes, and said that 21,000 more people are being sent in, including 20,000 from the Altreich [old German Reich, within the 1938 borders]. (Relocation and rehousing have already started. Several families in one room, 3.5 square meters a person.) He also said that he is negotiating to relieve the fuel-shortage problem. A change for the worse has occurred in the ghetto. What will come next?

Wednesday, October 8. Łódź.   I've received a letter from Lolek Łęczycki in Warsaw. He is recovering from a typhus epidemic that is raging there. Despite the disease, they had a painting exhibition. He writes that he will have an opportunity to send me something again.

I've started a campaign to pursue work and have mobilized a whole army of friends who are influential in various workshops and departments. Perhaps something will happen.

Thursday, October 9. Łódź.   Autumn has already begun, and it's cold as hell in the morning. Shivers run down my spine at the thought of winter. More and more I want to get a job, not to have to run around and not to freeze soon either.

Our [final] grades were read to us in school in the afternoon. I have all "very goods," except a B in gym. I've achieved the best results in my life and probably the best results in the school. As we've been told, in a few days we'll receive the graduation certificates with our grades in print. Then perhaps it'll be easier for me to get a job. But only the Devil can tell for sure.

Friday, October 10. Łódź.   In politics things are said to be very bad. The Germans have supposedly broken the Russian front with their 3-million-man army and are marching on Moscow. Hitler has personally taken command on the front. So it's to be another successful offensive. The Germans are really invincible. We'll rot in this ghetto for sure.

Nine hundred and some odd number of people arrived in the ghetto from Kowel Kujawski yesterday. It was the final transport from the Warthegau. Now transports from inside Germany are supposed to arrive. The Housing Department is working day and night.

Saturday, October 11. Łódź. Rainy autumn weather is already beginning. Even though there is a "highway," the road to Marysin is terrible. What will come next? No one really knows. Either I will get a job, or I will get stuck in those muddy holes in Marysin [the cemetery]. Although there is enough soup because a lot of boys don't come to school, and we can buy their portions, the basic situation is hopeless. The main thing is to make money to buy food and to have a warm corner. Oh, just to get a job! . . .

Sunday, October 12. Łódź. The first snow has fallen! An incredible sensation. Wet snow has covered everything in white, and people have pulled out all their winter rags. But I am not very warm in them at all. My shoes are so terribly soaked that I feel truly despondent.

I've submitted an appeal to Rumkowski again. This time in Yiddish. I ask in an elegant manner for a job and shoes. Perhaps this year something will come of it. I'm also working on all other fronts to get work.

A register of men for deportation to work in Germany has supposedly been compiled secretly on the basis of data from the Registration Department. Those to be deported are men fifteen to sixty years old who aren't employed in the ghetto. Being deported is not too nice a prospect. I'd like to settle myself in some workshop or in an office position as soon as possible.

Monday, October 13. Łódź. We won't get our soup in Marysin anymore, but somewhere else in the ghetto instead. Marysin has been entirely reserved for the deportees coming in from Germany. They are supposed to arrive any day now. The main ghetto area is also being reduced so we will be really crowded. In addition, they will cut off one more section and put the Gypsies there. Only the Devil can tell what else might happen here. They will probably totally destroy us.

Tuesday, October 14. Łódź. Our last day in Marysin. As of tomorrow we'll receive our soup at 31 Franciszkańska Street [in the central ghetto] in the former movie theater Bajka [Polish; fairy tale], which is now a synagogue. I wonder whether it'll be better or worse for us there.

Although Sunday's snow has almost disappeared, it's terribly wet, cold, and nasty. The first transport of deportees from Vienna will arrive tomorrow. They're said to be all Christians and Nazis whose grandmothers were proved to be Jews. They may yet set up an anti-Semitic association in the ghetto!

The first snow has fallen! An incredible sensation. Wet snow has covered everything in white, and people have pulled out all their winter rags. But I am not very warm in them at all. My shoes are so terribly soaked that I feel truly despondent.

Those to be deported are men fifteen to sixty years old who aren't employed in the ghetto. Being deported is not too nice a prospect. I'd like to settle myself in some workshop or in an office position as soon as possible.

Wednesday, October 15. Łódź. We are in Marysin once again because the Viennese won't arrive until tomorrow. I run to various "connections" and "protections" to get a job somewhere, but so far in vain. I'm beginning to fall into last year's mood again. On the one hand, I'm beset by fear of deportation to Germany; on the other hand, I'm afraid that I won't get a job after the German Jews arrive. I could already start working in the carpentry shop, but I have problems over there because they insist on a form from the School Department, which cannot be obtained anymore. I can't start working in the workshop where Podlaski is, either. There's been no answer to my request to Rumkowski, and there probably won't be any until the deportees are settled and "the old man" gets back to reviewing appeals. Will it ever happen, though? I doubt it. In any case, it won't happen soon enough.

Thursday, October 16. Łódź. We already ate in Bajka. Food there is no better or worse, but the portion is more honest (0.5 liter). The first transport of deportees from Vienna arrived in Marysin in the afternoon. There are thousands of them, pastors and doctors among them, and some have sons on the front. They've brought a carload of bread with them and excellent luggage, and are dressed splendidly. Every day the same number is supposed to arrive, up to 20,000. They will probably overwhelm us completely.

Friday, October 17. Łódź. Today seems to be the last time we will eat in Bajka. After our dinner the police arrived, and the next school group was not let in. A German was shooting in the air, and after that a transport of Czech deportees was brought in unexpectedly.* They, too, had wonderful luggage and cartloads of bread. I've heard that they have been inquiring whether it's possible to get a two-room apartment with running water. Interesting types . . . These "western Europeans" will soon learn the way some people live in the German Reich. But the fact that they're finding themselves in the same condition we are in won't help us a bit. I still can't get a job.

Saturday, October 18. Łódź. I've been to my "protector" in the carpentry workshop, but I got nothing. The workshop commissioner insists

---

* For a superbly detailed account of arriving in the ghetto in the transport of intellectuals and artists deported there from Prague, see Oskar Rosenfeld, notebook entries, in *Łódź Ghetto*, edited by Adelson and Lapides, pp. 167–70, 177–87.

that he won't hire me without the form from the School Department. I haven't succeeded at the saddlery workshop either. Of course, there's been no answer to my application to Rumkowski. Only the Devil knows how much longer I'll go on like this. It'll probably be harder to get a job now because transports from Berlin, Vienna, Prague, and Luxembourg arrive daily. However, they haven't taken Bajka away from us because the deportees have been packed into the school building at 27 Franciszkańska Street, in the former Mariavits' monastery.

Sunday, October 19. Łódź.   More Luxembourg Jews arrived today. They are beginning to crowd the ghetto. They have only one patch on the left breast with the inscription *Jude.* They are dressed splendidly (you can tell they haven't lived in Poland). They are buying up all they can in the ghetto, and all the prices have doubled. Bread is 12 to 13 RM; socks, which cost 70 pf before, are now 2 RM. Although they've been here for only a few days, they already complain about hunger. So what can we say, we who haven't had our stomachs full for more than a year? You can apparently get used to everything.

Monday, October 20. Łódź.   It seems that I will work in the cork workshop. Our teacher Szwarzfinger has received a request for six graduates, so perhaps I will be able to get in there. However, it takes more than a month to learn this "corkwork." Well, if there is nothing else for me, even this will do.

I went to visit the Czech Jews today. There are fine boys among them (among the Luxembourgers too). They were extremely well off until now, and are surprised at the filth here and are afraid of disease. A new transport from Vienna or Berlin has arrived. Almost all of them are Zionists, but "*rot*" [Red] are also everywhere. They're already looking for jobs. They're intelligent, clean, kind, and open. It's really a pleasure to be among them.

Tuesday, October 21. Łódź.   For now, nothing has come of the cork workshop. The School Department still doesn't want to give a [work suitability] confirmation, arguing that only those who are not suitable to continue [their] education should be given away to work. The fact that further education is out of sight and that I have to eat is considered irrelevant. Except for one regular and sometimes a few casual lessons, I don't have any others. I now make a maximum of 15 RM a month. To work as soon as possible!

Wednesday, October 22. Łódź.   I went with Father to the workshop to talk with Podlaski in the morning. He promised me that in two or three days he will set up a group of students, and that I will be included. He has advised me to learn saddlery making because I could earn up to 4 RM a day (experts make 4 to 5 RM a day). I'd like to start working as soon as possible, especially since all other opportunities seem to have failed.

The German Jews keep arriving: from Frankfurt am Main, Cologne, and also from Vienna and Prague (they live near us). Almost all are "big fish." At least so they look.

Thursday, October 23. Łódź.   I'll start my work in the saddlery workshop tomorrow. Rysiek Podlaski informed me about it today, while notifying five or six other boys from our class whom he placed there as well. So I will start a new notebook as a saddlery apprentice. My student career has been suspended, at least for a while. Will I ever again be a student? I don't know. I dare to doubt it. But perhaps? The main thing now is to make an income and survive poverty. Just to hold out, just to keep going. The war will take a long time, and our task now is to fight with all our strength to stay alive. The immediate goal: overcome the winter. I'm certain that a wonderful, shining life is still waiting for us.

We live in constant fear

The cover of diary notebook 3.

*W*ednesday, March 18. Łódź.   Our bread ration has been reduced, and vegetables don't arrive anymore. Hunger is ever more terrifying. The less there is to eat, the more people talk about covered tables and reminisce about the "good" prewar times. At work, food is almost the only topic of conversation (the food we had before the war, naturally). Nadzia was told to come to Chopin Street [Leather and Saddlery Workshop]. She will probably start working on Sunday.

Thursday, March 19. Łódź.   I went to the head office today, directly to old Podlaski. I asked him to assign me to a newly created group of apprentices, and obtained his permission quite easily. All he asked was if 2.50 RM a day was worth it for me. So I will become a group leader, probably starting on Sunday.

Winter has returned. Thick snow fell today, and it's really freezing cold. We have no way to get out of this cold. To say nothing of the hunger.

Friday, March 20. Łódź.   Father has finally received part of the latest workshop ration: meat, potatoes, cabbage, and beets. The rest next week. The workshops are supposed to receive a major supply of food for Easter, but nothing is known officially yet. It's still freezing. We began washing our completely dirty winter clothing yesterday with very active help from Father. Lice have shown up lately, just as they did at the end of last winter. We boil the clothing in tubs on a gas stove in the laundry room at night. The deportations continue.

Saturday, March 21. Łódź.   We worked from one to five today. At the workshop I have been officially appointed by Podlaski as a group leader, together with two other young saddlery makers, Szmaragd and Skoczylas. Nadzia will also be in my group.

The news that an additional 15,000 persons will be deported immediately burst like thunder in the ghetto this evening. Everybody says that now everyone will go, one by one, to the last ghetto dweller. There is a terrible frost again.

Sunday, March 22. Łódź.   For the first time I worked as a group leader. The three of us have a group of about forty-five workers. We distribute crochet hooks, needles, and thread among them, and have learned how to thread a needle and make clothes. All I have to do now is practice

The news that an additional 15,000 persons will be deported immediately burst like thunder in the ghetto this evening. Everybody says that now everyone will go, one by one, to the last ghetto dweller.

sewing on petersham and then on leather. My job is easy. I work only until 7:30, pick up my own bread ration, and am guaranteed 2.50 RM; in a word, the change of job has been very advantageous. Furthermore, the path to a future "career" has opened for me. "Mein Leben—was willst Du noch mehr" [German; My life—what more do you want]?

A ration of 2 kilos of rutabagas and 1 kilo of carrots per family (!) has been issued. The ghetto population has been divided into three categories: "A," "B," and "C." "A": workshop workers and clerks; "B": clerks and ordinary laborers; "C": the rest of the population. Meanwhile, hunger and deportations continue; sun and freezing cold.

Monday, March 23. Łódź.   We have received 24 kilograms of briquettes for our March ration. We have also received rotten rutabagas and carrots. I am extremely glad that Nadzia now has a job, and that she has the 15 decas of bread and 5 decas of sausage. Now Mom has her soup all to herself.

In the afternoon the Germans placed closely spaced armed sentries around the ghetto, and trucks full of soldiers and policemen were driving around. Nobody knows what it meant. Fortunately, everything returned to a normal, calm, blessed state after half an hour.

Tuesday, March 24. Łódź.   A rumor has spread that the decision to liquidate the ghetto has been made. They will supposedly clear Litzmannstadt* of Jews before May 1, so the deportations have been intensified (1,100 persons are sent out each day). Even clerks are said to have been taken. In the evening people were saying that only five workshops will be left (saddlery makers, tailors, metalworkers, dry-cleaning workers, and shoemakers), and their workers will be left without their families. Meanwhile, there are still no food rations at all. A loaf of bread already officially costs 100 RM, but you can't get one for even that much. The work with my group is very pleasant. A day or two more and the group will be able to start paid work. In spite of the light work, I am beginning to lose the rest of my strength at a terrifying rate. I almost fainted when I was going down a stairway with dish water in the morning. And there is still a long way to go until the end . . .

Wednesday, March 25. Łódź.   Before noon—certainty of deportation. In the afternoon—encouraging news, namely, the announcement by a German from the Bałuty Market† made to Podlaski during an inspection that the deportations will end, and substantial rations for the population and workshops will supposedly be issued very soon. I felt awful today. I read, but I can hardly learn anything, only a few English words. Among other things, I'm now reading excerpts from Schopenhauer's works. Philosophy and hunger: quite a combination.

Thursday, March 26. Łódź.   Rumkowski posted announcements cautioning against believing rumors that say the deportations have stopped, because they are continuing. Again total confusion. The deportations are in progress, while the workshops are receiving huge orders, and there is enough work for several months.

---

* Litzmannstadt was the German name for Łódź, after General Karl Litzmann, who fell in a battle near the city in World War I.
† Both Jewish and German ghetto administrations were located on this main square.

It was a lovely spring day today. How fortunate that I didn't have to fire up the stove. For now, I have an easy and rewarding job. The group is sewing very nicely, and it has already received materials for piecework. (Nadzia also sews very well.)

Friday, March 27. Łódź.   A series of rations has finally been issued: 3 kilos of potatoes, beets, sugar, margarine, coffee substitute, saccharine, and *Fruchtsuppe* [German; fruit soup]), and a ration of meat (30 dkg).

Many people are being deported. Only those employed in the workshops are exempted, but their families are deported if they are large. A certain percentage of clerks is also being deported.

Saturday, March 28. Łódź.   After two and a half years without hearing them, alarm sirens woke us several times last night. We didn't hear any planes, though. The ghetto is so absorbed in its internal problems that the night alarms were barely discussed during the day. From neighbors who are being deported, we have bought an étagère (my prewar dream), a kitchen table with storage space under it (for underclothes that up to now were lying about in sacks), and a few other trifles for the house. The price: two packs of cigarettes. After work, I went with Dadek Hamer to see our old friend from the building, Józik Wolman. We played cards for a while. (I hadn't played for two years. What a nonsensical way of spending time!)

Sunday, March 29. Łódź.   Over a dozen new apprentices have joined our group. Among them grownups, relatives of various high-ranking persons in the workshop who can save themselves in this way from deportation. The pace of the deportations has increased. A "mandated" number of people is supposed to go before April 3, and after that we will see . . . The holiday week has begun, but not at all in a holiday manner.

Monday, March 30. Łódź.   We've received our food allocations of 14 kilograms of vegetables. New "apprentices" keep coming into our group. They sew hooks on *Sturmgepäck* [German; army backpacks]. The deportations continue. Many workshop workers whose families have received orders to leave, while they themselves were exempted, are going voluntarily with their families. Apart from the deportations, several groups of persons left for Warsaw in recent days, taken out by their relatives (for big money). They travel comfortably in cars with a lot of luggage. Tomorrow: a general housecleaning, washing, and putting on bed-linen. After the dirty end of the winter, a cleaner spring. May it only be possible for us to remain here.

Tuesday, March 31. Łódź.   There were two alarms again last night, but nothing followed. I worked like a horse today, cleaning. Mom can hardly walk, so all the work fell to me and Nadzia. In the evening: general washing up, and my clean, fresh bed. Just like before the war. I miss "only" a glass of hot milk and noodles. The deportations continue.

Thursday, April 2. Łódź.   The first day of Passover. The police have spread the word that the deportations have stopped. The group that was supposed to go today has come back to Marysin. May there be no more deportations, and may something substantial arrive to eat. Potatoes are the main thing. To eat, think, study, write, and work. Just to get to the end! . . .

Friday, April 3. Łódź.   The deportations have been halted again, but nobody knows for how long. Meanwhile, winter has returned with thick snow. Rumkowski has posted an announcement that there will be a cleaning of the ghetto on Monday. From eight in the morning to three in the afternoon, all dwellers from the ages of fifteen to fifty will have to clean apartments and courtyards. There won't be any other work anywhere. All I care about, however, is that there is soup in my workshop.

Saturday, April 4. Łódź.   Snow and cold again. One more allocation of vegetables, 10 dkg of margarine, and 10 dkg of meat has been issued. Meanwhile, the heads of the workshops and other big shots have received splendid holiday gifts (sardines, white matzoth, sugar, margarine, wine, matzoth flour, briquette fuel, meat, and so on and on). So lives this petty bourgeois world.

Sunday, April 5. Łódź.   Tremendous anxiety pervaded our household because before the holidays Father took a bit of bread away from me. I had not spoken to him until today (he has quite a nature! I felt ashamed before Schopenhauer's spirit), but at Mom's request and with my own conscience begging, I finally decided to forget the whole thing. Maybe now, in spite of the war and hunger, everybody at home will live "fairly."

Rumkowski has made another announcement about tomorrow's cleaning. The matter must be quite serious. Meanwhile, spring is not coming. Clouds, frost, snow, rain; together or separately. And in politics, all's silent, silent . . .

Monday, April 6. Łódź.   I worked in the courtyard from eight until about twelve. I have never messed myself up in shit so much before. We gathered into one pile all the waste that had been thrown out into the courtyard during the entire winter. Now administration carts are supposed to take it away. In spite of my loafing, I had to work very hard.

At 4:30 we went to the workshop just for some soup. Potatoes supposedly arrived at Marysin today. They also say there won't be any more deportations in April. May it be true. What's more important, however, is whether there will be anything to eat! Just to be able to at least half-stuff my insatiable belly. I don't even dare to dream about being satiated in the ghetto. That has to wait until after the war. Meanwhile, I'm running out of the last bits of matzoth (Nadzia doesn't have any left, and Father will finish off his portion by tomorrow). Help! Something to eat! . . .

Thursday, April 7. Łódź.   No rations or hope for anything to eat. Rumkowski is said to have visited the kitchens and cooperatives yesterday. He laid into everyone, left and right, and came to the conclusion that much too much is being stolen and some remedy has to be found for it. I suspect, however, that the populace will in fact be the ones who suffer from the effects of this "remedying."

Today was the most lovely spring day. On such a day the poverty and hopelessness of the ghetto situation can be seen in all its "splendor." As though out of spite, there is no encouraging news from the outside, no "action" in the world. It looks like everything has become bogged down for ages to come. For us, at least.

Wednesday, April 8. Łódź.   A lovely, warm day again. There are still no rations, and the soup at the workshop is becoming more and more watery. Vegetables are supposedly arriving, but nothing is distributed. No one knows what will happen. Tomorrow we will finally receive bread. I have almost forgotten that such food exists. But I have not forgotten hunger. Nadzia begins work today with the other group. She will be able to earn a little more. She gets very little now.

They have called all the day workers to come to the head office for a meeting tomorrow at eleven. I wonder what they have in store for us. There are constant changes everywhere, but nothing is improving and there is nothing to eat.

Thursday, April 9. Łódź.   At three, Rumkowski gave a speech in the yard of the head office. His speech made a gloomy impression because the expected ration for the next three weeks was issued, and there are only six kilos of potatoes per person in it, 2 kilos of vegetables, half a kilo of flour, 40 dkg of sugar, and 20 dkg of margarine. That's it for all of April! Rumkowski, for his part, admitted that there is less and less food, and there is going to be even less, and he wants what little food there still is to get directly to the populace. Therefore, he intends to dissolve the workshop kitchens and give the appropriate allocation directly to each home. I don't think that the situation will be any better then. It's the stick or the club again. He also announced that because we lack strength, we are going to work only seven hours a day. He spoke a lot, but didn't say anything important. The demagoguery of a man sick with megalomania.

Friday, April 10. Łódź.   I got Podlaski to agree to take my mother on as a machine operator, but it didn't work out because a sewing instructor concluded that she was too weak. There isn't any other work for her.

Yesterday and today we have had nothing to cook. We finally received a loaf of bread yesterday, but it is terribly sour, dark, and small. The truth is that if only we had enough of that bread, at least we could eat our fill! There is a new position now at the workshop: curator of working youth, appointed by the School Department. We have Wolman, the Yiddish teacher in Marysin. He called a conference with the group leaders and management for tomorrow. Nadzia will be in my group. I was at the workshop today at 9:00 A.M. to prepare everything.

Saturday, April 11. Łódź.   After three o'clock we had the conference with Wolman. He offered me a job as his secretary, and talked about the relations between the foremen and the apprentices in the ghetto workshops. He made a series of proposals that were actively discussed. It was decided that in order to "bring the youths a moment of escape from meditations over food," lectures will be arranged.

Sunday, April 12. Łódź.   Work was great today. A small group (twenty-three people for the time being), calm, silence. Podlaski, who supervised us in the evening, was very appreciative of our work. We will receive a new assignment tomorrow. Maybe this week I will receive my daily wages because we would not be well off if we are paid a commission based on our group's productivity.

Monday, April 13. Łódź.   Hunger becomes more and more routine. There is no other news.

Tuesday, April 14. Łódź.   A new fashion has developed in the ghetto: potatoes are boiled and eaten in their skins. They say we're profiting both in quantity and in calories. The taste is a bit strange, but we've quickly become used to it. In the workshops the soup is worse and worse, and the cutlets are smaller and smaller. There are no rations, and no hope for any either. The hunger is intensifying. The weather is rainy again; it keeps pouring, and it's cold.

Wednesday, April 15. Łódź.   Mother went to the workshop yesterday and today, but they didn't let her work because she is too weak. Podlaski promised some lighter work for her, but for now there isn't any. Today they were seizing unemployed men and women able to work on various public projects. They say that the Germans will tour the ghetto to make certain that everything is really working well, as Rumkowski has assured them. They still have the time and the men to do all these things.

Thursday, April 16. Łódź.   The sun is finally shining again, and the Jews have regained hope. Again "S'yz git" [Yiddish; It's good] has become everyone's cheer: "Wus hert men?" "S'yz git" [What's the news? It's good], or "My zugt, s'yz git!" [People say, It's good].* However, nobody knows anything certain. Damn it! There is no political news, which usually proliferates in the spring! The work at the workshop makes me more and more exhausted. In my group I have discovered a guy whose parents run a small shop with leather goods and stationery articles, and at the price of waste paper I will be able to exchange my useless old books there for good ones.

Friday, April 17. Łódź.   In exchange for my old books I bought a history of Hebrew literature, two Hebrew short stories by Breuer, *Jeremiasz* in Hebrew by Lazarus, and an article in Yiddish by Żytłowski on

---

* In the Yiddish vernacular that developed in Poland during the Holocaust, the expression "S'iz gut" took on a sardonic meaning, heralding impending trouble. In the Kraków Ghetto, the famous Yiddish folk poet Mordkhe Gebirtig wrote a song entitled "S'iz Gut," and in the Lwów Ghetto, the following joke was popularly told: the last two surviving Jews from the ghetto were now also being sent away to be executed. On the way, one asked the other, "So what do they say?" Responded the other, "Men zugt s'iz gut" (They say it's good). See Nachman Blumental's Yiddish lexicon, *Werter un Wertlech Fun der Churbn-tkufe* (Words and Expressions from the Time of the Holocaust) (Tel Aviv, 1981). Dawid's transliterations from Yiddish vary widely from the accepted literary norms. So "S'iz gut"—a contraction of "Es is gut"—appears in his diary as "S'yz git." And where he wrote "My zugt," the literary norm would be "Men zogt."

the theory of Marxism.* I still want to read and to study. I borrow books, make plans and have projects, but there is nothing that I can turn into tangible reality. I used to blame it all on the winter, but it's quite warm now, and those winter obstacles are gone. Unfortunately, hunger is the real reason for my "laziness."

A meat ration of 10 dkg per person has been issued. In addition, 3 kilos of vegetables, and 10 kilos of slaggy coal per family. Systematically we are being pushed closer to death.

Saturday, April 18. Łódź.   A lovely day. But only insofar as the weather is concerned. I went to see various friends, but as a result I became so tired that I know I won't make another such tour any time soon. I saw Engel, who is going to leave for Warsaw (recently a few hundred people left for Warsaw by bus), and I also went to Wolman's. He read me a passage from his latest poem about Hitler. A very powerful and delightful thing. Wolman is, however, already completely broken by hunger and has stopped writing. Today he gave two lectures for the youths in the workshop, but the effort exhausted him terribly. In some respect Wolman's case makes me less lonely and despondent because I can see I'm not the only one who is being killed spiritually by hunger (physically, it is killing everyone).

Sunday, April 19. Łódź.   A new thunderbolt from the blue! A huge announcement has been posted about an examination beginning tomorrow of all the unemployed ghetto dwellers aged ten and over. It'll be conducted by medical commissions. There is a penalty for not showing up. The sick will be brought by stretcher bearers. Enormous panic hit the ghetto. All those who have unemployed family members are running like crazy to get them a job somewhere. The Arbeitseinsatz [Employment Department] issued 10,000 work cards today (it's all a matter of connections). When I came home Mom threw herself at me, crying. She is the only one in our family who is threatened now. Our side of the ghetto goes first. It will last for four days. People from our street will be examined on Wednesday. The Germans, Czechs, and those who are working and have cards from the Arbeitseinsatz for work are excused from the examination. We learned about it in the workshop.

* Chaim Żytłowski (1865–1943) was a well-known Jewish philosopher and social activist. He participated in the Russian Revolution and later became active in socialist and literary circles in the United States.

Father's true nature revealed itself today. He is becoming more and more crazy. He surely wants to get rid of Mom because he has not even lifted a finger to do anything to find her a job. He just keeps on shouting, annoying everyone at home.

In the evening I went to Podlaski's. I somehow managed to get him to promise that he would try to do something for Mom tomorrow. Perhaps he will be able to put her at a machine. The most varied rumors are spreading. They say that the healthy people will be sent away for work, and that the sick will either go too, or be left here, or be shot. Everything is possible. Meanwhile, almost all my friends have "somehow" taken care of their family perils. I can't wait until tomorrow to find out what's going to happen with Mom's work. I've heard that all those who were sent out of the ghetto are supposedly in a camp similar to the Łódź Gypsy ghetto.* I shudder at the very thought of it.

Meanwhile, the sun gives so much warmth that it's easier to work in the shop. As of today we group leaders will probably get a commission from the productivity. Oh, if only there weren't this situation with Mom. Poor, broken, weak, dear, unhappy creature! She has had enough trouble in the ghetto already, and quarrels and conflicts at home (there are many of them). According to Father, they're caused by my "indifference" to the family or, more precisely, to him. May we be able to save her! We will settle accounts with Father after the war. Feeling worse, Mom decided this week to give him only 25 dkg out of each loaf of her bread (instead of the former 50 dkg). He doesn't like this idea, but he calculated that if there is no Mom he will get even less. I brought the Warsaw addresses to Engel. Maybe he will really go, so I will let them know what is going on with me here. Meanwhile, Mom is in danger.

Monday, April 20. Łódź.   The ghetto has gone mad. Thousands of endangered unemployed persons are struggling for work in every possible way, mostly using connections. The German medical commission has begun its work. All those examined by the commission get an indelible stamp on their chests, a letter whose meaning nobody knows. Meanwhile, Rumkowski has decided to employ as many people as possible. The School Department keeps issuing forms to children. After filling them out, they don't have to go before the commission. Everyone em-

---

* A Gypsy camp, which was located by the Nazis beside the Jewish ghetto, was quickly wiped out by diseases resulting from the lack of sanitation.

ployed in the straw workshop* in the winter is getting a job there again. The Arbeitseinsatz is issuing thousands of work papers releasing people from having to appear before the commission.

Father has seen Podlaski about registering Mom on a good employment list. The outcome will be known tomorrow. Mom can hardly walk because of her despair. Father stomps about, constantly shouting. Meanwhile, the weather is so lovely—warm and sunny—no trace of snow or mud. The buds on the willows have burst into bloom, and the grass has turned green. "Spring, spring, a happy thing! ... "

Tuesday, April 21. Łódź. Mom has finally been taken care of. A few hundred persons received notes to report to the workshop for an examination today at two o'clock, among them Mom. They waited for several hours, lined up in military style in the workshop yard. The [Jewish] commission consisted of Rumkowski, Jakubowicz,† Podlaski, Celigman, and two policemen. They asked how many persons there are in the family, how long and where each person has worked. Some were told to wait to be assigned a job, while others were told to go to the German commission. They approved the people with families in which most of the members have work. Mom has been accepted. Tomorrow she is supposed to get an employment card, and she doesn't have to appear before the German commission. There are rumors that soon the entire ghetto population will be "stamped."

Meanwhile, a group of children who had gone to the School Department for forms were seized and taken for "stamping," to fill the quota of people to be examined in the scheduled district today. Because so many people are being employed everywhere, rumors have spread that soon no one will be exempted from the German examination. We live in constant fear and worry. It's interesting that we now talk less about hunger. (Less, but it's still on everyone's mind.)

Wednesday, April 22. Łódź. Mother has finally received a note from the Arbeitseinsatz with a job assignment in our workshop. The note's dated April 19, and it relieves her from the obligation to appear before

---

* The Germans had the Jews produce straw boots to be worn by troops in the bitter winter on the Russian front.

† Aron Jakubowicz (d. 1981), the second-ranking official in the Rumkowski administration, was chief of ghetto industry and trade, and liaison with the Nazi ghetto overseer, Hans Biebow. He survived the war, having been sent by Biebow to a work camp in Germany along with a group Jakubowicz was allowed to select to be saved from death at Auschwitz.

the German commission. In the workshop, they said that she will start work soon. Meanwhile, thousands of people are getting job assignments in all sorts of ways, and Rumkowski has to seize children for the examination, sending them in from a camp in Marysin; he also seizes people from the old-age homes.

An announcement has been posted saying that people must not believe rumors claiming that everyone over sixty years old is relieved of the obligation of reporting for the examination.

Thursday, April 23. Łódź.   Last night the police visited apartments looking for anyone who had shirked the obligation to appear before the commission. Those who had not reported and had nothing to justify their absence were deprived of food coupons. Yet there are fewer and fewer candidates for the examination, so roundups are even being carried out in the streets.

Roundups of those who tried to hide from the examination are going on night and day.

Another group left for Warsaw by bus. I wonder if Engel was among them. The conditions in Warsaw are supposedly excellent: the ghetto is open, everything can be bought for money, work is easy to find and pays well. Meanwhile, we are dying here.

Friday, April 24. Łódź.   Mom hasn't started her job yet. The situation is becoming dangerous again because the police demand an employment card when they check papers, and a card from the Arbeitseinsatz is not enough anymore. There are arguments at home again. Father takes kilograms of potatoes to the workshop, where he cooks them just for himself; then there is nothing to eat at home. Mom is silent, as always. She just grumbles. I pretend that I don't want to interfere, but everything is electric with tension.

We don't have any more fuel, so we had to chop up one of the chairs for firewood. Last evening I felt a terrible dizziness that continued all night and did not stop all day. I could hardly stay on my feet in the workshop. Nor did I read or write anything. It must be from exhaustion and general weakness.

Today the German medical commission visited our workshop. They are people from another world; our rulers, masters of life and death. In no way does their appearance suggest that their end is near. The hopes of the Jews for an end of the war this year are being dashed again. A new winter will be coming in the ghetto.

Saturday, April 25. Łódź. I went over to Milgrom, whose father is the head of the Arbeitseinsatz office, to ask him to assign my mother to our workshop. He is a very nasty man. He said that he cannot do anything. Also Rysiek Podlaski claims that no more people can be employed in the workshop.

There will be one more examination tomorrow. This time for the people who began employment in the workshop only last week. Some of them will be dismissed; of course, not the ones with strong connections. All my friends are surprised that my mother doesn't work in our workshop, considering the custom of hiring relatives. But I'm having such a tough time here with Podlaski, and Father's ill-will also plays a

They are people from another world; our rulers, masters of life and death. In no way does their appearance suggest that their end is near.

role perhaps. My bread has begun to disappear again. I blame it as always on Father, who has taken to stealing from us again at every turn. The arguments become more vehement and bitter each time. My dizziness is almost gone, but I can't read too much or it returns immediately.

Today was a nice cold day. And in politics, nothing is new.

Sunday, April 26. Łódź.   Commission members visited all the workshops today. They reviewed the newly employed workers.

An unexpected ration of 15 dkg of tiny fish per person has been issued. The fish already stink a little, but are still causing a sensation. I have never seen such tiny fish, even in an aquarium. They were a bit bland, but good. I wish there were more.

Monday, April 27. Łódź.   A ration for the first ten days of May was issued in the afternoon (15 dkg of sugar, 25 dkg of wheat flour, 10 dkg of honey, 20 dkg of salt, 10 dkg of margarine, 20 dkg of sauerkraut, soda, baking soda, matches, and citric acid). A ration of fuel has also been issued for all of May (8 kilos of briquettes per person, and 2 kilos of wood per family). It's cold again; constant clouds, wind, but no rain. In politics there is nothing new.

Tuesday, April 28. Łódź.   Rumkowski has posted announcements that people who have failed to appear for "stamping" are supposed to register today at Młynarska Street to complete the "stamping" program. We know now that the Devil is not as black as they paint him. The stamp [in fact] comes off the body, and after all, we now live day by day.

We have received our rations, but after giving me a few kicks, there is almost nothing left. What the hell! There will be a new ration in ten days.

It's getting much colder. Hitler reportedly gave a speech ordering the Germans to get ready for winter. He announced that he is personally taking over military affairs. However, there is no new information from the front. No news about an offensive or any movement. Nothing. Even if there is something happening out there, we know absolutely nothing here. Complete silence.

Wednesday, April 29. Łódź.   It's really bad at home. There is no fuel, and we are eating our May ration of potatoes in April. No one knows what will happen in May. Nothing good, that's for sure. Again I don't have any will, or rather any strength, for studying. I want to do something, but everything is exceptionally difficult for me, so I just stick to reading most of the time. Time is passing, my youth is passing, my school years, my power and enthusiasm are all passing. Only the Devil knows what I will manage to save from this pogrom. I'm slowly beginning to lose my hope of coming back to life or even of holding onto the one I'm living now.

In the afternoon an announcement was posted that as of Monday regular deportations of the unemployed German and Czech Jews will begin (1,000 people a day). They can appeal, however. New struggles for work will begin. Only those who earned a Cross of Merit can remain in our paradise here. One thing's for sure: it's not boring.

Thursday, April 30. Łódź. The weather is still very cold, and it's getting even colder. Is next winter coming already? Niutek Radzyner came to the workshop and "conferred" with his boys, my former school friends and others, in a stairwell. They are apparently up to something (perhaps finally something serious? I hope so!). I've been excluded from everything, secrets and nonsecrets, as "a traitor and a heretic, egotist, coward, and weakling." I don't care. May the war just end.

The unemployed were taken straight from their beds to the camp at Czarnieckiego Street.

We received our pay for last week—no commission yet, but it was based on a higher daily rate of 3 RM. I got 20 RM and 16 pf. They deducted 4 percent for taxes. Nadzia earned 7 RM last week. Meanwhile, there's nothing new in politics except for the bombing of Germany. Tonight they will be seizing people from their beds again. Maybe they will take us soon. I would not like it, damn it all!

Friday, May 1. Łódź. An announcement has been posted that all the German and Czech Jews, even those who have jobs, will be deported. What a prospect for us all! In the streets trading has begun in clothing that the German and Czech Jews are getting rid of in all haste. They don't want money, but food. A splendid new suit costs 6 kilos of potatoes; a pair of shoes, ¾ kilo of bread; trousers, 5 dkg of sausage. I wouldn't, however, give away a dekagram of food for even the best clothing because, like everyone else, I feel myself getting weaker at a terrifying rate.

Saturday, May 2. Łódź. Mom received a notice from the Arbeitseinsatz to come today for a job assignment. We thought that she would get assigned to our workshop, but they assigned her to public works, at the disposal of an administrator at 16 Drewnowska Street. Of course Mom went immediately for help to Moniek Wolfowicz, who promised to do something about her case tomorrow. Public works would finish Mom off in a few days. Father wanted to see Podlaski about the matter, but I'm sick of him after his many refusals to employ Mom.

The Jews are saying again that things are getting better as far as politics is concerned, and that the war will be over pretty soon. Idiotic talk! Everything has conspired against us. Even the warmth doesn't want to come this year.

Sunday, May 3. Łódź.   I'm working in the afternoon again. The saddlery makers work three shifts now because a few hundred more have been accepted at the workshop for training.

When Mom came back from her work today, she could hardly move. She looks terrible. They clean various yards, and, though they work quite slowly, it is extremely hard for her. Moniek Wolfowicz cannot offer us any help. I intend to talk to Milgrom once again. Perhaps he will try to give Mom some other work.

The first groups of German and Czech Jews have received notes to report for their departure. The barter trade is prospering in the streets.

Monday, May 4. Łódź.   Total hunger has again begun in the ghetto. Almost everywhere the potatoes and vegetables that were issued for the entire month of May have already been eaten up. There are no new rations; people eat their bread ration in two days, and later they subsist literally on only the soup provided at work. Money is of almost no value anymore. Those bedeviled Germans and Czechs are paying any price [for food] and the local Jews are following suit.

Rumkowski supposedly gave a speech to the workshop directors during supper in the kitchen for the intelligentsia yesterday.* He announced that several tens of thousands more workers from the surrounding areas will arrive in the ghetto. Then he said that we are not in any worse a situation than the Germans in the city because, after all, there are *Zusatzkarten* [German; coupons for additional food portions] for us. Finally, he announced that he has revived the *Beirat* and Hebrew cooperatives because the workshop directors and doctors work harder than the

---

* At this stage in the ghetto's history, various soup kitchens served particular segments of the population.

rest of the population and they mustn't starve. He also warned against malfeasance in the workshop kitchens and had announcements posted in the workshops about electing workers' delegates to inspect the kitchens. Meanwhile, it's cold again, and in politics there is nothing new. No allocations of potatoes are expected in May. It's going to be sheer paradise.

Tuesday, May 5. Łódź. It was snowing, and all the roofs were frosty in the morning. Could it be next winter already?

I talked to Milgrom about Mom. He promised to talk to Father. Perhaps it will be possible to arrange something. Otherwise, Mom's health and even her life are in danger. If only she could get under some roof and have some kind of sitting work because she can hardly stand on her feet.

The hunger is becoming more and more horrible. The price of a loaf of bread has reached 400 RM. Rumkowski has announced that the situation will deteriorate even further because there are no more potatoes, vegetables, "lard," or even sugar or honey. In the workshop almost no one has any strength to work.

Workers' delegates have arrived for an inspection of our workshop kitchen, and we can notice a number of margarine globules in the soup that were not there before at all. That's because the margarine, sugar, and flour were all eaten in the kitchen before the soup was served. But all this *Glück* won't satiate anyone. The agony of hunger begins.

Wednesday, May 6. Łódź. Milgrom hasn't arranged anything for Mom. I went to see Frydrych today, but he can't do anything either. I really don't know what to do.

Everyone works less and less. We all loaf completely. Time is passing to no avail. There is no news. The silence of death.

Thursday, May 7. Łódź. Deportation of the German Jews continues. The barter is quieting slowly because no one has any food to exchange anymore, and those who still have it have finally wised up and prefer to eat it themselves. I have a new problem now. Father came from a doctor with the news that there is something wrong with his right lung. The doctor told him to have an X ray, eat every two hours, and lie in bed for some time, and gave him other similar directions that are impossible to carry out in the ghetto. Nadzia, too, saw a doctor because she has abscesses on her feet and sides: "The result of bad nutrition."

Meanwhile, the *Beirat* doctors and chemists have received huge allotments: ½ kilo of butter, a kilo of meat, 80 dkg of oatmeal, 60 dkg of barley, flour, and other products. Social divisions in the ghetto become more and more scandalous. But we are in such a state of exhaustion that now I understand what it means not even to have enough strength to complain, let alone protest.

Friday, May 8. Łódź.   Everyone is waiting most impatiently for the next ration (the previous one was issued for the period until May 10). Again it will be only enough to have a little bite and then have two or three bits to cook.

Father has had an X ray, but he doesn't know the results yet. Mom keeps working because otherwise she would lose soup. The number of deaths in the ghetto has started to rise again at an incredible rate. People get swollen, and each day you can see someone else with the characteristic bags under their eyes, distended eyelids, cheeks, and chin; their legs become swollen, and in some cases their hands too.

The prices are insane. A portion of soup in the workshop is 20 RM (but you really have to look hard for a fool who wants to sell it). Hundreds of high-ranking clerks, and hundreds of other officers and officials, if only they have the slightest opportunity, steal and gobble terribly in the kitchens, bakeries, in food-supply offices, at the police stations, in the prison administration in Marysin, on the vegetable-market squares, in the cooperatives. They eat everywhere they can, at our expense, at the expense of the rest of the ghetto population. The sixteen workers from the tailor workshop who demanded the introduction of the two seven-hour shifts have been moved by Rumkowski to collect feces, which means a quicker end for them.

Saturday, May 9. Łódź.   There is a new scandal that will require all kinds of gods and devils for vengeance. The next ration has been postponed until [May] 15, supposedly to stop the sale of food to the German Jews. Rumkowski is very angry about such trade. The decision will contribute to the deaths of several thousand more persons in the coming days. Either Rumkowski has gone completely mad, or the Germans are really not sending any food to the ghetto. I flew into such a rage that at six I went to the concert on Krawiecka Street. It is organized every Saturday both for those who are completely satiated and for those who are completely hungry. The concert was overcrowded. There wasn't anything special there, but for an hour and a half I somehow distanced myself from the prepossessing reality of the ghetto. However, the music was just better background for meditation on the theme "what I would be eating now if there were no war . . . "*

Sunday, May 10. Łódź.   I work in the mornings. It's still cold, even though the sun has started to come out again. There are still no new food rations, and supposedly there won't be any until the end of the week. Father is feeling bad and has a high temperature. Yesterday he bought half a kilo of potato peels and boiled them for himself, but today he doesn't even have this. Mom, though she got tanned, is simply wasting away before our eyes. Nadzia is still having problems with abscesses. Today, for the first time, my co-leader, Rywek Skoczylas, congratulated me on having gotten fat—that is, that I already have big bags of "fat" under my eyes. So now we are taking our place in the line to Marysin, to the cemetery. Those with connections may go straight there without standing in line, but in this case the "well-connected" eagerly give their place to others, and time after time they move back. Beggars take precedence in this line . . .

Monday, May 11. Łódź.   The situation is horrible. Work in the workshops has almost stopped, and strikes are expected because no one has any strength to work. Father says that he coughed blood today. He definitely wants to leave the ghetto with the deportees. They say it's possible to do this. Almost no one (except for the circles made up of "the haves") has anything to eat. For a great number of people, the workshop soup is their only meal now.

Rumkowski has decided to issue new rations before [May] 15 after all! He did that in a very demagogic way. Tonight he posted announcements about a new ration for the following ten days (up to May 20), but it won't be issued until Wednesday at two in the afternoon. He shut the mouths of those ready to strike, who will be placated even by this pittance. In the meantime, he will manage to send off the German Jews, and will get rid of the food trade. Finally, he will fill the ghetto treasury with money (which is being accumulated by the people who have nothing to spend it on, while the administration has none to pay the wages). The ration will include 10 dkg of sausage, a kilo of potatoes, a kilo of beets, 30 dkg of wheat flour, 10 dkg of margarine, 15 dkg of sugar, 20

---

* The ghetto's house of culture was located on Krawiecka Street. Here symphony concerts, theatrical revues, literary readings, and art exhibitions were held, most of which opened with a speech by Rumkowski exhorting the ghetto dwellers to work more and gossip less.

*[W]e are taking our place in the line to Marysin, to the
cemetery. . . . [I]n this case the "well-connected" eagerly give their
place to others, and time after time they move back. Beggars take
precedence in this line . . .*

dkg of salt, 10 dkg of imitation honey, *Fruchtsuppe*, 13 dkg of imitation
coffee, 10 dkg of rye flakes, 7 dkg of potato flakes, vinegar, and baking
soda. It's just wonderful, except that many people will kick the bucket
before Wednesday.

Tuesday, May 12. Łódź.   Today we managed to create some confusion
when we were getting our dinner in the kitchen. As a result, Rysiek
Skoczylas, who was arranging the scheme, had six soups; I, as a "guest,"
had two extra soups; and several dozen more workers had one, two, or
three extra soups each. We were a little afraid that we might be assigned
to collect feces for this action, but we made it work somehow. I don't

think we will be able to get away with it next time because too many people know about it now. Here's how the trick worked: the kitchen workers agreed that a group leader should come inside and receive a calculated amount of sausage on his group's card. Then the group leader put the sausage portions into the bowls into which the soup was poured. The soup was poured as long as there was sausage, so a person could make several rounds with the same portion of sausage.

Prices went up again: a kilo of potatoes: 100 RM. A loaf of bread: 900 to 1,000 RM. Soon you will be able to become a millionaire in the ghetto and die of hunger on your bed of money.*

Wednesday, May 13. Łódź.   We couldn't "arrange" anything in the workshop kitchen today. As I had expected, Father got hold of my bread again. I will have to wait until Thursday to get back the 12 dkg that he borrowed.

In the workshop everything is awkward; nobody cares about anything; everyone just loafs, and all we do is wait for soup and after that for quitting time. Mom cooked only *Fruchtsuppe* this evening. It would be all right as a compote, but it has to serve as mid-day meal and supper as well. I can hardly drag my legs now, and they get terribly swollen in the evening.

People are saying today that the Germans are supposedly attacking or even taking over Leningrad, and that they have begun using poison gases.

Thursday, May 14. Łódź.   We've received our ration (through connections), and managed to restore ourselves a little again. I also had an extra soup, some of which I gave to Nadzia.

The weather is already warm, but rainy. Only now are the trees beginning to bloom. The deportations of the German Jews are over. In order to fill the required quota (mostly workers have been left in the ghetto), certain Jews from Łódź have been added. Two hundred men have volunteered to go to Poznań for road construction.

Friday, May 15. Łódź.   Also today we managed to "earn" extra soup in the kitchen (Nadzia had one, too). But this fun will soon end because

---

* For a graphic description of the relationship between bread prices and deportation from the ghetto, see Józef Zelkowicz, "Bread in the Year 1942," in *Łódź Ghetto: Inside a Community Under Siege,* edited by Alan Adelson and Robert Lapides (New York, 1989), pp. 245–50.

as of Sunday our group will be working only two shifts again. So we will be getting soup directly at the workshop, and our visits to the kitchen will end. But the main thing is not to worry. Maybe we will find some other way.

My group is now sewing so-called *Mantelriemen* [German; belts for an army coat]. We can make a good profit, but no one feels like sewing.

Saturday, May 16. Łódź.   The workshops did not receive sausage today. There was only soup. No one knows whether there will be sausage tomorrow. A loaf of bread cost only 200 RM ! today, and we could buy four saccharines for 1 RM.

We are expecting the arrival of several tens of thousands of men from neighboring towns. The first group is supposed to arrive today or tomorrow.

I went to a concert on Krawiecka Street again. Today the concert was much better than the one last week.

At home we all finally calmed down because Father learned from the doctor who had received his X-ray that there is no shadow on his lung. Father hasn't eaten more than his daily portion of bread since Thursday, and he says that he is going to behave like this from now on. For the time being we have something to eat for the next few days, but we have already started looking for a new ration. I just hope there won't be any postponement again.

In the evening Rumkowski posted announcements warning against carelessness in blacking out the windows in apartments and workshops. The smallest lit sliver in a window means the death penalty now. However, there has been no bombing yet. Complete silence.

Sunday, May 17. Łódź.   The first transport of Jews from Pabianice has arrived. Separately men, separately women, separately children. They are coming impoverished and tired, but they don't look bad. Like the German Jews, they have a patch with "*Jude*" inscribed on their chests, but on their backs a patch like ours, only on the left side.*

It is rumored that because people are hoarding money, and because of lower production in the workshops, all prices in the ghetto will go up

---

* According to official ghetto chronicler Bernard Ostrowski, after his visit with the bereaved women of Pabianice, "There were plenty of orders (for new work) in Pabianice. . . . [B]ut that did not protect the Jews against wholesale deportation. Fear for our ghetto's fate is keeping everyone up at night. Our last hope is our Chairman; people believe that he will succeed, if not totally, then at least in part, in averting the calamities that now loom ahead" (Lucjan Dobroszycki, *The Chronicle of the Łódź Ghetto* [New Haven, Conn., 1984], pp. 177–87).

by 100 percent. Again, there was no sausage in the workshop today. They say that if there isn't any on Tuesday either, that will mean there won't be any sausage at all anymore.

It was pouring all day long, but it cleared up late in the evening. In politics there is nothing new.

Monday, May 18. Łódź.   The new ration for the last ten days of May has been issued. Everywhere tremendous happiness.

The second transport of Pabianice Jews has arrived. There is still no sausage in the workshops, and most likely there won't be any at all. My legs have begun to weaken at a terrifying rate in the past few days. I can hardly walk at all. Climbing up and down the stairs makes me particularly tired, but I can't avoid the stairs in the workshop because my group works on the third floor. We are running on the last of our energy.

Tuesday, May 19. Łódź.   It is rumored that new deportations will start on Friday. The "Germans," "Czechs," Jews from Pabianice and Brzeziny, and some of us [Łódź natives] are supposed to go. The Jews from Pabianice had been "stamped" there and divided into two categories: able vs. unable to work. Only those able to work were sent here.

The weather is finally warmer, though not enough to warm me up. I suppose I will have to wait for that until the war is over. Despite the Jews' most optimistic hopes and moods, the war seems to have absolutely no intention of ending this summer.

Wednesday, May 20. Łódź.   We have received our new food ration. So there's something to nibble and spread on bread for two or three days again. There are rumors that we will have a small additional ration for the holiday. (Tomorrow is Erev Shavuot.)

Tomorrow the first group of deportees is going. They are the Jews who have just arrived from Brzeziny. After that, others will go. There are rumors about an enormous ghetto for all the Jews from the Reich, but only for those who can work.* Nobody knows what the Germans do with the children and those unable to work. The Pabianice Jews also know nothing about their elderly, their sick, and their children. Children

---

* Rumors spread in the ghetto that the Jews of Europe would be sent to Madagascar, for instance. Rumkowski confided to associates that he expected to be appointed by the Nazis to run a permanent Jewish slave state after the war. Raul Hilberg details the phases of consideration and planning behind the Madagascar plan, "the last major effort to 'solve the Jewish problem' by emigration," in *The Destruction of the European Jews* (Chicago, 1961), pp. 128, 138, 141, 258, 260–61.

Nobody knows what the Germans do with the children and those unable to work. The Pabianice Jews also know nothing about their elderly, their sick, and their children. Children were torn away from their mothers in the most brutal way. We are not considered humans at all; cattle for work or slaughter.

were torn away from their mothers in the most brutal way. We are not considered humans at all; cattle for work or slaughter. No one knows what happened to the Jews deported from Łódź. No one can be certain of anything now. They are after Jews all over the Reich. But nowhere is the hunger like it is here.

Thursday, May 21. Łódź.   Three tiny additional rations were issued, one after another, which made the ghetto much happier than they should have. In the morning a ration of 5 dkg of candy was issued; in the afternoon, a ration of 20 dkg of sugar (!), 7 dkg of margarine, and 5 dkg of ersatz coffee; and in the evening, a ration of 15 dkg of meat. The expected price increase has indeed taken place. By this means, Rumkowski wants to squeeze out the accumulated cash and increase production in the workshops. Anyhow, I had a great day today because I received a 20-dkg portion of sausage—prolonging life again for a while. And so it goes, day by day, ration by ration, deportation by deportation until the end of the war, or departure to Marysin, or perhaps until we go into exile.

Friday, May 22. Łódź.   Jews from small towns keep arriving. They have had it better everywhere else than here.

The garden plots in the ghetto have turned green. You can already get spinach and chives. The weather is finally warm, though not enough to satisfy me.

No one knows what happened to the Jews deported from Łódź. No one can be certain of anything now. [Depicted in a secret scrap book kept by the ghetto's Statistics Department. The text reads: "Like a stone in the water, they disappeared. 45,000 from the ghetto."]

Saturday, May 23. Łódź.   A circular arrived in the workshop saying it is mandatory to salute all Germans in uniforms who pass through the ghetto, even if they're in cars; if a commission arrives in the workshop, we should greet them by standing up. I wonder whether the order is the result of a good or bad political situation in Germany. I think it's the latter. Until now the Germans didn't care about Jews saluting them. Meanwhile, there is nothing to eat again. The soup in the workshop is hopeless. As for sausage, one shouldn't even dream of it. People are getting swollen at a terrifying rate, while Rumkowski is demanding greater and greater productivity . . . The less you eat, the more you should work. There is no shortage of hands to work, so they can press people as much as they want.

In the afternoon I went to see Niutek Radzyner because I heard that he was sick, and I wanted to talk to him for a while. He is in worse condition than I expected. He has had a high fever for three weeks. It's probably pleuritis. I couldn't exchange a single word with him. I'll visit him again soon.

Sunday, May 24. Łódź.   I work in the mornings again. Being on the morning shift is much worse than working the afternoon one because there is nothing to do for the rest of the day. Last week I studied a little, but now I'm so weak that I can't do anything. I can't write either. Recently I have had a few talks, discussions really, with Kazik Biremwajg, my former schoolmate in the ghetto, who works in my group now. He is an orthodox *radzynerowiec* [Polish; follower of the Hasidic rabbi of Radzyń] and a poet-humorist. My views left him surprised, terrified, and . . . curious. He comes over to talk with me more and more often.

A ration of 7 kilos of briquettes for June has been issued. Tomorrow I will receive 20 dkg of sausage. In spite of these rations, the situation in the ghetto is becoming tragic again, since there are no vegetables or potatoes or even pickled beets at all. The soup in the workshop is absolutely hopeless. If it weren't for the fact that together with Rysiek Skoczylas we perform quite courageous "operations" in the kitchen, and in effect we have an additional half or whole portion of soup, I am not sure if I could drag myself to the workshop. In politics nothing is new.

Monday, May 25. Łódź.   There are no vegetables in the June ration, not even potatoes. Now Rumkowski won't have to bother himself that people have eaten their potatoes too early; we won't even have a chance

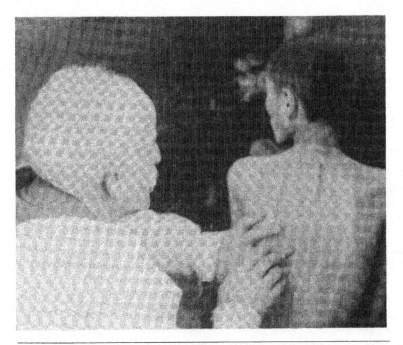

A person becomes thin (an "hourglass") and pale in the face, then comes the swelling, a few days in bed or in the hospital, and that's it. The person was living, the person is dead. . . .

to see them this time. The situation is worsening, and there is no hope for the end.

They keep relocating the Jews from small neighboring towns (Brzeziny, Ozorków, and others) into the ghetto, while the deportations from the ghetto have been stopped. Even that chance for getting out of the ghetto has been taken away. Death is striking left and right. A person becomes thin (an "hourglass") and pale in the face, then comes the swelling, a few days in bed or in the hospital, and that's it. The person was living, the person is dead; we live and die like cattle.

Tuesday, May 26. Łódź.   An unexpected additional ration has been issued: 25 dkg of sugar, 7 dkg of artificial coffee, 5 dkg of margarine, caustic soda, soap, and matches. Again, a prolonging of life for a day and a half.

I went to see Radzyner in the evening. He feels much better. I revealed part of my views to him, and we discussed them for quite a long time without any result. Jerzyk [Rapaport] was also present. I understand those people less and less, if what they say is to be believed. They show a continual, sober readiness to fight, die, suffer, and so on and on; quite in the manner of the Middle Ages. After coming back from Niutek's, I quickly wrote down the most important thoughts of my theory about pure egoism and the sanctity of human life so that I would have an outline for our next discussion. If I had something to eat, maybe something more substantial would grow out of my notes.

Wednesday, May 27. Łódź.   In the afternoon an announcement was posted about the voluntary registration of men between the ages of eighteen and fifty for work in Poznań. Father, who has been warning us for a long time that he would go (though at other times he shouted that we, and particularly I, shouldn't wish for his departure), has now registered in the Arbeitseinsatz to leave. Tomorrow at one o'clock he is supposed to appear before a medical commission. I, too, considered the possibility of leaving, but because of my weakness and lethargy caused by hunger, I don't think I have enough strength to go. Besides, I would miss my books and "letters," notes and copybooks. Especially this diary.

Today I went to the concert on Krawiecka Street again. It was the first concert worth seeing in the ghetto: a Beethoven evening. The whole of select society gathered, bloated and dressed up. The gap between various classes of people in the ghetto grows wider and wider. Some steal to feed themselves, others feed themselves officially, while the rest are swelling up and dying of hunger. The deported Jews from Pabianice and elsewhere flee from here to work in Poznań as though they are escaping from hell. The kingdom of Chaim Rumkowski. Nothing like it exists anywhere else in the Reich.

Thursday, May 28. Łódź.   Father says that he went through the medical examination today, but they did not accept him because he works in the shop. (It will not be cleared up until Sunday whether they will also accept the workshop workers.)

We are cooking the last remains of our May ration. We have only candy that we received today and that I am just finishing. There isn't any trace left of Tuesday's tiny ration. And so one must live and not die until the liberation.

I, too, considered the possibility of leaving, but because of my weakness and lethargy caused by hunger, I don't think I have enough strength to go. Besides, I would miss my books and "letters," notes and copybooks. Especially this diary.

Szyjo Sonnabend's father and a stretcher bearer from our workshop died yesterday. In both cases the "sickness" had taken three days and consisted of a swelling of the limbs, body, and heart; fever for half a day, and that was it. Meanwhile, in politics there is nothing new.

It was the first concert worth seeing in the ghetto: a Beethoven evening. The whole of select society gathered, bloated and dressed up. The gap between various classes of people in the ghetto grows wider and wider. Some steal to feed themselves, others feed themselves officially, while the rest are swelling up and dying of hunger. . . . The kingdom of Chaim Rumkowski.

Friday, May 29. Łódź. The *Beirat* and the medical cooperative are continually receiving enormous allocations, while other people faint and collapse on the streets all day long. Eating potato peelings has become a new fashion during the past two months. Doctors were giving out coupons to sick people for a kilo of peelings, and such enormous lines formed for them that they stopped issuing peelings to "strangers," and only kitchen workers and "connected people" receive them now. Just like all other "ordinary" people, I feel worse and worse, and if the situation continues even a little longer like this, I am out. I don't feel the heat so much, but I sweat more and more.

Saturday, May 30. Łódź. The "internal situation" at home is becoming extremely tense again. After two weeks of relative calm, during which Father divided his bread into equal daily portions, he became spoiled again. Last Thursday and again yesterday he devoured his whole loaf of bread, and today on top of it, half a kilo from Mom and Nadzia. I also don't know why he hoards all the money. He takes away all of Mom's and Nadzia's pay, and doesn't want to give us money for anything. Today he bought our ration of sausage and ate over 5 dkg of it on the street (Nadzia was with him), so everyone's share of sausage was short. He has also managed to borrow 10 dkg of bread from Nadzia already. (Stupid girl. I take my portion of bread to the workshop with me now.) Father also bought his whole portion of meat today, and, having received a liter of whey at the dairy store for a whole family, he cooked it only for himself and lapped it all up. As a result, the rest of us have nothing to cook at home anymore, and are going to bed without supper. Nor did Father go to the workshop today; he was roaming around the city all day long. He certainly must have spent a great deal of money. Mom looks like a cadaver, and the worries at home are absolutely killing her. If only he seriously wanted to leave! No, no way, though. Instead, he's taken to stealing from us and harassing us, as though that will help him. We didn't buy our kitchen ration today because he didn't want to give us any money, and I don't want to give away my last few marks because then we would be left without a single penny, should it come to

---

[P]eople faint and collapse on the streets all day long.

the worst. The situation is horrible and the person who is suffering most, physically and emotionally, is Mother.

Sunday, May 31. Łódź.   Father showed us that he has all the money with him, so I have given away my last pay to buy our ration. Father says that because he will probably leave, he plans to exchange "Chaimkas" [ghetto currency nicknamed for Chaim Rumkowski] for German marks in order to have something to take with him. Well, that's something different. In any case, when I came back from the workshop in the evening, I discovered that I was short several spoonfuls of [artificial] honey and that Mom was short even more than that. There is no one to borrow bread from, so once again there are arguments and tension.

Today for the last time we had soup at the workshop. They made what's commonly called swill. As luck would have it, I had three portions. Otherwise, I wouldn't have made it back home. The women giving out the soup were quite generous to us group leaders, and were "doling out" the soup most favorably.

Rumkowski gave a speech today and said that 20,000 more people would arrive in the ghetto. Then he warned people against taking walks in the ghetto, told us to work diligently, etc., etc. Food, of course, is not mentioned anymore. I've heard confidential information that's spreading around to the effect that they have brought shipments with clothing* back into the ghetto that they are supposedly†

---

* These shipments were the baggage of deportees sent out of the ghetto and asphyxiated in gas vans near the village of Chełmno. According to the official ghetto Chronicle entry for May 30 and 31, "The people of the ghetto are tremendously puzzled by the arrival of these shipments" ("Large Shipments of Baggage," in Dobroszycki, *Chronicle of the Łódź Ghetto,* pp. 190–91). Sorting the bundles, ghetto workers repeatedly found letters, currency, and identification cards, which confirmed that these were the goods of their own deportees.
† The notebook breaks off.

The bloodthirsty Nazi beast

*T*hursday, *June 4. Łódź.* Fortunately the "Greiser" cloud has passed. Greiser visited the ghetto, toured many workshops, and was reportedly very happy with our *Arbeitsgebiet* [German; work district].* The visit was over by the afternoon, and after it, bread was issued. Rumkowski was running around the ghetto in a very merry mood, and perhaps because of that a new ration was issued in the evening: 25 dkg of sugar, 10 dkg of margarine, 10 dkg of coffee, the *Fruchtsuppe* powder, and 8 dkg of candies. There is still a lot of work in the workshops. We're running out of *Mantelriemen* and are supposed to receive a new article, *KTG* [German, *Koppeltragegestell;* carrier attachments for army belts].

The weather is very lovely. In politics something is supposedly starting to happen again. However, nothing specific is known.

Friday, June 5. Łódź. I've restored myself a bit again with the latest ration. I only wish that I had something to cook. We finally received coal. Wood is so scarce that the wooden objects and furniture that we gathered during the period of deportations have already been chopped up.

I'm reading Żytłowski in Yiddish now. It's very interesting. I'm also doing a little in languages and history. The pace is awfully slow because hunger hangs over everything.

England has supposedly started some sort of an offensive. However, nothing specific is known. Meanwhile, the winter is approaching . . .

Saturday, June 6. Łódź. Food supplies will get a bit better now because the ghetto reportedly has made quite a good impression on Greiser. Potatoes have been arriving continually since yesterday.

Last night several hundred deportees from Pabianice were taken out for labor in Poznań. New volunteers' registrations are being accepted. Father has stopped mentioning his departure completely, probably to spite me. Meanwhile, my strength is definitely deserting me. I'm sweating all the time, both during the day and during the night. I can't walk any farther than to the workshop and back, even when they issue a ration. I am failing fast.

---

* "The populace knows and understands that this is not an ordinary inspection but concerns . . . the question of its very existence," asserts the ghetto Chronicle entry on this date. "After the inspection by the authorities, the Chairman remained in a good mood. The distribution of a supplemental, 'sweet' ration was viewed as a token of the ghetto leader's excellent humor" (Lucjan Dobroszycki, *The Chronicle of the Łódź Ghetto* [New Haven, Conn., 1984], pp. 199–201).

Food supplies will get a bit better now because the ghetto reportedly has made quite a good impression on Greiser. Potatoes have been arriving continually since yesterday.

Sunday, June 7. Łódź.   A kitchen ration for the second third of June [10–20] has been issued: 2.5 kilos of potatoes, 40 dkg of flour, 40 dkg of sugar, 10 dkg of pickled tomatoes, 10 dkg of peas, 15 dkg of margarine, 25 dkg of salt, 5 dkg of powdered soup, 15 dkg of imitation coffee, and a few other trifles. There's no honey or marmalade, but even so this ration is better than the previous one. They also say something about an additional ration of potatoes to be issued in a few days. In any case, today we'll go to sleep without supper.

  Tomorrow a transport of 250 persons will go to Poznań. The same number is to be sent every week. If they run out of volunteers, they'll take people by force. A roundup was organized yesterday at the food market. Some forty traders were arrested. Apparently something is happening in the ghetto again. It cannot remain calm for long.

Monday, June 8. Łódź. Nadzia is sick and seems to be in serious condition because she has hardly been able to eat for two days. This is one of the most dangerous symptoms in the ghetto.

The situation in the workshop has changed. Production keeps increasing. Everyone needs money, so everyone is increasing their efforts. My last pay amounted to 24.66 RM. A kilo of sugar costs 40 RM; bread, 100 RM. Summer passes, winter approaches, years pass, so does my youth, strength, and life. Meanwhile, the war goes on and there's no prospect for change.

Tuesday, June 9. Łódź. More and more men are being sent out by force for labor in Poznań. Last night they were taken from their beds, from the streets, and even from workplaces. Only workers in certain workshops are released. The transports are departing at an accelerated rate. The interesting thing is that those who registered voluntarily have not been called up so far.

I went to see the variety show on Krawiecka Street. They are playing it now for a second time. Except for ghetto jokes, there's nothing worth seeing. Only the dances were pretty good. But the most important thing is that for two hours I could stop thinking about food or hunger.

Wednesday, June 10. Łódź. In politics there's nothing new. Total silence again. Apparently all news about the English offensive, bombings, heavy fighting on the front, etc. were lies. There's nothing to give us hope for a quick end to the war.

Thursday, June 11. Łódź. The days are passing imperceptibly, and there is no change in sight. Although the food-supply situation has improved and for the preharvest time is not that bad, the specter of winter approaching appears before everyone. Everyone knows perfectly well that they won't survive the winter. Pessimism is building everywhere: "Either the war will end before the winter, or we will."

Friday, June 12. Łódź. Tomorrow we'll receive coupons for a quarter a kilo of cottage cheese. All these allocations, rations, and coupons seem like injections administered to the moribund to prolong life only briefly.

*I went to see the variety show on Krawiecka Street. They are playing
it now for a second time. Except for ghetto jokes, there's nothing
worth seeing. Only the dances were pretty good. But the most
important thing is that for two hours I could stop thinking about
food or hunger.*

One buys them, gives them a lick (sometimes there's something to cook,
sometimes to eat with bread), and after that there's emptiness in the
apartment and stomach and again waiting for a new ration. Even
though the stubborn optimists claim that the war will end before the
winter, nobody believes them anymore. I've never believed them.

Saturday, June 13. Łódź. Last week was marked by various stomach ailments: thousands of cases of poisoning, stomach swellings, diarrhea, loss of appetite, nausea, and so on. They say it's from sausage or from fresh chestnut bread. Nadzia has already recovered, but now Mom has a problem with her stomach. Father and I, as always in stomach matters, are holding on perfectly well, but for the everlasting shortages and the everlasting hunger.

Father works in the garden plots now in the afternoon. He gets 50 pf an hour. In the cutting room they earn close to nothing.

In the workshop we took a photo of ourselves (Rysiek Skoczylas and his older brother, an instructor; their sister; a fine Bałuty character, Moniek Knobel;* and I) in memory of our career in the saddlery workshop in the ghetto. I only wonder if we'll live to look at this keepsake photo.

There are rumors about a far-reaching alliance that has supposedly been concluded between England and the United States, and about a twenty-year pact with the Soviets.† However, the news interests me now only from one point of view: whether it will bring the war's end closer. The war has to end soon because we simply don't have the strength to last much longer.

Sunday, June 14. Łódź. I'm working afternoons again. The *Mantelriemen* have been finished, and now my group begins to sew *KTG*. Although I lay in bed until twelve today and even slept a bit, I felt as though I had a fever all day. Today in the workshop I wrote, under the influence of the awful state of my mind, "Hallucinations of a Person Dying of Starvation," several tiny pages of confessions and hallucinations. The constant struggle of hope against despair will kill me ultimately. An old filled tooth has flared up again, and I constantly suffer

* Rysiek Skoczylas (b. 1925) and his brother, Izrael (b. 1916), are presumed to have been deported to Auschwitz. Their fate is unknown, as is that of their sister. Mojżesz Knobel (b. 1924) was also deported to Auschwitz and is believed to have survived. Dawid's description of him as "a fine Bałuty character" suggests a kid from the slums who might now be described as "street smart."

† There were many elements of truth in the reports Dawid was picking up. The Atlantic Charter, signed by Churchill and Roosevelt in August 1941 and endorsed a month later by the Soviets and fourteen other anti-Axis nations, called for a new world order aligned against tyranny and aggression. The Arcadia Conference, held in December 1941 and January 1942, extended that resolve. The twenty-year British–Soviet friendship pact was signed in London on May 26, 1942. Less than a month later, the United States and Great Britain expanded their earlier agreements by establishing joint production, supply, and food committees, and resolved to coordinate their campaigns against Germany.

from unbearable pain. Tomorrow I will see the dentist, a visit I've been postponing as long as I can. In politics there's nothing new.

Monday, June 15. Łódź.   Last night roundups were organized again for men and boys who are to be sent out immediately for labor in Poznań. I stayed awake for several hours because of the toothache and heard them visiting apartments, "hunting for game."

I went to the dentist. She cleaned my tooth and will fill it tomorrow. Fillings are very expensive, but I have to complete the treatment. It's been a long time since I was in the central area of the ghetto, and today for the first time on Brzezińska Street I saw a streetcar carrying workers and clerks to Marysin. This is a prehistoric contraption like all other cars in the ghetto, open on both ends. You pay a mark for a twelve-ride ticket. Streetcar tracks are also being built to the coal market so that briquettes and coal that will be arriving by the streetcar can be dumped directly onto the square, "cheap and neat." The ghetto is organizing everything for years to come. I only wonder who all this is for, because ordinary mortals won't survive much longer, and the parasites won't be able to live without our work either. Anyhow, nobody seems to think about that at the moment.

Tuesday, June 16. Łódź.   Last night I had an incredible toothache, and in the morning my mug was really swollen. [It was] fortunate that the dentist had not filled the tooth because an abscess is festering there and the tooth has to be removed.

We are now sewing a new article: *KTG.* It is very complicated work, and the poor children are really sweating. Instructors are trying to shirk the work and put everything on us group leaders, but I have succeeded in restraining them. I was in another world today, however, because the tooth was bothering me all the time.

All hopes about additional rations have proved to be only dreams. We won't receive any addition to our rations. A new ration of meat or sausage is also out of the question. In politics there's nothing new.

Wednesday, June 17. Łódź.   Last night I had no pain, but my face became so swollen that the tooth can't be removed now.

Late in the evening, Father brought home lovely clothes that he bought from a policeman who works in Marysin for the ridiculously low sum of 35 marks. The police, assigned to work with the arriving transports, have picked the newcomers so clean they are able to sell their

surplus plundered clothes. We have money because we can't buy anything to eat with my last pay except dinners and bread. Father also
bought socks for Mom, himself, and me for 10 RM. I will finally have
something to wear because the clothes I have on now are deteriorated.
The only thing I still don't have is shoes. The clogs I'm wearing won't
last much longer. However, shoes are almost impossible to get outside
the *Bekleidungstelle* [German; clothing-distribution site]. You have to
have extremely powerful connections to buy anything there. High-
ranking clerks, their families, relatives, and friends are the ones who
benefit from the *Bekleidungstelle.* Meanwhile, the rest of the population
either has traded away their food to the German Jews for clothes or are
half-naked and barefoot. The social order is excellent here, as is everything else.

Thursday, June 18. Łódź.   My group is already in full swing sewing
the *KTG.* This is painstaking and demanding work, so careless saddlery
makers keep receiving returns to be corrected. Juvenile workers get their
bread in a house next to the workshop. I eat with them there because it's
much more comfortable for me. But I'm still just as hungry. I keep losing
breath and often have to go outside to get some air. My face is still
swollen.

I went to bed without supper because we have nothing to cook at
home. We won't get our food rations before Saturday. Perhaps tomorrow we'll be able to borrow something to cook.

Friday, June 19. Łódź.   It's cold again after several weeks of tolerably
warm weather. The mornings are extremely cold, and for most of the
day it's cloudy (though it's not raining). Everything's insufficient, typical
of wartime. Even summer lacks the warmth of the sun.

My toothache is already completely gone, and the swelling has gone
down a bit. The dentist told me that there's a chance to cure the tooth
without removing it. In politics there's nothing new. The summer's ending, but there's still no help for us.

Saturday, June 20. Łódź.   We finally have the ration. I also got the
photo taken a week ago. It came out fine, realistically showing our
hungry ghetto countenances. It's only from this photograph that I realize what condition I am in. "The hourglass on the mug," as they so
rightly say in the ghetto.

In the workshop, we received bread and butter (for 20 pf). There was so little butter that you could barely see it. Let the Devil take it! That's the way we live, day to day, minute to minute, meal to meal. How much longer, how much longer?

Sunday, June 21. Łódź.   Today the three of us received our worker's food rations and, in addition, salad and cottage cheese. Mom hasn't received her coupons for food yet. Father insisted on weighing out his portion of sugar and butter, but Nadzia and I shared ours with Mom. As far as weighing and sharing portions is concerned, the situation is becoming critical at home. Naturally most of the trouble is caused by Father, who cheats at every opportunity (while considering himself the one who is being cheated). I'm dreaming about the end of the war for one more reason: I want to become independent and to start my own new life, free of arguments and screaming in my parental home. But our separation seems a long way off. More likely we'll all kick the bucket in the ghetto.

Monday, June 22. Łódź.   It's been a year since the German–Soviet war broke out, but there is still no hope for its prompt end. The Jews have been promising for several weeks that offensive actions by the Allied superpowers will start today, but it seems to me that the beginning of the end remains unfortunately far off. Meanwhile, an absolutely reactionary period has begun in the ghetto. Rumkowski, without a thought about adding something to eat for the starving population of the ghetto, has set up the so-called *Beirat 2*. It is an additional cooperative for the police, instructors, and all kinds of higher-ranking clerks, who, together with those belonging to the "B 1" and "L" (doctors), receive special allocations of food on a regular basis. So much for the official version. Unofficially, the stealing of food and filling of pockets by people working with food is becoming more and more outrageous. The big shots eat, so to speak, in advance. There are people in the ghetto who have already set aside little fortunes for after the war, particularly the Jewish Kripo agents. Our authorities are also feeding themselves all right. All this robbery is being conducted with increasing indulgence and greed while the starvation increases around them. We can see how one person's hunger feeds another's appetite.

The dentist has filled one of my teeth, but the one that's been sore has yet to be cured. I paid 5 RM again into an account for the future filling. If they are going to bury me in this ghetto, let it at least be without cavities in my teeth. Should I, however, get out of here, I'll need to have my teeth in good shape to be able to bite without any problem, to bite all the way!

Tuesday, June 23. Łódź.   It's still damned cold. The sun shines, but you can't go out without a coat. I'm deteriorating more rapidly. Even reading is difficult for me. I can't concentrate on anything for long. Time runs from one meal to another. The shop, work, eating, sleeping, then the same all over again. In politics there's nothing new.

Wednesday, June 24. Łódź.   There's something wrong with my tooth again; it will have to be removed. I'm going to pot, and I feel completely indifferent. Life is more and more horrible, drab, and totally worthless.

Thursday, June 25. Łódź.   The sun was somewhat more "human" these past two days, but today it's cold again. Harvests will probably be awful this year. No food arrives in the ghetto: no vegetables, not even the poorest greens.

Ever greater productivity is being demanded in the workshops. Instructors, the police, and other gangs of loafers receive additional food coupons while the rest of the population is dying of hunger.

A tuberculosis epidemic has broken out. Many people have fever, spit blood, and heigh-ho to a hospital or directly to Marysin [the cemetery].

The Germans are reportedly winning on all fronts again. As we can see from the orders sent to the ghetto, they are indeed preparing for winter [warfare]: clothes insulated with cotton-wool or feathers, and white uniforms for snow are already being made in the ghetto. The ghetto gives the Germans more and more, while they send us less and less food. What's left of our life's blood is being extracted from us. They don't care about us at all in the long run. And the war will drag on.

Friday, June 26. Łódź.   Still no improvement of any kind. We keep working and starving, with no prospects for even the slightest change. The workshops are being enlarged, new ones are being built, and the cemetery is being expanded. Our workshop has opened a new training section for children in two small houses not far from us.

I have learned that Engel and Kałuszyner finally went to Warsaw. I wonder whether they've given my regards to Lolek Łęczycki. Stefan Kałuszyner is said to have gorged himself so much on the first day after

Our workshop has opened a new training section for children in two small houses not far from us.

his arrival in Warsaw that he got a high fever and had to stay in bed for over a week. But he certainly felt satiated, a feeling I haven't experienced in two years. I can't even study anymore.

I've been to see Niutek Radzyner, who still hopes to win me over to coming back to his Party and joining its actions. He gently tried to convince me that I won't have a clear conscience if I sit doing nothing, but if he only knew how little I care about all of it now! And how lazy I am about going somewhere or doing something. I can't even read anymore, and writing is entirely out of the question. Will I ever feel well and strong again?

Saturday, June 27. Łódź. A ration for the first third of July has been issued. It made the ghetto people's blood run cold. There are 2.5 kilos of potatoes, 20 dkg of flour (35 dkg previously), 12 dkg of sugar (40 dkg previously), 10 dkg of rye flakes (15 dkg previously), 12 dkg of margarine, 10 dkg of [artificial] honey, caustic soda, soda, vinegar, and matches; no vegetables or canned food—a horrible decrease from the previous allocation. People are already hanging their heads completely because when July begins like this, then how will we be able to get through the winter? Death from hunger is becoming obvious for most people in the ghetto.

Sunday, June 28. Łódź. Tomorrow, Flug's and my groups are moving unexpectedly to 72 Łagiewnicka Street. Three other groups from the head offices will also come. A new division of the Leder-und-Sattler [German; Leather and Saddlery (workshop)] is being set up there. I'm very pleased with this change because we're getting good, roomy premises on the second floor (as opposed to the fourth floor at 4 Chopin Street, where we were located until now). Moving my group to the new building honors us, but what's the use of it when it doesn't provide anything to eat or bring any new hope for a quick end to the war?

Monday, June 29. Łódź. We have worked at the new premises. If only we had something to eat. But the location is not bad at all. We have two rooms for saddlery makers and a room for the *Vorricht* [German; preparatory section].

We will now be issued 1.90 kilos of bread for seven days. The Germans are reportedly no longer sending in any food for children under ten or for the elderly. There's horrible hunger in the ghetto. There are absolutely no additional rations, and nothing can be bought on the streets anymore (perhaps only a kilo of small beet leaves). July will be horrible.

Tuesday, June 30. Łódź. Because he registered earlier, Father received a summons to depart to Poznań today. He was supposed to sleep overnight in the [prison] camp on Czarnieckiego Street, but a friend, a commissioner, exempted him. Father is also trying to secure an exemption from the departure altogether because he's lost his wish to wander. He'll probably succeed.

I had a horrible toothache again. I'll definitely have to have the tooth removed.

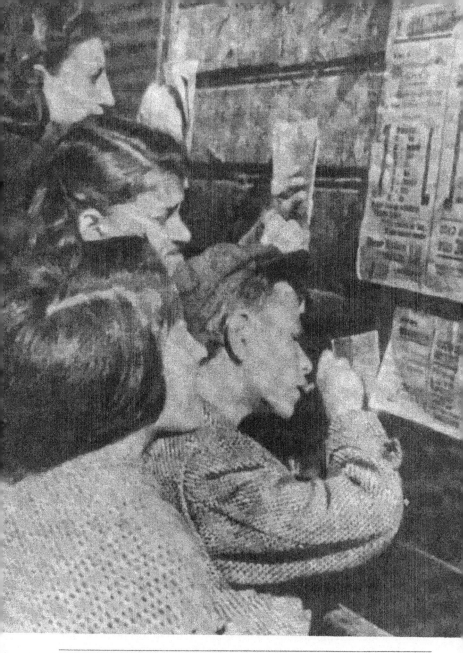

A ration for the first third of July has been issued. It made the ghetto people's blood run cold . . . a horrible decrease from the previous allocation. . . . [W]hen July begins like this, then how will we be able to get through the winter? Death from hunger is becoming obvious for most people in the ghetto.

Wednesday, July 1. Łódź.   I didn't sleep a bit all night. I was running around the room, writhing in pain that didn't cease for a moment. Early in the morning I went to the dentist. She couldn't remove the tooth because a solid abscess has formed there and my face was too swollen. She just ordered me to take a preventive remedy, and to come tomorrow to have the abscess lanced. Meanwhile, I suffer horribly. I think I have a fever. I'm terribly weak and can't do anything. I escaped from the workshop after an hour of being there, and went to bed immediately. Nadzia brought bread home for me. The swelling is growing worse.

Thursday, July 2. Łódź.   This morning I went to another doctor, a stomatologist, Dr. Szmulowicz. He cut my gum and told me to remove the tooth after the swelling goes down. My folks at home won't let me go to the other dentist anymore, believing that she's the cause of the entire problem. I stayed in bed again almost all day long (I went to the workshop only to pass along my ID card for bread). I sleep almost all the time, unless I'm too troubled by the pain. Pus is flowing out through the cut in my gum so I have to wash my mouth with peroxide every once in a while. I feel weaker and weaker. Meanwhile, the Germans are taking over Sevastopol and have now captured nearly all of Egypt. Our chances of surviving the war are diminishing at lightning speed.

Friday, July 3. Łódź.   Father has received the exemption and doesn't have to report for departure to Poznań. We've eaten almost our entire ration (naturally, with the greatest contribution on Father's part), and all that we have to cook will now last for only two more days.

It's still cold and foul. Today by chance I read the *Litzmannstadter Zeitung.** (It is printed in the Latin alphabet.) With a thousand words of description, they report the capture of Sevastopol, their victorious march in Egypt, victories on the seas, and on and on. After reading this newspaper, you lose any remaining shred of humor or hope. These are irrefutable facts against our futile, stupid rumors.

---

* According to Dobroszycki, "In the Łódź ghetto people were not allowed to possess or even read the *Litzmannstadter Zeitung,* the official organ of the occupying authorities. The Polish clandestine press did not reach the ghetto either. . . . The Łódź ghetto truly was hermetically sealed" (*Chronicle of the Łódź Ghetto,* pp. xxii–xxiii). This prevalently held view that the Łódź Ghetto was "hermetically sealed" seems substantially contradicted by the fact that this German-language newspaper, published for circulation in the city and forbidden in the ghetto, in fact persistently made its way into the ghetto and was avidly read and talked about. Dawid's Communist underground somehow received it regularly.

Saturday, July 4. Łódź.   Mom brought radish leaves for me from work. They have come into fashion in the ghetto lately for cooking (they cost 3 RM a kilo). The soup she made with them was quite all right, though I doubt that it has any nutritional value. I'm so weakened that immediately after work I go to bed and sleep, which has never happened to me before. I don't read at all. Tomorrow I will go to a doctor for an examination and perhaps the removal of my sore tooth. The Germans push on.

Sunday, July 5. Łódź.   I've finally gotten rid of that tooth. (It was the first time I've had a tooth pulled.) The doctor removed it "professionally" in a hospital, without anesthesia and, what's more important, without charge. There is almost nothing to cook at home. Raddish leaves are our essential food.

I'm so weakened that I lie all day long as though I were dead. I don't read and don't want to do anything. Slow death has begun.

Monday, July 6. Łódź.   The weather's finally hot. I can't feel the heat, however, and don't broil as others do. My weakness and sleepiness increase many times over.

The work in the new workshop has already stabilized. Yesterday and today we were sewing *Sturmgepäck,* and as of tomorrow we'll do the *KTG* again.

Tuesday, July 7. Łódź.   Today in the workshop we received only dry bread. Depression prevails everywhere. All I eat now is a daily portion of bread and a plate of radish-leaf "soup." I'm unable to think of anything.

Wednesday, July 8. Łódź.   A ration for the second third of July has already been issued. It's almost identical to the previous one, except that now there's 1.5 kilos of potatoes instead of 2.5 kilos (there are 10 dkg of peas in return).

Splendid fish arrived in the ghetto yesterday. It was distributed among "B 1" and "B 2" (doctors, *Beirat,* police, and instructors). The remains were dealt out today among fortune's darlings with connections. In our family Father received 45 dkg for 1 RM. The fish was delicious, though cooked without any seasoning. What a pity that we eat it only once in three years!

I read in a newspaper that the Germans have captured Voronezh and are moving ahead in Russia. In Africa, they don't have any new advancement, but through all of their words runs arrogance and the confidence to drag the war on through the winter. That will finish us here in the ghetto.

Thursday, July 9. Łódź. New vegetables have finally started to arrive in the ghetto, though in small quantities. There's lettuce, beet leaves, and small carrots. Naturally the privileged classes receive them first.

There are allusions again to deportations and to more Jews being brought in from surrounding areas. Transports of Jews from Kalisz have already arrived. Children, the elderly, and those unable to work are supposed to be deported from the ghetto soon.* Meanwhile, the number of people who have the strength to work diminishes greatly. Everything's running out. I can't go upstairs or even stay on the street for long. Weak legs are the best indication of exhaustion from starvation.

Friday, July 10. Łódź. I'm more and more saddened by Mom's appearance. The long distance to work has withered her completely. Father has also declined badly recently. Last week I saw Mrs. Deutsch, who also feels very bad. Most people are just cadavers, walking shadows of their former selves. The hope for an end to the war in 1942, so alive at the beginning of the summer, has now completely disappeared. The prospect of our liberation moves farther and farther off, becoming more and more unattainable.

Saturday, July 11. Łódź. I saw Wolman, for whom I arranged a certain transaction. He is very dejected because a doctor told him that he is on the verge of consumption. Even so, he assured me with a smile that he would like very much to survive this war.

I also met Calel, who is working as a messenger on the vegetable [market] square, where he stuffs himself with various vegetables. He has a fever and receives injections of calcium for his lungs, which are "out of order." I shiver at the thought of what may be happening in my own lungs. In politics there's nothing new.

Sunday, July 12. Łódź. I've been more and more nervous recently. As though out of spite, I keep meeting people who enjoy all sorts of cou-

---

* Dawid reports the prospect of this loss two months before Józef Zelkowicz would report in September that the events "struck like a bolt of lightning" ("In These Nightmarish Days," in *Łódź Ghetto: Inside a Community Under Siege,* edited by Alan Adelson and Robert Lapides [New York, 1989], p. 320).

pons, allocations, additions, vacations, boardinghouses in Marysin, and so on, and who tell me about their *Glück* in their good-natured naïveté. One can arrive at the quite obvious conclusion that about 20,000 people in the ghetto eat what could be used to issue double-quantity rations for the rest of the population. The additional food coupons for instructors, *Beirat*, clerks, management, and special individuals (issued by the food supply dignitaries for "one-time use") contain more products than ever. The parasites in the kitchens will grow fatter while the workers will receive a little cloudy, troubled water. This is the joy reserved for the big shots in the departments and those who have "connections." Meanwhile, the coupons for the rest of the population get worse every time. Damn it! I wish I could burn up that whole gang once and for all!

Monday, July 13. Łódź.   I received my food ration only today. This time I had a fierce argument with Father, who is becoming greedier and more rapacious for every little morsel; he cheats in a stupid, intricate way everywhere he can, which upsets me terribly.

Tuesday, July 14. Łódź.   Enormous quantities of new vegetables keep arriving in the ghetto. A few dozen carloads of beets reportedly have arrived. However, I haven't yet had a chance to taste even a beet leaf, to say nothing about a beet itself.

I felt awful today, which scares me because I'm aware of the growing number of cases falling ill with the most common sickness in the ghetto, so-called water in the lungs: high temperature, sharp pain, sometimes a cough, sweating, then X ray ("swelling and shadows in the apexes" [of the lungs]), injections, medicines, the hospital, and then the cemetery. At the same time, the ghetto dignitaries are gorging, unafraid of death from exhaustion or tuberculosis. The gap between the haves and the remaining ghetto population is becoming wider, more insolent, and extreme. I remember the sentence that was supposedly spoken by Rumkowski last year that he can't save everyone, so instead of having the entire ghetto population exposed to a slow death by hunger, I'll save at least "the top ten thousand."*

Wednesday, July 15, Łódź.   Beets are already out of sight, but we haven't received a single gram out of all those transports that arrived.

---

* Ghetto survivors have corroborated in interviews and memoirs that Rumkowski openly declared the goal of saving 10,000 lives—coincidentally about the number who did survive.

Foul weather continues, days are becoming shorter, nights longer and colder, and in politics there's nothing new.

Thursday, July 16. Łódź.   The ghetto is running out of potatoes. They will be served in several workshops for the next two days, but there will be no potatoes in the next kitchen ration or for those who work. The balance in the ghetto will be maintained: on the one hand, some food is arriving, but on the other, products are disappearing. Not to overeat, that's the important thing.

Friday, July 17. Łódź.   The German newspaper I sometimes read is hopelessly boring and says nothing except to continually assure *Endsieg* [German; final victory]. I can't find hope anywhere for a quick end to the war, or for even the smallest victory on the part of the Allied powers.

The death rate keeps rising in the ghetto. Many of the teachers from the former *gymnasium* have died, or are dying, or are incurably sick. I keep hearing about all kinds of previously unknown diseases that put people down after a short struggle. All immunity is disappearing, and any little thing can become a cause of death. In the cemetery, graves are dug as piecework for several dozen funerals in advance. Meanwhile, winter is approaching. Who will survive it? It's very doubtful that we will. Nevertheless, spending one more winter in the ghetto becomes an inevitable and implacable prospect. No, the war will not end this year.

Saturday, July 18. Łódź.   Today there was no work in the workshop because of sulfur disinfection there against insects. Tomorrow, too, we won't have work for the same reason. In school such a break would be a great thing, but here it's a painful hole in our stomachs because we will not receive any food except soup.

For the first time in an eternity we've had homemade *cholent* from 1.5 kilos of potatoes, 10 dkg of peas, 10 dkg of barley, and flour we gathered during all of last week when Mom was bringing leaves from the "plantation" where she works. We baked it in the bakery on a special coupon we had bought from a rabbi. It was delicious, but then . . .

Sunday, July 19. Łódź.   The disinfection continues, and the weather is becoming even nastier: clouds and rain all the time. I can barely see the sun.

I was transferred as a group leader today to a group that works in the afternoon. I will not have any partners here. The previous group leader was transferred to [the workshop at] 21 Franciszkańska Street, where his rule with a firm hand is expected to be very useful.

Monday, July 20. Łódź.   I've met with Niutek. We understand each other better, but we're also decidedly and consciously growing very distant from each other. He is now a complete dogmatist, ready to slaughter and be slaughtered. His world has already been fulfilled; his actions are clear and decided for the rest of his life; a life subordinated to an idea. Nothing exists for him but the idea he is pursuing.

Our former political organization of school youths has developed colossally during the past year, having greatly surpassed the bounds set for it at that time. Naturally, Niutek is in its vanguard, independent and critical of other authorities in the ghetto.

As for me, my egoistic individualism has led me in a completely different direction; I've taken on other goals and tasks in life for myself. My political views, which have never been as extreme as those of Niutek, haven't changed, though. After the war everything will be revealed. Meanwhile, we huddle down quietly and struggle for life; to endure and survive.

Wednesday, July 22. Łódź.   The ghetto keeps developing. It is, rather, a factory called Gettoverwaltung [German; Ghetto Administration], a company of German capitalists, and perhaps of Rumkowski and Jakubowicz, exploiting the ghetto as an industrial center that keeps extending the scope of its activities. The number of workers in the workshops and on the internal posts in the country of "Der Älteste der Juden" is growing. Currently a whole block of buildings adjacent to our workshop is being reconstructed to accommodate the enlarged metal workshop and new sections of the saddlery workshop. All kinds of new workshops are also being created in various spots in the ghetto, reaching out their tentacles now for the last reserves of children (even those younger than ten) and adults who are barely able to work.

Meanwhile, a death sentence (the third one in the ghetto, I think) by hanging was carried out on a square near Bazarna Street today. This time two young men who supposedly escaped work in Poznań were hanged. Naturally, Jews performed the execution.

A ration of a kilogram of potatoes has been issued. Optimists assure: "Rumkowski receives enough food from the Germans." We know it, but is this food for us or does he keep it only for himself and his circle? ...

Thursday, July 23. Łódź.   In politics there's nothing new, but either as a result of a somewhat better food situation or as a result of some mysterious mystical calculations, the spirit of the Jews in the ghetto has risen a bit again, and they maintain that the war will end this year. There are no specific events to support this claim, but perhaps the belief will somehow help.

Meanwhile, sickness and death rates are in incredible "record" form in the ghetto. A supposedly healthy person goes to bed for a day or two and by the third day is on the way to Marysin as a corpse. Swelling from starvation, tuberculosis, or any other symptom is not even mentioned anymore. The person died, that's all.

Friday, July 24. Łódź.   I have to worry again about Mom. She is subject to layoffs after finishing work in the garden plots. Tomorrow she'll work there for the last time. Again, a loss of food coupons, soup, and pay. I hope that Mom will get a job somewhere else.

I still try desperately not to give up, to read, to work on something, but I make almost no progress. I'm somehow horribly, continuously exhausted and lazy. I'd like to do everything, but I can't get to anything. Meanwhile, the end of the war is still very far away.

Saturday, July 25. Łódź.   I went to Mrs. Deutsch's in the afternoon. I met a Dr. Fred Goldschmidt there, an already swollen former prosecutor. His wife read excerpts from his book to us (it is supposedly already very thick) about the ghetto. He writes only in German; the book is of great literary value, and consists of numerous sketches, poems, short stories, and pictures. He's extremely prolific (until the war he wrote hardly anything) and writes incessantly in spite of the horrible conditions.*

Mrs. Deutsch is completely listless. She stares straight ahead vacantly and is incapable of any serious conversation. I'm totally depressed after the visit and feel more lonely. Except for Wolman's, there's no other place I can go. All intellectually superior colleagues, acquaintances, or friends have parted from me for reasons of principle (Niutek Radzyner, for example), or died, or declined mentally. Is that what's ahead for me too? Only the Devil knows.

Sunday, July 26. Łódź.   Were it not for all kinds of scraps of rags that Father takes secretly out of the cutting room, sawdust I once got for a

---

* Fred Goldschmidt's manuscript does not appear to have survived.

fuel coupon, wood that is slowly chopped out of our "furniture," and other kinds of minor fuel materials, the 28 kilos of briquettes given monthly by Rumkowski wouldn't be enough for four of us to cook our rations for even two weeks. The people who have either gas in their homes (even though it's rationed) or friendly connections in places where they can cook on gas (*Gasküchenstelle*) can consider themselves lucky. There are also people who cook on electricity, but electric cookers are no longer available. And that's the way we live, from one meal to another. My discomfort deepens; I can literally feel all my strength vanishing.

Monday, July 27. Łódź.   I didn't receive my portion of bread today. Some corrupt practices have supposedly been discovered in bakeries, and a whole lot of commissaries, bakers, and policemen have been arrested, but meanwhile bread is not being distributed. Even though Mom cooked something in the morning, I feel the lack of my daily 13 dkg of bread acutely. I had no idea that I'm already so weakened.

Perhaps it was under the influence of feeling extremely ill, combined with some kind of inspiration, that today in the workshop I wrote what seems to me a quite strong Yiddish poem, "Lebn wil ich" [I Want to Live] and a few small pages for *Alarm*. The latter [written] perhaps under the influence of alarm sirens that have been going on repeatedly during the last few nights (no air raid has followed, though).

In politics there's still nothing new. Jews are being deported from the Warsaw Ghetto (10,000 persons a day). Pogroms and shooting at the deportees are part of the events. Their chairman committed suicide.* In any case, those in Warsaw haven't gone through as much suffering as we have. And here it's not over yet.

Tuesday, July 28. Łódź.   The daily ration of bread has been reduced! The mood in the city is horrible. To make matters worse, there are no vegetables, and the soup in the workshop is awful. Even though a new ration of sausage and meat (10 dkg per person) has been issued, it doesn't console anyone.

After two days of not working, Mom got work gardening again

---

* Adam Czerniaków (1880–1942), Rumkowski's counterpart in the Warsaw Ghetto, took poison on July 23, 1942, rather than carry out Nazi orders to deport most of his population, including the ghetto's children; immense deportations ensued, liquidating all but a final 10 percent of the ghetto population at Treblinka. Dawid's diary entry corresponds precisely to the date the official ghetto Chronicle notes the "alarming news" from Warsaw.

today. This time the plot is much closer. Maybe she will not lose the coupon for the next ration (because of those two days without work) after all.

There is no political news. Constant hopeless, stifling silence.

Wednesday, July 29. Łódź. We've been informed that Mom will not lose her ration because she was working on July 20.

I suddenly felt sick and dizzy in the afternoon. Nothing could bring me back to consciousness, so breaking my principle, I ate half of my portion of tomorrow's bread. The past two days have been days of first-class hunger. The cooperatives have been closed (supposedly because of cleaning), and no food was issued.

Enormous bombings of Germany are reported. If only something comes of it.

Thursday, July 30. Łódź. I showed or rather read to Wolman the poem I composed the day before yesterday (I revised it on Tuesday). He thinks that "there is heart in it, but the form is still extremely primitive." He advises me to study Jewish literature seriously, and to write only in moments of absolute necessity. I'll try to follow his advice if I only have the strength to read. After yesterday's incident I'm very much weakened, and as though out of spite, there's nothing to eat at home.

Saturday, August 1. Łódź. After work I went to see Mom in the garden where she now works. She sits crouched on an upturned pot, and prepares clean soil under beet seedlings. If I were in her place, I would gorge myself.

We have received 5 dkg of yeast, which recently became a medical and nutritional remedy. Doctors now prescribe yeast coupons for all kinds of sicknesses, but it helps us about as much as cupping can help the dead. The death rate's rising every day.

The work in our workshop is said to be coming to an end. On Chopin Street and in the head offices they've been without work for almost a week now, and our *KTG* sewing is also said to be ending. There are no new orders. Is this a good or a bad sign?

Sunday, August 2. Łódź. August is beginning with nice warm days, but it won't be for long. It would be too good if the sun were shining for us. The Germans are said to be at peak readiness for the expected English–American offensive. But when the hell will it happen?

*After work I went to see Mom in the garden where she now works.
She sits crouched on an upturned pot, and prepares clean soil under
beet seedlings. If I were in her place, I would gorge myself.*

There's been a warning posted that there'll be no more potatoes in
August, so we shouldn't eat the ones we received last time too quickly.
Hunger is becoming ever more horrible.

Monday, August 3. Łódź.   The mood in the ghetto is slowly improving
with weak hopes and dreams. Although there's still no specific reason
for encouragement, folks are lifting their heads and speaking about a
quick end to the war. Perhaps we won't have to spend one more winter
in the ghetto. After all, we can conclude on the basis of the little bits of

news that are reaching us that the world is in the process of colossal political and social change, and is on the eve of events of extreme importance. And perhaps it's already been decided on the other side of the front to strike hard and to finish the Germans off for good—if not for any other reason than at least to open closed European markets for American industry. Meanwhile, trembling with fear for what remains of our strength, we anxiously calculate our abilities and chances of getting out of this trap. Perhaps we'll make it after all!

Tuesday, August 4. Łódź.   Niutek came to our workshop to see Szyjo Sonnabend (Niutek maintains only friendly relations with me). I, too, spoke with Szyjo. He understands quite well my "isolated-from-everyday-life" writing perspective, and he, too, is reluctant to take direct action. He asked me whether I'd like to make use of their organization to widen the influence of my works. I've agreed readily because this is the only way I can be useful to them. Everything I write is almost 100 percent consistent with their views, except, of course, for the essential difference in our opinions on personal attitude. In any case, Szyjo has agreed with me that an unshaken, sincere, honest, and in every way persuaded sympathizer like me is a hundred times more important for the organization than many a loud, even sincerely working activist who may, however, in actuality be a Kripo agent. In my view, I can give the society more while working for myself than many an activist who doesn't want anything for himself. The main thing is to survive.

Wednesday, August 5. Łódź.   In politics it's somehow silent again. The only thing I can glean from the newspaper is about the Russian offensive. Gentlemen democrats in the West continue to do nothing.

In India a National Congress that wants independence has assembled. Gandhi is its chairman. England is not giving in and is being supported by China, the Soviet Union, and the United States. Colossal changes are taking place all around the world, while we are rotting here in the ghetto. What a delight it must be to be free and satiated now, and to take in the history happening before our eyes!

Thursday, August 6. Łódź.   We are greatly worried because the mother of my friend from the building, Olek Kamusiewicz, is sick. Just like Olek, she is completely swollen, already dying. Even though these days such a case is "nothing unusual or extraordinary," it has the most horrible impact on us because of our mothers' friendship and my friendship with Olek. Last year Olek's father died, swollen of hunger, and now it's his mother. Olek himself is also in quite serious condition, and none of us here can help him with anything.

Friday, August 7. Łódź.   Hanky-panky again at the workshop. I will get a new group on Sunday. My group's previous leader is coming back. I tried to persuade Podlaski to let me stay. I was supported by Rysiek and even the group delegation of juvenile and older workers, but nothing helped. Podlaski values this other person more than me, even though everybody hates him. I am so mad that I can't sit still.

Saturday, August 8. Łódź.   I'm now buying a second soup at the workshop. It costs 3 RM. I can't "organize" a soup at the kitchen. The others who have connections, however—even minor ones—get as much soup as they want. So there are always battles because you rarely find the 10 decas of potatoes you're entitled to. Of course, we can't measure the amount of flour and other ingredients in our soup. The people at the kitchen don't give a damn about it—while the big shots from the workshop stuff themselves with no restraint. We all just hope the war's end is near. Otherwise we're lost. Eighty percent of the ghetto population will not survive the winter.

Sunday, August 9. Łódź.   Mrs. Kamusiewicz has died. A day before her death a doctor stated that had she had 3 dkg of sugar and 10 dkg of meat a day added to her food for at least a week, he would have been able to keep her alive! But as in the case of 80 percent of the ghetto population, such treatment is a physical impossibility.

A ration for the second third of August has been issued. There are no green vegetables at all; only 1.5 kilos of potatoes, 10 dkg of sausage, 30 dkg of rye flour, 12 dkg of sugar, 10 dkg of oil (!), 25 dkg of salt, 25 dkg of ersatz coffee, and a few small trifles like soap, citric acid, paprika.

The weather is still undecided, as though it were deliberating whether to extend the summer or to recognize the autumn, which is already approaching. In politics there's nothing new.

Monday, August 10. Łódź.   At home wasteful consumption is being practiced, counting on additional food allocations (I don't know from where, perhaps from heaven). We cook two times a day, and potatoes are running out at a frightening rate.

A circular has been sent to the cooperatives that they should issue 10 more dkg of peas for 20 pf (per person). Even this will help a little. As long as there's something to eat, we'll get through to the end of the war.

Meanwhile, in politics everything's become silent again. The Germans continue to move ahead in a section of the Caucasus. Perhaps a breakthrough will occur in the beginning of autumn.

Tuesday, August 11. Łódź.   Day after day passes. One buys rations, eats the little food there is in them, starves while eating it, and after that keeps waiting obstinately, continuously, and unshakenly until the end of the cursed, devilish war; the workshop, home, meals, reading, night with bedbugs and cockroaches, and all over again without end, constantly losing strength, with diminishing efficiency of body and mind. We keep dreaming, waiting, and counting, always with the same negative result outraging all possible calculations and suppositions. We're fighting to survive until liberation, a goal as elusive as a phantom.

Wednesday, August 12. Łódź.   Transports of Jews have begun arriving in the ghetto from neighboring small towns, which are being totally "de-Jewed." Transports from Pabianice, Bełchatów, Turek, and some other holes have already arrived. In Turek, where the ghetto was based on agricultural production, a literal pogrom was staged (out of 2,000 residents, 150 have been left). All the new arrivals (no matter from where) say that until this moment they hadn't known what hunger meant. Our ghetto terrifies them; however, since they are in better shape than we are, they have better chances of surviving the war than we do. For the past year, they lived in constant uncertainty and fear for their fates. It finally ended with their deportation here without any luggage.

Thursday, August 13. Łódź.   Absolutely no food is arriving in the ghetto. We are running out of potatoes and will have nothing to cook after Sunday. Only those who have some kind of a plot or plow-field have a small chance of holding out through the oncoming period. No one knows why they aren't sending in food, because the crops have been quite good. Is it because of the intensified anti-Jewish campaign, or just a momentary technical holdup? In any case, a period of incredible hunger is beginning in the ghetto again.*

---

* To break down the Jews' resistance to boarding the trains, the Nazis typically intensified levels of hunger and starvation in the weeks immediately preceding major deportations.

Wednesday, August 14. Łódź.   Today, amid the greatest hum in the workshop, I wrote several more pages for *Alarm*. I've recently checked out Polish novels from the library (for 2 RM a month). I am also reading the second volume of Galsworthy's *Forsythe Saga* and Thomas Mann's *Buddenbrooks* in their original languages. I have no strength to study, however. I waded through the history coursebook until the first year of World War I; I can't go on any further. My foreign languages have again been "held in abeyance." Maybe now I'll be writing a little more. I wish I could pull myself together. The deepest pessimism is beginning to rule me again.

All the new arrivals (no matter from where) say that until this moment they hadn't known what hunger meant. Our ghetto terrifies them. . . .

Saturday, August 15. Łódź.   Today I ate a quarter of a kilo of dry ersatz coffee with sugar, which I still had from an old ration. I bought the coffee in private trade (2 RM for a kilo). Coffee with sugar, or saccharine, or without anything has been a basic element in my diet for a long time, but now, because of a production decrease in the workshop and an enormous drop in income as its result, I will have to give up all additional purchases.

Father came home from work with a 39.9°C [103.8°F] fever. He went to bed, but it goes without saying that if he is able to walk, he will go to work tomorrow. After all, it would be a waste of soup and perhaps of a food coupon as well!

Sunday, August 16. Łódź.   The weather's warm and relatively sunny; silent and still, but I feel it's the lull before the storm. I went to the concert hall at 3 Krawiecka Street for a meeting of *Luftschutz* services because on Friday I received a note to report there. Fail to report for this kind of a meeting and you risk twenty-four-hour arrest. There was a lecture on wounds, incendiary bombs, extinguishing, etc., in a word, on things about which I have heard enough, both before and during the war.

Trains full of fire-extinguishing tools like pumps, gas masks, sandbags, axes, etc. are arriving in the ghetto. They feed us this instead of food, which has run out in the ghetto and is not arriving anymore.

Lolek Milgrom has offered me a post as a regular clerk in the Arbeitseinsatz, where new clerks are needed, so educated and intelligent individuals are in demand. Lolek himself doesn't work in the shop anymore, and has been a clerk in the Statistics Department for two weeks. I agreed to his offer immediately, and asked him to arrange the job quickly. Everyone at home is also glad. I've been sick of the atmosphere in the workshop for a long time, and even though I am a group leader there, and thus have almost nothing to do, I will be happy to start in the new post where there'll be no worrying about income reductions, as there is with the piecework at the workshop, and where the work itself will be more pleasant, interesting, and will suit me better. We'll see what will come of it. Perhaps if I get better work, the war will end "out of spite! . . . "

Monday, August 17. Łódź.   There's finally a tiny spark of hope for us. The Germans report that Churchill has been in Moscow since [August] 13 and that the conference of superpowers that's been going on there has already divided almost the entire world of the future. Goebbels is reported to have given a speech in which he announced that the next weeks will be crucial and that everything will be decided in the East (the new call for the army: "Wir schlagen die Englander im Osten!" [German; We're defeating the English in the east!]); after that he spoke about murderous bombings of Germany and vowed that the Allies will not break the Germans. The uprising in Yugoslavia is spreading wider, and the Italians have suffered a major defeat there. The Germans who have been driven past the Caucasus will apparently have to lay their heads there because they will face the forces of the Soviet Union, England, and the United States. A Soviet offensive is in progress all along the Russian front. There are also efforts at an American offensive on the Mediterranean Sea. The Germans are preparing themselves to repulse enemy attacks everywhere, but they admit they are ready to lose on several fronts in order to win(!) on one they will choose. Most important is the hope for a general offensive.

There's been an incredible uplifting of spirits in the ghetto. The Jews are raising their heads again, but they're very frightened by the rumors circulating about the Germans' intention to finish off the Jews in Europe before losing the war.* Even so, everyone's full of rosy hopes. The assumption is slowly being made that the war finally may be over in 1942. May it be so! May we just have enough strength to last until that moment. If we receive only a few potatoes and vegetables, a bit of sugar and oil, a regular portion of bread and soup in the workshop, we may be able to pull through somehow. May the food supply just not get worse, and may the date of our liberation not slip farther away.

Tuesday, August 18. Łódź.   The guardian of the juvenile workers in our workshop, Goldman, a young and pleasing man from whom I have all the newspaper news and who's known for his extreme optimism, thinks that our liberation is only weeks away!

Pervasive exhaustion dominates the ghetto. There's no work in the shops (as of tomorrow we'll work for only four hours a day because of limited production), food does not arrive, and prices keep rising. Everybody is completely exhausted. All my friends have gone incredibly to pot.

Wednesday, August 19. Łódź.   Everybody lives now with the growing hope for an end of the war in 1942. In the evening the news spread

---

* Indeed, in the final months of the war in Europe, the Germans diverted some trains from the defense against the advancing Russians and committed that rolling stock into transporting the remaining Jews to the death camps.

(allegedly broadcast by England) that a general air offensive has begun in the west and in the east, and that the English, Americans, and Canadians have landed in France. The agitation in the ghetto seems identical to the agitation in Poland in August 1939, except that this time our waiting is filled with happiness and hope instead of dread.*

The newspaper reports that Churchill has returned to England after settling all disputed issues, and that Stalin has gone to the front. Feelings of eager excitement, anxiety, and the most pleasant yearning for liberation are slowly coming over me.

Thursday, August 20. Łódź. The news about the landing in France turns out to be true, except that the Germans are writing that they've beaten the enemies back into the sea. I went to see Niutek, who has yesterday's news from the English radio, which admits partial retreat but mentions further successes in other places. The mood in the ghetto is joyous and full of expectation. We forget that it's been two days since any food arrived, that the situation is becoming more and more serious, and that our imaginations are leaping too far ahead into peacetime.

A few friends and I spoke a lot today about the future, and we have come to the conclusion that if we survive the ghetto, we'll certainly experience a richness of life that we wouldn't have appreciated otherwise. May the moment of liberation come at last!

Friday, August 21. Łódź. Damn it, in politics everything has fallen silent again. The Germans are writing that the English offensive has failed and that they are expecting new attacks. There's no other news from the front; also nothing about any bombings.

I found out that my post in the Arbeitseinsatz is 100 percent certain, and all I have to do is to wait for my nomination and the call. Rysiek Podlaski will work there as well.

In the afternoon it was +39°C [103°F] in the sun. I don't feel the heat at all. But the fatigue, which is characteristic of all starvelings, increases a hundredfold in the heat. I can't study at all, and even reading fiction is arduous for me. I can leave home only if my legs don't fail me, and they are failing more and more often recently.

---

* Ships sent on this date to launch an Allied commando raid intended to test the German defenses were, in fact, spotted by a German trawler in the English Channel some twelve miles off the intended landing site at Dieppe, France. A radioed warning gave the Germans several hours to prepare a rain of steel and fire with which to greet the hapless would-be invaders.

Saturday, August 22. Łódź.   Last night a transport of Jews from Ozorków arrived in the ghetto. In politics there's nothing new. Even if there's something going on in the wide world, no news reaches us. Could it be that the promise of liberation will again end in disappointment?

Sunday, August 23. Łódź.   I don't know whether it's because of the heat or because of some other reason, but bedbugs and flies have multiplied in our home, just as they have everywhere else. We have swarms of them at home. I'm sure the bedbugs drink half a glass of my blood every night! As for the flies, we just can't get away from them. The radical remedy for these plagues would be to end the war. That would solve this and other important problems as well.

Jews from the small towns in the region are still coming. I have been visiting Goldman every evening to get information from the newspaper. He thinks the Jews have weak nerves and cannot contemplate the end of the war without creating a sensation. In yesterday's newspaper, there was news about bombings of the General Gouvernement [occupied Poland not incorporated into the Reich], especially Warsaw and eastern Germany. That's probably why there was an alarm two days ago.

Monday, August 24. Łódź.   I've received a summons to report to the Personalabteilung [German; Personnel Department] for a work assignment tomorrow.

The newspaper reports Brazil's declaration of war against Germany, a Turkish–Soviet treaty, and details about the Soviet offensive all along the front. "All quiet on the western front," however.

Tuesday, August 25. Łódź.   I've seen Franek, a chief of the Personalabteilung. I stood in a line there from eight in the morning to twelve, and barely managed to get to him. I immediately received the note to the Arbeitseinsatz as a *Büroangestellter* [German; office employee]. In the afternoon I went to Milgrom's office in the Arbeitseinsatz at 11 Lutomierska Street. He told me to come right to work tomorrow.

Wednesday, August 26. Łódź.   Today I worked in the Arbeitseinsatz as a clerk, a pen pusher. I work there from 7:30 in the morning to four in the afternoon. I'm very satisfied because I finally have the peace I longed for. I don't have to care about anything, and the thoughtless rewriting of data in the files doesn't require any effort. There's also none of the prisonlike atmosphere in the workshop, no screaming, less dust, and no

Leder-und-Sattler idiots. Above all, I don't have too much time left to stay at home and think of food.

I visited Goldman in the evening (as I have done every day lately), but there was nothing interesting in the newspapers. They still negotiate and prepare, but do not attack. Who knows how much longer it might take.

Thursday, August 27. Łódź. The heat is becoming intolerable. Although the thermometer indicates over +40°C [about 104°F] in the sun, I'm not too hot, only terribly stuffy; my exhaustion intensifies; bedbugs are everywhere. In addition, a cough has gotten hold of me in the past few days, and it worsens every day. I'm sure it'll drag on. I'm dripping with sweat at every meal, and I feel very uneasy. Could it be that I am also being finished off?

Jews continue to be sent into the ghetto from the surrounding small towns (Bełchatów, Wieluń, Sieradz, Zduńska Wola). They tell horrible stories about the murdering of thousands of Jews and bring only a few remnants [of their communities] into the ghetto. They were not allowed to take anything with them, and there are no elderly, children, or sick among them at all. Those able to work and those unable were killed without distinction. They had eaten well, though, like cattle fattened for slaughter. In the Arbeitseinsatz we now have a lot of work because the new arrivals are directed to our offices to receive work assignments. There is such a crowd here that I can barely get through when I come to work.

I'm helping to set up a new file of workers being deported for labor to Germany. I am learning very interesting things: letters and bills sent in by various German firms and work camps that employ Jewish slaves (*jüdische Arbeitskräfte*) from our ghetto. Their wages are minimal, deductions [for their expenses] enormous, and their working conditions must be awful because notifications keep arriving about sick workers sent to hospitals in Berlin, from where they are returned to the ghetto and are unable to work.

Friday, August 28. Łódź. A transport of Jews from Łask has arrived. They went through the same things as all the other transports. Only a small group has reached the ghetto.

Saturday, August 29. Łódź. I'm coughing more frequently. I think I'll have to see a doctor, which I would immensely like to avoid, but the point is to avoid sickness.

The German front line near Rzhev has been broken by the Russians. Although the Germans belittle the loss and boast of further progress in the Caucasus, it's evident that their "career" is being terminated. Whatever happens, there won't be any more German victories.

Sunday, August 30. Łódź.   The Russians are reported to be moving forward, and they keep seizing new areas. On the western front everything continues all quiet. Only Crete was bombed. Mexico, too, is said to have declared war against the Axis countries. Yet there are still no specific prospects for improvement for us.

Monday, August 31. Łódź.   The last day of the third year of the war. I don't think I will be noting any more war anniversaries because it will be either me or the war . . .

Tuesday, September 1. Łódź.   The first day of the new year of the war (the fourth year of the war) brought horrible news early in the morning that all the hospitals in the ghetto were being emptied by the Germans. In the morning the areas around the hospitals were surrounded by guards, and all the sick, without exception, were loaded onto trucks and driven out of the ghetto. Because we already know from the stories told by those brought into the ghetto how the Germans "deal with" the sick, a great panic has risen in the city. Scenes from Dante took place when the sick were being loaded. People knew that they were going to their deaths! They even fought the Germans and had to be thrown onto the trucks by force. A number of the sick in various conditions managed to escape from the hospitals the Germans reached later. The sick from the sanitarium in Marysin are also said to have been deported. In our office nobody could concentrate on their work (my job is to pay wages to the families of workers in Germany). They say that in other workshops and offices nobody worked at all. People are already beginning to fear for their children and the elderly.*

[Air-raid] alarms become more frequent at night, though there are

---

* Extensively detailed accounts of the forced deportation of the ghetto's sick, and subsequently the children and elderly, can be found in Dobroszycki, *Chronicle of the Łódź Ghetto,* pp. 248–52, and in the eloquent monograph by Zelkowicz, "In These Nightmarish Days," in *Łódź Ghetto,* edited by Adelson and Lapides, pp. 320–28, 336–47; "In These Nightmarish Days," in *A Holocaust Reader,* edited by Lucy Dawidowicz (West Orange, N.J., 1976), pp. 298–316; and "Days of Nightmare," in *Art from the Ashes: A Holocaust Anthology,* edited by Lawrence L. Langer (New York, 1995), pp. 200–214.

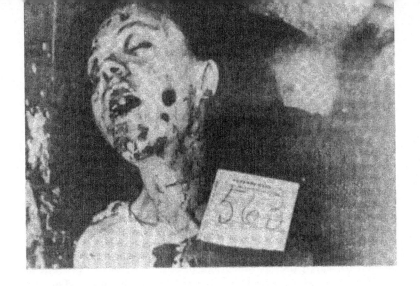

Scenes from Dante took place when the sick were being loaded.
People knew that they were going to their deaths! They even fought
the Germans and had to be thrown onto the trucks by force.

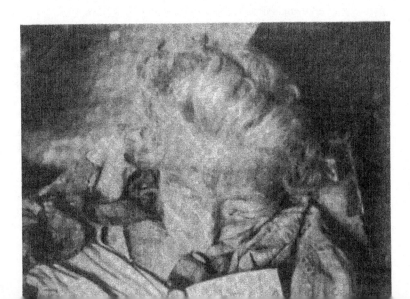

still no raids. I am beginning to believe more strongly that the last act of the war has begun. It's five to twelve. May we not be finished off first.

Meanwhile, more work orders arrive in the ghetto, and although some workshops (Leder-und-Sattler, for example) have almost no work, others (like the straw [boots] and carpentry ones) are receiving colossal orders.

Wednesday, September 2. Łódź.   The hospital tragedy did not end with yesterday's deportation of the sick from the ghetto. When the Germans found out that a number of the sick escaped from various hospitals, they demanded their return. Following the registers from the hospitals, they started to search the apartments of patients' relatives to fish out the fugitives. On this occasion, the Jewish police committed a kind of crime unknown before in the ghetto. The Germans demanded as a quota the number of sick registered on the hospitals' lists. The police, as a result of various orders from influential people, wanted to spare the relatives of powerful persons, so they invented a new way of dealing with the situation: they went to the apartments of the sick who had already been driven out and, as if out of the blue, asked where the deported person was. When the unfortunate relatives answered that they had already been taken, the police took hostages anyway, unless the alleged fugitive was presented. As a result, when the Germans sent in vehicles today for the rest of the sick, a number of hostages were included to fill the quota, while the "connected" ones stayed in hiding. The mood in the ghetto is panicky; everything's in suspense, and everyone's waiting.

Thursday, September 3. Łódź.   After two cold days, it's hot again. The newspaper reports the bombing of Warsaw and the Protectorate. The situation of the Germans on the eastern front is also clearly worsening by the minute.

Potatoes keep arriving in the ghetto, and as of tomorrow as much as 8 kilos per person will be distributed.

In the evening disturbing news spread that the Germans had allegedly demanded that all the children up to age ten must be delivered for deportation and, supposedly, for extermination. The situation in the ghetto is very much like the one in all the surrounding towns prior to deportations there, with the difference that there the deportations were sudden and unexpected, while here they are being arranged with the most sophisticated premeditation.

Friday, September 4. Łódź.   Yesterday's tragic news has turned out to be unfortunately true. The Germans are demanding all the children up to age ten, the elderly over sixty-five, and all other sick, swollen invalids, people unable to work, and those without employment. The panic in the city is incredible. Nobody's working anywhere; everyone's running to secure work assignments for those in their family who are unemployed; parents of the unfortunate children are trying to save them by any means. The Registration Office was sealed after the lists were made, so that all rescue attempts by falsifying birth certificates, registration books and other documents, or making up death certificates, etc. are failing.

The mood in the ghetto is panicky; everything's in suspense, and everyone's waiting.

Incredible scenes were taking place in our Arbeitseinsatz. Work assignments were issued in great haste, even though they already say that our efforts don't matter because there will be a general *Szpera* [curfew], [the German *Gehsperre* became *Szpera* in the ghetto] during which medical commissions will examine everyone to decide on their ability to work.

Today, despite incredible difficulties, I managed as a clerk to get a work assignment for Mom in the furniture workshop. Even so, I am very worried about Mom because she's terribly emaciated, shrunken, and weak. Nevertheless, she still works in the garden most of the time, is not sick, and even cooks, cleans, and, if there's need, does laundry at home.

Early in the morning, the office of the School Department was registering eight- and ten-year-old children for work, but at twelve it was announced that the lists had been invalidated. At 2:00 P.M. our office was closed, and we were all ordered to go home until further notice. Similarly, except for food-supply people, "fecesmen," police, firefighters, and various guards; all other departments, offices, administration agencies, etc. have been closed.

The mood of panic is intensifying by the second. All kinds of rumors are repeated from lips to lips that we should expect the worst. At four Rumkowski and [Dawid] Warszawski, the supreme director of a number of workshops, gave speeches on Firemen's Square (13 Lutomierska Street). They said that "the sacrifice of the children and the elderly is necessary," that "nothing could be done to prevent it," and asked us "not to hinder carrying out the deportation action."* It was easy for them to say that because they managed to secure from the Germans exemption from the deportation for children of workshop directors, firemen, policemen, doctors, instructors, the *Beirat,* and the Devil knows who else. In addition, all kinds of connections will be set in motion now (thousands of the well-connected elderly, the sick, and children will be saved), and the Germans who have demanded 25,000 people will receive in their place completely different persons who, though able to

---

* Sierakowiak's quotations are basically paraphrasings. For the verbatim text of Chaim Rumkowski's staggering speech, see *Łódź Ghetto,* edited by Adelson and Lapides, pp. 328–31. "They are asking us to give up the best we possess. . . . I never imagined that I would be forced to deliver this sacrifice with my own hands. . . . I must stretch out my hands and beg: Brothers and sisters, hand them over to me! Fathers and mothers, give me your children! . . . I must perform this difficult and bloody operation—I must cut off limbs in order to save the body itself!—I must take children because, if not, others may be taken as well, God forbid! . . . My duty is to preserve the Jews who remain. . . . The part that can be saved is much larger than the part that must be given away."

At four Rumkowski and [Dawid] Warszawski, the supreme director of a number of workshops, gave speeches. . . . They said that "the sacrifice of the children and the elderly is necessary," that "nothing could be done to prevent it," and asked us "not to hinder carrying out the deportation action."

work, will nevertheless be sacrificed to make up for the "connected" children and elderly.

Father's cousin, who has a three-year-old girl and wants to save her, came to us in the evening. We've agreed to let her stay with her child, and even to let her whole family come down. They were afraid to stay at their home, not to be taken as hostages for the child. As a result of the heat outside and stuffiness at home, which is caused by the presence of so many people, I could hardly fall asleep.

Late in the evening there was an air raid on Łódź, and several bombs were even dropped. Their sound had a blissful effect on the hearts of all Jews in the ghetto. May it just all end well.

Saturday, September 5. Łódź.   My most Sacred, beloved, worn-out, blessed, cherished Mother has fallen victim to the bloodthirsty German Nazi beast!!! And totally innocently, solely because of the evil hearts of two Czech Jews, the doctors who came to examine us. From early morning on the city was anxious: the news spread like a thunderbolt that at night they had taken the children and elderly to the empty hospitals from which they will be deported (3,000 persons a day!) beginning on Monday.

I, too, felt somewhat uneasy from early in the morning, chased by foreboding and unable to stay home because of heat and humidity.* After two, after we had thrown together a dinner soup, cars and wagons pulled in with the medical examiners, policemen, firemen, and nurses, who started the roundup. The house across from us (8 Spacerowa Street) was sealed off, and after an hour and a half three children were brought out of it. The screams, struggling, cries of the mothers and of everyone on the street were indescribable. Parents of the children who were taken away actually went insane.

While all that was going on, two doctors, two nurses, several firemen, and policemen entered our building completely unexpectedly. They had lists with the names of the tenants in every apartment. A frantic, unexpected examination began. The doctors (old, mean, and sour deportees from Prague), despite policemen's and nurses' objections, started an extremely thorough examination of every tenant, and fished out a great many of the "sick and unable to work," and the ones whom they described as *"fragliche Reserve"* [German; questionable reserve]. My unfortunate dearest mother was among the latter, but it's little consolation for me, since all have been taken to the hospital at 34 Łagiewnicka. What hurts most is the fact that they didn't search at all for those tenants who weren't in their homes, and that although there were over a dozen children in our apartment building, they didn't take even one of them. Our cousin hid with the children behind the bed, her

---

* Zelkowicz wrote, "It has begun. . . . People run through the streets like unleashed spirits. . . . They stand in line like condemned prisoners, stand and wait their turn at the gallows. . . . There is no ear that can hear the silent scream that deafens with its hardness and hardens with its deafening silence. . . . They run over the three ghetto bridges like a herd of hundred-headed serpents surging back and forth. . . . The sky constantly swelling and welling, soon to burst and spill out utter horror and utter reality. It has begun!" ("In These Nightmarish Days," in *Łódź Ghetto,* edited by Adelson and Lapides, p. 336).

family scattered, and everyone came out safe and sound. Meanwhile, my beloved mother has fallen a victim! Our neighbor, old Miller, a seventy-year-old man, uncle of the ghetto's chief doctor, has been left untouched, and my healthy (though emaciated) mother has been taken in his place! . . . The shabby old doctor who examined her searched and searched and was very surprised that he couldn't find any disease in her. Nevertheless, he kept shaking his head, saying to his comrade in Czech: "Very weak, very weak." And despite the opposition and intervention from the police and nurses present at the examination, he added these two unfortunate words to our family's record.

These doctors apparently didn't realize at all what they were doing because they also took our neighbor's son, Dawid Hamer, a young lad of twenty-four, who never had had anything to do with any sickness or doctor in his entire life. Later on, however, through the connections of his cousin, a commissioner, he was examined for a second time and was released in the evening. And what difference does it make to me that as a result of the above case those two doctors have been dismissed by the president and haven't been allowed to continue examining other people? What difference does it make to me that the entire hospital, its entire personnel, are indignant!? My mother has been caught, and I doubt very much that anything will save her.

After the doctors announced the verdict, and when Mom, unfortunate Mom! was running like mad around the house, begging the doctors to spare her life, Father was eating soup that had been left on the stove by the relatives hiding in our apartment, and he was taking sugar out of their bag! True, he was kind of confused, questioned the policemen and doctors, but he didn't run out anywhere in the city; he didn't go to any friends' connections to ask for protection. In a word, he was glad to be rid of a wife with whom life had been becoming harder and harder, thus pushing Mom into her grave.

I swear on this human life that's holy to me that if I only knew that my mother wouldn't have to die, that she'd survive the war despite the deportation, I could accept what has happened. Dear Mother, my tiny, emaciated mother who has gone through so many misfortunes in her life, whose entire life was one of sacrifice for others, relatives and strangers, who might not have been taken away because of her exhaustion had it not been for Father and Nadzia robbing her of food here in the ghetto. My poor mother, who always feared everything, yet invariably continued to believe in God, showed them, in spite of extreme nervousness, complete presence of mind. With a fatalism and with heartbreaking, maddening logic, she spoke to us about her fate. She kind of admitted that I was right when I told her that she had given her life by lending and giving away provisions, but she admitted it with such a bitter smile that I could see she didn't regret her conduct at all, and, although she loved her life so greatly, for her there are values even more important than life, like God, family, etc. She kissed each one of us good-bye, took a bag with her bread and a few potatoes that I forced on her, and left quickly to her horrible fate. I couldn't muster the willpower to look through the window after her or to cry. I walked around, talked, and finally sat as though I had turned to stone. Every other moment, nervous spasms took hold of my heart, hands, mouth, and throat, so that I thought my heart was breaking. It didn't break, though, and it let me eat, think, speak, and go to sleep.

Although there was a wagon waiting downstairs, victims from our house were walked on foot because the hospital was nearby. Old Mrs. Bay has been taken (her daughter has been scurrying around like mad, looking for connections), Mr. Szwalbe (fifty-five years old) has been taken, and many others as well. Our building has fallen victim either to vengeance by the examining doctors or to some other forces.

I've lost Mother. I write "I've lost" because I can hardly believe anything can save her. She doesn't have connections like Dadek Hamer, and that's why she has been taken as a victim for old man X, or for child of dignitary Y.

I was also examined very thoroughly (like everyone else, I was ordered to show my legs, in case they were swollen), but in effect I've been let go. Although until now I considered myself a confirmed egoist as far as life is concerned, I am not sure whether it would have made much of a difference to me if I had been taken with Mom and even died. After all, it's more than a human being can stand to listen to the words Mom uttered before leaving, and to know that she is an innocent victim. And there has been no help from anywhere. It's true that she's being held in a sort of reserve, but our dignitaries will give away even the healthiest reserve in place of their crippled connections. Cursed, capitalistic world!

In the evening Hala Wolman, the sister of my friend from the building, came to see us. She works as a nurse in the hospital, right where Mom is. She consoled us that Mom was scheduled for a second examination, and that as a victim of the crazy doctors she would be released. Promises, promises; only fools are taken in by fine promises. But I'm not taken in even by the finest promise or consolation, since I know that thousands of people destined for deportation have connections, and other victims have to be "reserved" in their place. Meanwhile, if Mom had only left home, nothing would have happened to her. And so, someone else's baby has been saved in our home, while my mother has been taken. Nadzia screamed, cried, suffered spasms, but these days it doesn't move anyone. I am speechless and close to madness.

Sunday, September 6. Łódź. Yesterday in the afternoon [curfew] notices appeared that from 5:00 P.M. until further notice people are forbidden to leave their apartments without a pass from the district. Naturally, excluding this and that, and such and such. They will evidently start thorough searches now. Last night was relatively calm around our building, but in other sections they took a lot of people. The raids are still carried out without the Germans' assistance or pogroms, which everyone fears (let even this happen, if it were to give me my mother back).

At half past six I brought a towel, soap, and a clean shirt to Hala Wolman for Mom, which she had requested through Hala just yesterday. Hala has promised to do all in her power to have Mom examined a second time and released. Father, whose conscience apparently spoke up a little overnight, hurried in the morning to two acquaintances for help, but hasn't secured any, naturally. Mom is sitting there, and nothing is happening. It's not even known whether she'll be examined one more time or not, and whether there is any chance for her release.

Last night passed without any air-raid alarm, and generally one can hardly find anyone counting on a miracle from the outside. The heat is still incredible. In spite of the curfew, people are running around the streets, looking for help for their unfortunates. The *Szpera* continues, though, and everything is closed.

After dinner rumors spread that the Germans are now accompanying the medical commissions, and that they decide who will be taken and who will not. There's been an order that all the children who were released be gathered in one of the hospitals, but although Rumkowski assures us that he guarantees "safe conduct" for these children, no one really believes him; even policemen, instructors, and managers are despairing now. Laments and shouts, cries and screams have become so commonplace that one pays almost no attention to them. What do I care about another mother's cry when my own mother has been taken from me!? I don't think there can be ample revenge for this.

On Bazarna Street a huge gallows has been built on which they will hang over twenty people from Pabianice who escaped from their town

Laments and shouts, cries and screams have become so commonplace that one pays almost no attention to them. What do I care about another mother's cry when my own mother has been taken from me!? I don't think there can be ample revenge for this.

On Bazarna Street a huge gallows has been built on which they will
hang several people from Pabianice who escaped from their town
before the deportation there. But the Devil knows how else these
gallows will come in handy.

before the deportation there. But the Devil knows how else these gallows will come in handy.

People who are hiding their children in garrets, toilets, and other
holes are losing their heads out of despair. On our street, which is just
beside the hospital, lamentation from funeral cars passing and from
processions of the victims goes on all day long.

In the evening Father got through to Mom in the hospital. They
wouldn't even let her appear before the commission, that's how awful
she is said to look now. Thanks only to Hala Wolman's intercession, she
is supposed to be examined once again, however. After eight, when Hala
had already come back from work, I went to her home. She didn't have
any specific information yet, but said that the situation looked very bad

[N]othing will fill up the eternal emptiness in the soul, brain, mind, and heart that is created by the loss of one's most beloved person.

anyway, and that she doubted Mom could be saved. If one doesn't have connections outside the hospital, at least with a police commissioner, one can't do anything inside. Father says that it's a real hell inside; everything is confused and in a horrible state. They say that Mom is unrecognizable, which makes her slender chances even less. At times such shudders and heart palpitations come over me that it seems to me I'm going insane or delirious. Even so, I'm unable to turn my consciousness away from Mom, and suddenly, as though I divide, I find myself in her mind and body. The hour of her deportation is coming closer, and there's no help from anywhere. Although there were some thunderstorms and lightning, and it even rained in the evening, it didn't bring any relief to our torment. That's because even the greatest rainfall can't wash away a completely broken heart, and nothing will fill up the eternal emptiness in the soul, brain, mind, and heart that is created by the loss of one's most beloved person.

There is
no way out

W*ednesday, November 11. Łódź.* I'm wearing short under-wear, so I'm really freezing, completely curled up and never warm enough. No one made a fire in the stove in the office this morning because there was no wood or anything else. However, since none of us was able to begin work due to the cold, we decided to use the former Welfare Department archives to build a fire.

Father has received his food coupon and bought bread with it. He is still insatiable. His swelling won't go down. Today he earned 5 RM carrying coal. I would like him to see Podlaski, so that he could start working for him or possibly somewhere else.

Hitler gave a speech yesterday. Among other things he said that those Jews who died aren't laughing anymore, while those who are still laughing will stop soon. The Americans have supposedly taken Algeria and Morocco. They are doing everything except coming here, damn them!

Thursday, November 12. Łódź. The news about the taking of Algeria and Morocco has been confirmed by the newspaper. They also write that the Germans have taken over that part of France they had not previously occupied, in order to protect it from an American invasion. They say that the real game will begin soon.

Meanwhile, freezing weather is not easing up. Father has already bought his allocation of potatoes, but regarding work, he hasn't secured anything. He is tyrannizing at home like never before. I don't protest. Let the Devil take it all.

The lights went out unexpectedly in our part of the ghetto in the evening. We lighted the apartment with a hastily assembled water-and-oil lantern. The lights went on again at eleven at night. My heart was racing, though nothing important happened.

Friday, November 13. Łódź. The freezing weather persists. We still have no coal in the office, but, fortunately, the reserve of paper will last a few more days. In politics there is nothing special. With Father there is no change; he doesn't have any work yet, except for bringing coal for Mrs. Hamer. He is swollen and very exhausted. Nevertheless, his menda-cious and deceitful nature is already emerging again. He is cooking up a storm, and the situation is beyond my control. Come what may! But the most worrisome thing is that we don't have fuel at all. Father says he will manage. We'll see!

I met with Niutek in the evening. He is trying to enlist me in his actions.

Saturday, November 14. Łódź.   I went to Wolman. He, too, has gone completely to pot. In politics there is nothing new that could help my hunger. In Africa the Krauts are getting a thrashing; in Russia the situation remains unchanged, while in Europe it's silent.

Sunday, November 15. Łódź.   Father is so swollen that he didn't get up all day. I really don't know what's going to happen. He has no work or income. Nadzia, too, has recently been earning next to nothing. It keeps raining, and in politics there is nothing new.

Monday, November 16. Łódź.   Relations at home have again become tense. Father has decided to cook only for himself. After all, he says, we have our soup at work. He's still lying in bed most of the time.

I met with Niutek today, but somehow we didn't talk about anything special. He is still deeply pessimistic about political matters, and he doesn't think that the war will be over soon. In politics there's nothing new.

Tuesday, November 17. Łódź.   Father is still lying in bed. The situation is becoming really irritating. When Nadzia and I are out, he cooks himself a whole bunch of potatoes and uses up a lot of briquettes (which we borrowed). Nor does he have the slightest intention of finding a job. In addition, his thievish old habits (stealing food from our portions) are coming into fashion again. I am terribly upset and will probably explode.

The conditions we live in are becoming more and more despicable. The bedding has been without linen for four months, and there aren't even any clean underclothes. With difficulty, I can have hot water and clean clothes once every two weeks. Of course, Father can't get rid of his lice and doesn't care about them anymore anyway. Soon our whole apartment will be "taken" by them. There is no comforting news from anywhere. Everything has fallen silent.

Thursday, November 19. Łódź.   A food ration for the last ten days of November has been issued. I had a fierce argument over the ration with Father, who had already managed to buy our allocation. A lot was missing when we weighed it. I told him everything I think of him and why I hate him. He doesn't care. He is still not looking for a job. Potatoes are disappearing at a terrifying rate at home. I can't do anything about it, though, and have to grit my teeth and remain silent. Whatever will be will be.

Friday, November 20. Łódź.   A ration of 4 kilos of potatoes and 2 kilos of radishes has been issued. The potatoes are rotten, but even so they taste fine. Tomorrow we are supposed to receive a coupon for 10 kilos of vegetables. Nothing is left from our previous ration of vegetables.

There's been no change with Father. He is spiting us and devouring all the food. Meanwhile, the weather's severely cold. At the office, it's cold despite the heating.

Saturday, November 21. Łódź.   The Germans are admitting in the newspaper that they have given up Bengazi. They are said to be getting a severe thrashing in Africa. There is also a lot of talk in the ghetto about a Russian offensive that either has begun or is about to begin. Italy is being heavily bombed. Despite all these events, the war will certainly take a long time.

At home the tension is growing, and sudden outbursts between Father and me are becoming more frequent. In spite of his dirty tricks, Father is still trying to keep peace with me, but I can't overcome my feelings and I look at everything indifferently. The office has become a paradise for me; each time I come home from work, I am filled with fear and disgust. *Tempora mutantur . . .*

Sunday, November 22. Łódź.   Today nearly resulted in a fight between Father and me. He drove me to the point where I threw a few radish slices at him because he wouldn't let me eat them in peace. You can't even suggest that he start working somewhere. He prefers to carry coal from Marysin for people and cook himself huge potfuls of food at home. He is still full of lice and doesn't even consider bathing to get rid of them. He sleeps in his street clothes and blows his nose on a dirty towel. There is no end to my suffering. Neither his willingness to wash my shirt nor his speed in buying all kinds of food rations and allocations are able to mollify me. I don't even mention his thievery and childish cheating in portioning out the food. As always, he fusses over every crumb and peel. In a word, he is a completely broken man.

Monday, November 23. Łódź.   Thick, fluffy snow has fallen. Winter has now set in for good. In politics there is still nothing special. They are thrashing each other in Africa and somehow can't put an end to it! There are also rumors (supposedly "from the radio") that an offensive has begun on the eastern front. Nothing specific is known, though. At home, the situation hasn't changed in any way.

Tuesday, November 24. Łódź.   Enormous supplies of cabbages have begun to arrive in the ghetto. Coupons for 2 kilograms are given out at workplaces, and, in addition, an allocation of 3 kilos per person is given at the markets. However, despite all those transports of food that are arriving, I am constantly as hungry as a dog, and for the thousandth time I can see that the rations we receive cannot satisfy our hunger.

New people are still being accepted for the Sonderabteilung [German; Special Department]. Also, a picturesquely uniformed women's police force has been formed to combat the adolescent peddlers of saccharine and toffee. The policewomen wear coats and ski pants of light green and gray cloth, and a sailor's hat of the same color with the police insignia on it. They have armbands and nightsticks, but they haven't used them too often so far.

Meanwhile, Rumkowski is disappearing from the ghetto's political stage. All the workshops and offices already have rubber stamps without the "Der Älteste der Juden" inscription.* And at the food-supply offices, Gertler† has become the only decisive figure. But the war and the development of the ghetto continue to thrive as ever.

Wednesday, November 25. Łódź.   The newspaper reports that the Russians are breaking the German front southeast of Stalingrad. Of course, the Germans promise that the final victory will be theirs. In any case,

---

* In the wake of the deportations in September 1942, Rumkowski was left with tremendously reduced influence. The Nazis had found it necessary to use their own troops to carry out the deportations and resorted less and less to working through their appointed Jewish administrator.
† Dawid Gertler (1911–1977) was the head of the Special Unit, or Sonderkommando, of the ghetto police force, the Jewish Administration's own secret police. Through the ghetto's early years, he was often considered Rumkowski's chief rival for favor with the Nazis. His unit oversaw the distribution of food in the ghetto. Abruptly, on July 12, 1943, he was arrested and taken out of the ghetto in a mysterious episode that still had the people talking months later. Repeatedly, he was rumored to have returned. But the Nazis had in fact deported him to Auschwitz. He survived the war. Until today, what soured them to Gertler remains a mystery, though survivors generally relate accounts that he had been smuggling food into the ghetto and had bribed Gestapo and Kripo agents. For more on the "Gertler psychosis," which prevailed in the ghetto after his disappearance, see Lucjan Dobroszycki, *The Chronicle of the Łódź Ghetto* (New Haven, Conn., 1984), p. 359.

something is beginning to happen in the east. Meanwhile, the winter is here in full force. Everything works just like it always has in the ghetto: typhus is raging, and the scrap from our "ghetto/factory" is taken away to the cemetery.

Thursday, November 26. Łódź.   The weather is already wintry. Snow, thaw, wind, and the same old tune over and over again. Only to hold out until the spring.

[A] picturesquely uniformed women's police force has been formed to combat the adolescent peddlers of saccharine and toffee. . . . They have armbands and nightsticks, but they haven't used them too often so far.

Friday, November 27. Łódź.   The Germans are finally admitting in the newspaper that the Russians have begun a general offensive and have broken the front on the Don River and on the Kalinin–Taropec line. The joy in the city is incredible. Naturally, fear quickly follows that the Germans will take vengeance on us when their defeats grow in number. But who cares! Just let the good news keep coming.

Saturday, November 28. Łódź.   Winter has set in for good. Snow and extreme freezing resemble the North Pole. The newspaper writes that the Germans have taken over Toulon and that Hitler has ordered the dismantling of the French army. Other than that, there's nothing interesting.

At home the situation hasn't changed. Father remains unemployed; he only carries coal from Marysin and cooks at home. His relations with me have improved, though.

I went over to see Wolman; despite his hunger, he keeps on writing little by little.

Sunday, November 29. Łódź.   I have received an unexpected 35 RM welfare payment from Bande, a member of the *Beirat* commission who works in my room. He is an exceptionally honest and helpful man, albeit very religious. He took an interest in my situation, and, knowing that neither Father nor Nadzia has any income, he put me on his list for the one-time emergency assistance that is available in the ghetto for the sick, unemployed, aged, etc. The submission of names of candidates for assistance has been entrusted by Rumkowski to "men of conscience," and Bande is one of them.* The money will be very helpful to us.

As far as the weather is concerned, I don't think today can be compared with any day in recent history in Łódź. In the afternoon and evening there was a gale roaring like I had never seen before. When I went to see Goldman (who was out anyway), I literally flew in the air for the first time in my life, carried by the wind. I had to fight the wind on all fours, falling down time after time. So, what kind of weather must it make on the Soviet front, 30-degrees-below-zero cold in an open field, under fire!? Brr . . . However, the Germans are still holding on, fighting and oppressing us! . . .

Monday, November 30. Łódź.   I've been reading very little lately, but I've written a few Polish poems at the office in the past two weeks. I

---

* The ghetto Chronicle notes an I. Bande among the men regularly conferring with Rumkowski. See Dobroszycki, *Chronicle of the Łódź Ghetto*, p. 478.

think I've already mastered the form to some extent. At home, I do absolutely nothing. With Father there's been no change.

Tuesday, December 1. Łódź.   The last month of 1942. Dreams of the war ending this year belong to the past now. We are up to our ears in winter, which has barely begun. Father has finally received an official dismissal statement from Leder-und-Sattler. Tomorrow I will try to get him a job assignment. Maybe this time it will work out.

Wednesday, December 2. Łódź.   I have received an assignment for Father to Holzwolle-Fabrik [German; excelsior factory]. It seems to me, however, that nothing will come of it because on hearing the news, Father said that he doesn't like the commute to Marysin or the work in that shop. But except for public works in the ghetto or demolition outside the ghetto, there's nothing else available.

In politics there's still nothing new. Winter is here in force. The snow is just like in the winter of 1939 and 1940. At home it's dirtier, colder, and wetter, yet washing's out of the question. Father is incredibly dirty and full of lice. Since his return from jail, he hasn't washed himself even once.* I am still holding on. Nadzia has already been infested.

Thursday, December 3. Łódź.   There has been an incredible snowfall in the city. In the face of the enormous masses of snow that fell during the night, crossing the bridge became an acrobatic stunt. That's why with the colossal crowd of people rushing to their jobs at eight o'clock, it took me about an hour to get through† (as of today we start work at eight in the morning, not at 7:30, as before).

As for Father, things are completely hopeless. He went to Marysin today and came back with nothing because he says that the distance is too great and the work is too hard. He prefers to stay at home and wolf down the potatoes he cooks for himself in colossal quantities every day.

In the afternoon I met with Niutek. I went to see him simply because I had nowhere else to go. Goldman moved out, and I could not bear staying at home. I regretted the visit immensely because I hate to be considered an intruder. I just took advantage of the opportunity to read today's newspaper, which, however, contained nothing new, except for Mussolini's silly and empty speech. Again the same old slogan: until spring!

---

* The reason for Majlech Sierakowiak's incarceration must have been reported in the previous notebook, which has not survived.
† Terrible pedestrian traffic jams resulted during the morning "hour rush," as exhausted ghetto dwellers climbed the many stairs of the bridges spanning the restricted thoroughfares.

Friday, December 4. Łódź.   It keeps snowing. The fuel allocation for December has been issued: only 10 kilos of briquettes per person this time but also, for the first time in a year, there are 3 kilos of wood. There are no new food rations.

Saturday, December 5. Łódź.   The ghetto is facing very important local events. Rumors about deportations intensify, but there are also "counter-rumors" saying that Biebow has supposedly received an Iron Cross in Berlin for our ghetto, in return for which the workshops are supposed to work ten to twelve hours a day in order to increase production. Meanwhile, there is a huge demand for men between the ages of eighteen and forty to demolish houses outside the ghetto in the part of the city that has been recently detached from the ghetto. The supervisors of our workshop, Fuchs and Sienicki,* are running around and "catch" suitable men. A hundred persons have already been taken.

In the afternoon I went to Frydrych's. He recovered from typhus, and, thanks to the *Beirat* and other special food coupons, has restored himself well. Later on I went to Wolman's. After his wife and child had left, we had a very serious and honest conversation. Seeing that I clearly understand the unbearable relations at his home, his discord with an unsuitable wife and his being robbed of control over the child, he unburdened his sorrows and dreams to me about dispelling this unbearable and painful atmosphere. This was something I was just waiting for, and I came back at him with a confession of my suffering at home and my wish to sail out of this now intolerable port. We also talked about various friendly subjects concerning his and my plans. After that I had to go back home, where, in the meantime, Nadzia had had a real row with Father, so the supper was cold. Because of the entire situation we don't talk at all anymore . . .

Sunday, December 6. Łódź.   Recently I've been possessed by a wish to forget myself in intensive reading, but I can do it for only brief moments. I can read in the office only when I have less work to do, and when there is nobody around. The book lies in a drawer, which I close immediately whenever there is the least rustle outside the door. It's better than not reading at all. At home, because of the cold (you can't even sit still) and the lack of light by the bed, reading is out of the question. I am currently reading Żeromski's *Dzieje grzechu* [Polish; History of a Sin], which I

---

* Bernard Fuchs and Akiwa Sienicki were heads of the ghetto's Department of Labor. Fuchs survived. Sienicki's fate is not known.

checked out from the library. I want to brush up a bit on classicism, and on the purity and beauty of the Polish language. I also have a play by Ibsen that I found in German, and [Romain] Rolland's *Beethoven*, in Yiddish. I have finished Żytłowski in Yiddish, Strindberg in German, and various other volumes. But I don't have enough patience and strength to put my thoughts together. Oh, when will the end of all this suffering come at last? When?

I went to speak with Niutek. He told me quite clearly that I have no more reason to come to his place and "referred" me to Fredek Taub, through whom I am supposed to remain in touch with him. Had it not been for the fact that I can't stand the atmosphere at home and that I have nowhere else to go, I wouldn't have gone there at all, particularly because I hate staying where I am not welcome and where I don't feel comfortable.

Monday, December 7. Łódź. The political situation is worsening again. The Allied forces' offensive in Africa has been stopped by the Germans, who are starting a counteroffensive there and, they say, on the Russian front as well. There is no chance the war can end this winter. All we can do is wait and hold out, provided, of course, that "circumstances beyond our control" don't make it impossible. Meanwhile, there has been a thaw and people can breathe more easily.

The situation with Father remains unchanged. I asked Baum, an old friend of Father's, to recommend Father to the commissioner of the carpentry workshop since he was a cabinetmaker before the war (Baum is on the [carpentry workshop] commission). Perhaps something will come of it in a few days.

Tuesday, December 8. Łódź.   8°C [39°F]! There is almost no trace left of the enormous weight of snow that accumulated recently. The joy because of this is enormous. One more day has been won!

I have received an additional 15 RM welfare from Bande, which makes it a full 50 RM. It will be put to good use, since we've been left without a single penny. Father just sits and cooks as if nothing were happening. Not a single word about going to work. I am silent, which drives him crazy. He would like to have normal relations at home. So would I.

Wednesday, December 9. Łódź. The weather is warmer. I had nowhere to go today, so I went to Frydrych's again, where at least there was some coffee and a slice of potato coffee cake to eat.

Father bought the latest food ration for the next ten days. Again there are 3 kilos of potatoes and 5 kilos of cabbage, 20 dkg of meat, and 15 dkg of sausage.

Thursday, December 10. Łódź.   Considering it's December, the weather is still ideal. With a letter that I managed to secure from Baum, Father went to [Szoel] Terkeltaub, the commissioner of the carpentry workshop, who issued the "Employee Requested" form for Father. Maybe this time it will turn out for the good.

At the office I received ⅓ of a can of pickled meat (30 dkg). Even though I was told that this meat should be cooked, at home we ate it straight from the can. The first time in my life I ate canned meat. Just to get by! Until the spring!

Friday, December 11. Łódź.   Father brought his paperwork to my office today, and we went to see Sienicki ("the minister of labor"), who immediately gave him a skilled worker's assignment to the carpentry workshop. Father has almost accepted that he has to work, and we now have "peace" and normal relations at home. If only Father could get rid of his terrible scratching; he is completely covered with lice and scabs. Nadzia didn't go to work on Tuesday so she could do laundry. Perhaps next week, when the clothes have dried, the situation will improve somewhat. Meanwhile, the weather is excellent. The temperature is between 4 and 8°C [40–46°F].

Saturday, December 12. Łódź.   With the ID card from the Clothing Department that I arranged yesterday, I have received a pair of socks and a pair of gloves (for the three of us!). In order to become eligible for other things (clothes, underclothes, and shoes from the deportees from nearby towns) that have been arriving in the ghetto for several months, one needs special coupons issued at workshops or by the director of the Bekleidungsabteilung [Clothing Department].

Father was at his new job for the first time. He has been appointed a warehouseman and quality inspector in the children's bed department.

The weather is still warm. Another week has passed.

Sunday, December 13. Łódź.   According to the German sources, the English and Americans, and in part the Soviets as well, have been completely halted, and the Germans have begun a counteroffensive.

Three Jewish girls were executed on Czarneckiego Street. They were said to have escaped from the labor camps in Germany, and were caught when they were crossing the perimeter of our ghetto. They were taken out of a room and shot like dogs in the hallway. Meanwhile, a ration of 10 dkg of fish and ½ kg of carrots per person has been issued. The "fish" are several centimeter-long, salted gudgeon that stink for a mile. Too bad there is so little of it.

It was cold again today. Winter is coming back.

Monday, December 14. Łódź.   Father has received a coupon for 10 kg of wood scraps. Our fuel situation will improve a bit again. There is no other news. It's cold again.

Tuesday, December 15. Łódź.   There are rumors about some commission from the Red Cross that is supposed to visit the areas occupied by Germany—to examine the situation of the conquered nations, and the condition of the Jews in particular. Supposedly there's been an outcry in the world about the persecutions and murders of the Jews in Germany. Perhaps because of that outcry, we've been receiving a bit more to eat recently. How content and happy my dear, never-forgotten little Mom would now be! There's not one single event I don't immediately associate in my thoughts with her. Sometimes when I think about my sorrow, I am afraid I will go crazy. Did it really have to happen?

I haven't gone out to read a newspaper or to see any friends recently. If there's good news, it will reach me by itself. The weather is so-so.

Wednesday, December 16. Łódź.   I've received 5 kg of kohlrabis. There are rumors about various imminent additional food allocations. We will see. There'll be probably some news before spring.

Thursday, December 17. Łódź.   The weather is warm again, but I feel worse. I've had a headache for two days. The main thing, however, is to hold out and enjoy every bearable passing day of winter.

Friday, December 18. Łódź.   An unexpected food ration for the third part of December has been issued (25 dkg of marmalade, 50 dkg of flour, 4 kg of potatoes, and 5 kg of turnips).

There are a lot of rumors going around the ghetto about a storm of protest that erupted abroad as a result of terrible persecutions of the Jews in Germany in the recent months. A joke is even circulating about how an exchange of Jews for American Germans is supposed to be arranged.

Whatever you say, bad rumors have silenced, and people talk now about how they expect improvement in the status of Jews in Germany. The Rollkommando has been dissolved.*

Saturday, December 19. Łódź.   Unfortunate events have taken strong hold of us, and won't ease their grip. It has turned out that Father acquired scabies in jail. He has been "cultivating" it, carelessly blaming lice for the itching. Because we chopped up our only wooden bed for fuel, Nadzia has been forced to sleep with Father in the bigger bed, and so she, too, has been infected with this devilish disease. I am now living in fear about myself because our crowded conditions don't allow for a separation of the sick from the healthy. When I begin to feel terrible itching and pick my skin in the evening, cold shivers run down my spine. Father accepts everything blankly, and in spite of his work he is failing more and more. Nadzia will see a skin doctor tomorrow. It's clear that before this war ends, we will have to suffer a number of plagues.

Sunday, December 20. Łódź.   Nadzia went to the doctor today. He prescribed "scabies water" for her, which she is supposed to apply two times a day for four days. After that period, and after she has washed herself and changed her underclothes, she is supposed to see the doctor again. Father will need to do the same. Meanwhile, he is unable to go to work and loses his soup there.

The weather is still excellent, except that in the morning and evening there's dense fog. In politics there's nothing new.

---

* The term *Rollkommando* was rarely used outside German military, police, and SS circles; appears little in the literature, but became all too well known in communities, such as the Łódź Ghetto, that had experienced partial liquidations. Rollkommando units took part in the harrowing deportation of 15,000 children, sickly, and elderly from the Łódź Ghetto in the "Nightmarish Days" of September 1942, according to Lucjan Dobroszycki (*Dziennik. Dawid Sierakowiak* [Warsaw, 1960] fn 178). The title was applied to German mobile units based in a particular region and directed to move through surrounding towns and villages, "cleansing" them of Jews and others. Holocaust scholar Raul Hilberg interprets the young diarist's entry as an indication that word had reached the ghetto that the Germans were phasing out their operation in Chełmno-Kulmhof, where Jews from the Łódź region were gassed and burned. Testimonies reflect that deportations to Chełmno were almost over by October 1942, and by December, when Dawid wrote this entry, the Germans were basically finished killing deportees there, but still had bodies left to burn. On December 1, 1941, Colonel Joachim Jaeger described in a report the operations of one Rollkommando unit composed of eight to ten men that worked its way through the Kaunas region of Lithuania. See Raul Hilberg, *The Destruction of the European Jews* (New York, 1985), vol. 1, p. 294. These details are elaborated extensively in subsequent French, German, and Italian editions, and in forthcoming Romanian, Italian, and Japanese editions.

Monday, December 21. Łódź.   Father also went to the doctor today. The doctor gave him the same advice he gave to Nadzia. He also ordered that the persons in close contact with the sick must use the medicine. I took advantage of this instruction and applied the sulfurized hydrogen salve from head to toe.

Tuesday, December 22. Łódź.   The Germans admit in the newspaper today that they've been forced to withdraw to "previously selected positions" because the Soviets broke the front. We don't know anything else.

Wednesday, December 23. Łódź.   At 5:30 in the morning a fire broke out in the woodworking factory on 6 Bazarna Street (a former hospital). The building, its new and old machines, the entire supply of wood, and manufactured goods have burned. The German Fire Department, with the help of the Jewish Fire Department and people mobilized from the nearby streets, was fighting to put out the fire until late afternoon. The director and several dozen of the workshop's employees have been arrested. The entire ghetto is panic-stricken; we only hope the Germans won't consider the accident sabotage and decide to act accordingly. So far it has been calm.*

Thursday, December 24. Łódź.   I've finally received a coupon for shoes (I filed an application for it two months ago). I cannot use it now, however, because I don't have cash. I wrote an application for a loan at the beginning of the week. Bande took it from me, and promised to have it approved directly in the Secretariat for Requests and Applications. My clogs are completely finished, and boots or shoes would be very nice to have. But what can I do?

Friday, December 25. Łódź.   The first Christmas of the war without snow. The weather is already becoming cold, though. In politics there's nothing new. Huge battles are reportedly going on, but we know nothing specific. Bande has had my loan application approved, and I will be able to receive the money on Sunday. In all likelihood it will be a monthly stipend (80 RM), to be paid back in ten months. I will be able to buy shoes for myself, for Nadzia, too, and some clothes, possibly

* Those interrogated were subsequently released. The official ghetto Chronicle attributes the blaze, which was fueled by benzene and other chemicals used on the premises, to an electrical short circuit.

underclothes, for Father. Too bad no food can be bought for an afford-able price. At home, we are eating the last bits of our rations. But who cares! Just to hold out until spring!

Saturday, December 26. Łódź.   Winter has won after all. It was really freezing in the morning.

There was *cholent* in the kitchen at our offices today. Such an event usually causes a total revolution at work. Most of the low- and high-ranking clerks rush like wild fire to get this devine delicacy. (They've had enough of what they call "unbearable" soups.) The ones who can have their fill of the soup through various manipulations, connections, and official privileges show their thoughtless animal-like natures when they stampede for the *cholent*. One more coupon, one more portion please—Oh, *cholent*, that *cholent*! Meanwhile, at our home, as in half of the homes in the ghetto, serious hunger is setting in. All we have left to eat is 5 kg of potatoes. We cook one meager soup a day.

In politics there's nothing new. Meanwhile, Rumkowski, as he did during past periods of hunger, again organizes concerts, shows, and various kinds of jubilee feasts. So today, for example, there was a jubilee dedicated to the tailor and textile workshops; on Krawiecka Street there will be a real ball for the *Beirat*, the higher-ranking clerks of these workshops, which will, of course, bring about a further reduction in the rations for the rest of the population. The black hearse is becoming extremely popular again.

Sunday, December 27. Łódź.   I have received a loan from the Supple-mental Assistance Office, resulting from my application being approved by the Secretariat for Requests and Applications. So in the afternoon I went to the Clothing Department to find shoes. I couldn't find any, though, because an ordinary mortal is simply shown a few pairs of good-for-nothing shoes with the comment, "There is nothing else for you," and that's it. Since I don't have any connections there, I will wait for a while; perhaps another shipment of old Jewish shoes will arrive in the ghetto again.

It was minus 3°C [27°F] today. Everyone is waiting tensely for the next food ration, which will decide the fate of our stomachs for the first ten days of January.

Yesterday at Krawiecka Street, "the old man" said that he will give 5-kilo rations to the workers in the "jubilee" workshops. It is again *a beau geste* on us. Gertler, as a defender of the masses, is said to oppose the idea, but the masters will get the approval while the flunky will go away with nothing.

Monday, December 28. Łódź.   The ration for the first ten days of January has been issued. There are no potatoes at all in it, only 5 kilos of vegetables and a bit of marmalade. The dejection in the city is terrible. I am completely depressed. The prospect of cold and hunger fills me with indescribable terror. I remember scenes of suffering in the previous years when the state of my health and strength was much better, and yet I was hardly able to stand the torment. I am also afraid that Father's animal-like self-indulgence will return (he has recently been eating almost as much as he wants, so he has calmed down somewhat). Today we went to bed without supper because Nadzia portioned out our remaining potato scraps for tomorrow and the day after tomorrow.

The black hearse is becoming extremely popular again.

Nadzia and Father have had their scabies cured for now, but because we can't change the bedding, it will probably come back again.

Tuesday, December 29. Łódź.   In the morning it was minus 7°C [20°F]. In the afternoon the temperature eased up, and it began to snow. I called on Niutek and after that Fredek [Taub]; I agreed to cooperate with their organization as a very close sympathizer, an "apprentice of the order." Fredek also took my notebook with my latest poems and the beginning of *Alarm*. He is going to be the first critic of my work and will also decide about my value to the organization and about our further cooperation.

Wednesday, December 30. Łódź.   We have had our last potato in a watery soup. As usual in the times of hunger, I have to turn to forced, intensive reading to drive away the sense of deprivation with this "opiate." My brain seems to have become much too exhausted.

Roosevelt supposedly said in some speech that in 1943 the Allies will show what they can do. Soon will come the assurances that the war is 100 percent certain to end in '43. And everyone will believe that for another year. Provided they stay alive that long.

Thursday, December 31. Łódź.   The last day of the old year. New Year's Eve, so solemnly celebrated in Poland. Hunger is spreading in the ghetto, while the wealthy classes indulge themselves to the utmost. The higher-ranking clerks in our office are organizing a real feed for themselves today. There will be vodka, soup, cakes, salad, and sausage! One can only try to imagine what the "real" rulers will be having! Gertler's gang, the market gardeners, the police, Kripo men, wagon drivers, Gestapo men, bakers— in one word, all those who gorge themselves from official and unofficial sources in the ghetto—they can all revel now. Relations in the ghetto are becoming more and more typical of wartime: on the one hand, wealth, frolic, and satisfaction; on the other hand, poverty, hunger, and death. Old clogs and beautiful knee boots; warm apartments and wet, cold hovels; red, healthy necks and pale, bony "hourglasses"—these are the symbols of the class structure in the ghetto. Meanwhile, the war goes on. The year that was expected to be the last of the war is ending. Few people count on 1943 now. There's been too much disillusionment and sacrificed life, and too many tears.

Friday, January 1, 1943. Łódź.   We are entering a new year, the fifth calendar year of the war. We are completely ignorant about events going

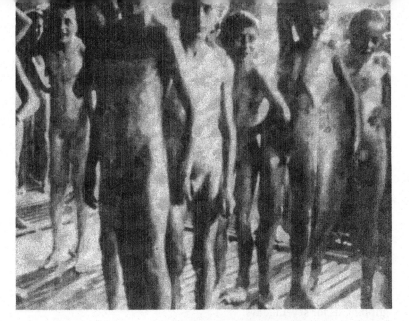

Old clogs and beautiful knee boots; warm apartments and wet, cold hovels; red, healthy necks and pale, bony "hourglasses"—these are the symbols of the class structure in the ghetto.

on outside the ghetto, dejected about our satanic misfortunes, and we are falling deeper and deeper into black despair and disbelief. There are no prospects for the better, many for the worse. We are in an epoch of hunger, cold, death, and fear. A few dozen people from Czarnieckiego Street [the Central Prison] and even from the police stations have been deported to an unknown destination.

Last evening a fire broke out in the Wäsche-u. Kleider-Abt. [German; Laundry and Clothing Department] (1 Dworska Street), and today the Textilfäbrikations-Abt. [German; Textile Manufacturing Department] was ablaze (77 Drewnowska Street). My flesh crawls at the very thought that the Germans may want us to bear the consequences of these events.

Despite various rumors, there haven't been and, most probably, there won't be any new potato rations. Hunger is raging permanently. Winter, too, has set in for real. Snow and freezing weather have been gripping us for several days.

Yesterday's New Year's ball for our office "soup eaters" and *"cholent eaters"* ended at four in the morning, so they did not come to work until noon today. They "enjoyed" themselves very much. After all, it was New Year's Eve!

Saturday, January 2. Łódź.   Yesterday Father fell very badly and couldn't go to work. I had to report it to the workshop (Father works as a doorman there now). I hope he hasn't broken his leg. Tomorrow a doctor will come.

I didn't go anywhere in the afternoon. Yesterday I went to Fredek's. He hadn't yet read all of my writing and promised solemnly to bring it back to me when he does.

I go to bed earlier if possible because it's really cold at home. Everything is beginning to mold again because of the moisture. We don't cook suppers anymore, so I eat my last meal (rutabaga soup and sometimes a piece of bread with radishes) at four o'clock. However, I read more and more in bed. Every cloud has a . . .

Sunday, January 3. Łódź.   The doctor we requested for Father hasn't come. Supposedly he will come tomorrow. Meanwhile, the weather is even colder, and hunger is worsening. All we cook at home now is a bit of soup made of rutabagas and flour. In the evening there is only one plate for everyone. In politics there's nothing new. The newspapers have died completely.

Monday, January 4. Łódź.   Father's leg turns out to be broken at the ankle, and the doctor wrote a note to the surgical hospital to put it in a cast. He hasn't even bandaged it, though. Meanwhile, there is "tension" again at home. Father thinks that nobody cares about him and that we don't want to save him. He forgets how he acted when Mother was being taken away to perish. I usually remain silent and leave home, provided I have enough strength to drag myself out somewhere.

I have received my writing from Fredek. As far as the poems are concerned, he said that their content surpasses their form, "which remains immature." He liked my poem "Oh, Gods, Where Is Your Might? . . ."

Tuesday, January 5. Łódź.   Father is still at home. I went to get some shoes, and this time I bought myself a pair of Hasidic shoes. (In order to be able to make the purchase, I had to have a recommendation from one of the saleswomen, who turned out to be an old friend of Mother's. I paid 16 RM.)

Today it was minus 4°C [24°F]. More snow is accumulating. Winter's in full swing.

Wednesday, January 6. Łódź.   In the morning Father started a serious argument with me. He doesn't care if the entire ghetto collapses, as long as he is taken to the hospital. I went to see Hala Wolman, who promised to intervene to try to find room for Father at the hospital.

Thursday, January 14. Łódź.   It is minus 8°C [18°F], but I'm so cold it feels as if it were minus 20 [−4°F]. It's terrible at home. Nadzia went to the hospital to make an inquiry. Father has had his leg put in a cast already, but he will have to stay in the hospital for a few more days. He keeps on sending requests for food. Nadzia sent him the 25 dkg of her bread she usually gives him, and that's it. We couldn't give him any of our watery soup. He is not the kind of father worth giving up our health for, as our unfortunate mother did. My blessed, beloved, unforgotten in any moment of the day or night mother!

My feet have been frostbitten in my new shoes, and I walk now like a cripple. Getting up in the morning is torture again. In the morning the temperature in our room is below the freezing point, and it's a miracle we haven't yet caught cold. Nadzia stays in this cold all day long! So after she finishes cooking dinner, she goes to bed immediately.

Friday, January 15. Łódź.   I went to Lolek Milgrom's and borrowed Dostoevski's *The Idiot* from him. I've been reading quite a lot in Yiddish recently. I spend little time in the office now, so I read mostly in bed at home. Otherwise, I do nothing. Just to get by, until the spring.

Saturday, January 16. Łódź.   After work I dropped in on Turbowicz and borrowed our last Hebrew-school textbook from him. I want to read a little in this language, which I am beginning to forget.

In the afternoon I went to Wolman's and borrowed the first volume of Peretz's works.* I have a whole collection of books at home now. I don't know when I will manage to read them. In politics there's nothing new.

Sunday, January 17. Łódź.   In the ghetto, all kinds of additional food coupons are being issued (permanent, temporary, bonuses, additions, etc., etc.), whose incredibly high number is directly proportional to the intensifying hunger. There are the so-called CP [Polish, Ciężko Pracujący; hard-worker] coupons, B (*Beirat*) coupons, B 1 (second-rate *Beirat*), B 2 (the police, guards, higher-ranking clerks, etc.), B 3 (coupons for one-time use by clerks and sometimes workers), the coupons issued personally by Rumkowski, Gertler, Jakubowicz, Hiksow, Praszkier, and all sorts of other Gestapo and Kripo men.

The system of additional food coupons has grown into a colossal machine, the so-called *Diät-Ladovum*, and consumes an incredible amount of goods that an average ghetto dweller has almost no chance to see (for example, horse fat, carrots, sugar, rye flakes, sago [a thickening agent], artificial honey, etc.). However, the few dozen chosen ones who have the entire production of the ghetto at their disposal can live in better conditions than did many a Łódź factory owner before the war. There are feasts and balls organized in the ghetto that 90 percent of the Germans wouldn't even dream of. In addition, there has been a reduction in the number of clerks and so-called black workers in the bakeries recently, to put all kinds of protégés in their place. (In the bakery one officially receives 50 dkg of bread a day and a loaf a week to take home.) The Sonderabteilung has become enormously powerful and controls almost the entire food-distribution system in the ghetto now. They did manage to put an end to the thievery and introduce some order, but all this has been done by Gertler at the expense of colossal food allocations

---

* Isaac Loeb Peretz (1852–1915) was an extremely popular Polish-Yiddish writer. He is considered one of the founders of modern Yiddish literature.

for his policemen and undercover agents. They feed themselves as much as they wish, and live the good life, while the gray mass of the "unconnected" population . . .

Last night there was an alarm, but no air raid followed. The Western crooks [Allies] are as silent as they were before. I've already lost all hope for an early end to the war. A few days ago, Wolman came to my office, worried by the fact that I hadn't come to see him for over a month. He, too, is in a pessimistic mood. He keeps on writing, but the hunger is troubling him. I would like to have my legs healed so that I could go see him again. As long as I don't croak, I will have plenty of time to go to him because the war will definitely take a long time.

Thursday, February 18. Łódź.   On my way back from the office, I met Rysiek Skoczylas, who works as a conductor on the ghetto streetcar. He gave me a lift all the way home. For the first time since my arrival in the ghetto, I used some kind of transportation. Maybe I should think of it as a sign of the coming end of bad times?

Again fifty persons from Czarnieckiego Street have been sent to Germany. "For labor in Germany," they say, but nothing certain is known.

Friday, February 19. Łódź.   The Germans admit in the newspaper that they have given up Kharkov. There is also Goebbels's speech complaining about the seriousness of the situation, acknowledging Kharkov, getting down on the Jews, and asking ten questions that are supposed to prove that the morale of the nation is still excellent.

I received an affirmative reply to my application for a loan, and have already received 80 RM. It was only today that Bande took the application for a food coupon for Father from me. I had our typist type it. Perhaps aesthetic appearance is of some importance.

On my way back home I dropped into a small grocery shop near our office to get a few candies on the occasion of having received the loan, and to create a bit of joy at home. In the shop I noticed an old school friend of mine from our first years in "Jabne,"* Elek Opatowski, sitting by a table. The youth has become involved in all kinds of underground activities, and in the beginning of the ghetto he was famous as a tough guy and a golden lad of shady character. Nevertheless, he is a guy with a heart of gold, which he proved today. The moment I saw him, he was eating quite a piece of bread on which he was spreading lard (5 RM a

* Students attended Jabne Jewish elementary schools throughout Poland before 1939.

dekagram!). Without saying a word, he cut a piece of bread for me, spread lard on it, and literally forced me to eat it up. We had a long conversation, and when we were leaving the joint, he slipped 10 RM into my hand because he was moved by my situation and Father's illness. "You'll return it when you have enough." In a moment he was gone. I was shocked, not so much by this piece of bread or the 10 marks, but by the fact that such a déclassé guy would do such a thing. I would like to be able to repay him some day for what he did, because he's truly worth remembering with gratitude, though he didn't ask for that at all. Anyway, it's interesting what different kinds of people there are in the ghetto.

Saturday, February 20. Łódź.   I went to Wolman's. Even though I can hardly walk because of the damned wound on my leg, I just can't stand staying at home. The scabies is worsening. I have plenty of scabs on my body, and my tortures are horrible. I absolutely have to see a doctor.

In politics there's nothing new. The weather's excellent.

Sunday, February 21. Łódź.   I dragged myself to an outpatient department, but I didn't get a ticket to see a doctor.

I learned about the death of my Aunt Rajca. She had water in her lungs and contracted tuberculosis. I didn't tell Father about it, not to upset him.

In the afternoon Nadzia and I went to 24 Limanowskiego Street, where we bought 12 kilos of wood for 1.30 RM a kilo. This was a good deal, since a kilo of wood in a store usually costs 2 RM. In politics there are high hopes, but nothing specific is known.

Monday, February 22. Łódź.   We've run out of vegetables, and now Nadzia is cooking soup for three people out of half a kilo of potatoes and about 5 dkg of the groceries.

My scabies is even worse. I'm sure that I also have a skin inflammation on my penis. I'm definitely going to a doctor tomorrow.

Tuesday, February 23. Łódź.   I saw a doctor. He prescribed an ointment to apply over my entire body. However, it soon turned out that the ointment is not available anywhere in the ghetto, so I had to go back to the doctor to have him change the prescription to another ointment. After that I went to a pharmacy on Rybna Street, where Mr. Blausztajn is a manager, and he promised to use his connections to prepare a quarter of the prescribed ointment for me. (I have also learned from him that Kuba had pleurisy and water in his lungs.) Because the medicine couldn't be ready sooner than seven o'clock, I dropped in on Kuba. I had not seen him in nearly a year, but nothing has changed there and his life continues in the prewar manner. A company of friends, all wearing knee boots, was gathered; they played bridge, having fun not feeling hungry.

In the evening I applied the ointment all over myself. Unfortunately, it is brown and made a Negro out of me. I wonder how I will look at the office tomorrow because I won't dare wash myself without the doctor's permission. I am supposed to repeat the application for five more nights, then wait twenty-four hours, and wash myself the following night. On the eighth day I'm supposed to see the doctor again. The entire treatment may very likely be for nothing because Father is still full of scabs from head to foot, Nadzia has them too, and after a few days I will probably become infected again.

Wednesday, February 24. Łódź.   Today I was tormented with shame at the office because of my black hands. However I slept well and had no itching all night.

The hunger is intensifying at home. We don't have any food left from the latest food ration anymore, and our soups are really meager. I told Nadzia to buy an additional 40 dkg of sauerkraut for 6.40 RM. The hundred RM I received from Bande have already been used up, and I've made the first bite into the 80 from the loan. Father is feeling much worse, and there is no help for us from anywhere. Bande hasn't yet acted on my application for a food coupon for Father.

Thursday, February 25. Łódź.   The day has brought more terrifying news. In the newspaper, the Führer solemnly vows to exterminate all the Jews in Europe!

I met with Niutek and Fredek, whom I informed about my activities. Niutek asked me to make a certain small inquiry in our office, which may be of some use some day. In addition, he livened up my spirit, told me to hold on, and expressed his prognostication that the war would soon be over.

I have also seen the doctor again to renew the ointment prescription so that I can complete the treatment. He told me to wash my hands during the day to be able to work normally.

Friday, February 26. Łódź.   In the evening at the office I read excerpts from *Alarm*. Everybody liked them very much, in terms of both the expression and the subject. Were it not for my nasty illness, I think I could write a bit more now. Meanwhile, I can't write or even read.

Every morning I apply the ointment from head to foot, but it hardly helps at all. The bedding on which I lie is incredibly dirty, and the feeling of disgust for the conditions I live in exceeds imagination.

Podlaski has promised to employ Nadzia again in his workshop. He told her to come to see him on Monday.

Father has become indifferent to everything now. He has difficulty breathing, speaks very little, and eats less and less, though his stomach is not sick. A doctor was supposed to come to us today, but he hasn't come, and promised to come early tomorrow morning (he couldn't make it today because of the overwhelming number of visits).

Saturday, March 6. Łódź.   My unfortunate once-powerful father died today at four in the afternoon. He became very weak last night, and by the morning he lay almost unable to move. Breathing was becoming increasingly difficult for him. He couldn't pass urine at all, and spoke very little, though he was completely conscious and aware of everything. The doctor didn't come until half past eleven and diagnosed a total weakening of the heart muscle. He prescribed immediate injections of strychnine, but it's been half a year since such injections could be bought in the ghetto, and now they can be obtained only in very small amounts through strong connections in the Sonderabteilung, where they are procured by Gertler. Nadzia called in Uncle Szlamko, who took the prescriptions and tried to buy the medicine, but he couldn't help either. For dinner Father managed to eat a few dry boiled potatoes with beetroot soup, but Nadzia had to feed it all directly into his mouth.

At three o'clock Nadzia went down for salad and cheese, and I stayed alone with Father in the apartment. Suddenly, at about five to four, Father asked me to arrange the pillows more comfortably for him. I did that. Father bowed his head and lay without any movement, breathing very shallowly. From my own bed, I kept watch on him constantly and suddenly I thought I saw him stop breathing. For a few minutes, numb with fear, I couldn't believe it myself, and it was several minutes after four when I called one of the neighbors. The neighbor tried to move Father's head on the pillow, but, terrified, she discovered that Father was already dead. When Nadzia came with the salad and cheese, she rushed screaming in tears to Father, but it was already too late. We sent for our uncle, who came to us later in the evening. No one else from the family has shown up.

Sunday, March 7. Łódź.   Just like Nadzia, I lay sleepless all night. She lay on my bed in her coat and street clothes.

In the morning Uncle settled the formalities with the doctor and the Burial Department. About one o'clock, while I lay turned to the wall, Father was washed in our apartment according to the ritual. At three the hearse arrived.

I have become so agitated that I have a high fever again. I am nervous and frightened in the extreme. I can't even take my temperature because I tremble so much I can't place the thermometer in my armpit. I even called in a medic for 5 RM. After examining me, he said that the fever most probably comes from an infection in the little wound I still have from the frostbite. However, he found my lungs in good condition. He also prescribed a medicine and an ointment, and told me to stay in bed, which I won't be able to do because I think I will go crazy if I stay home one more day with my thoughts, fears, and recollections.

Nadzia, Aunt Esler's daughter, came to us today and promised that she would give me linen to cover my unbearable bedding. Only Uncle and Chaim Esler came to the cemetery. Nobody came to see us at home in the evening, and we were left alone for the night again.

Monday, March 8. Łódź.   I still lay in bed today because the fever persists. I am so agitated, however, that almost everyone advises me to get up and go to work without checking my temperature. I will do so. Tomorrow I am absolutely going to work.

Fuchs, Aunt Esler's brother-in-law, came to see me today before noon. I told him to sell Father's summer coat, which we had given him for retailoring. Let him keep what's due for his work and give us back the rest. We will have a few marks at least.

We have been left Father's kilo of bread, a little piece of cheese, three teaspoons of sugar, and about 2 dkg of oil. We are not selling any of it. Together with my latest ration of butter, cheese, and powdered milk, we now have quite a substantial amount of food. Only my fever, sadness, and the fact that I still have to stay in bed are killing me with heart palpitations. I wake up at night with my heart either racing or beating very weakly, and I can't go back to sleep for a long time. I can't wait for tomorrow to go to the office.

Nadzia has met with Podlaski. He told her not to come again for a while because he has no job for her yet. Nevertheless, she will go to see him tomorrow again, ask him one more time for a job, explaining that she can't wait at home. Oh, if only I were on my feet again! Just not in this bed, which has become the symbol of a grave in the ghetto; only not to stay in this cursed apartment, where there is no cure or help. Maybe I will succeed in cheating the fever if I am on my feet. I hope so!

Tuesday, March 9. Łódź.   I did as I had said. I said to hell with the thermometer and went to the office today. I continue to have a fever, though. There was a surprise waiting for us at the office, which quickly became news in the entire ghetto. Biebow from the Gettoverwaltung visited our department with Fuchs, and they toured the whole office. As a result of the visit (Biebow also inspected the Personnel and Economic Departments), all the clerks, men and women less than forty years of age, will be dismissed from the offices and will have to find employment in the workshops or in public works. Old and exhausted workers will be employed in their place. In almost every room, there was an argument because there were way too many young, made-up, and nicely dressed workers there. Biebow also dismissed the three directors in our workshop—Andres, Uryson, and Sienicki—and has given all the managing power to Fuchs. Sienicki, who has Rumkowski's special protection and is fat as a bull as a result, has simply been fired. Uryson and Andres have been reduced to positions of ordinary clerks. Even though all these changes are hurting me no less than they hurt the persons who have been dismissed, I don't think that clearing the offices of this healthy, dressed-up, arrogant, and well-connected rabble will do much harm.

Biebow has also carried out a kind of purge in Rumkowski's secretariat on the Bałuty Market. The "Eldest" has completely fallen. He has fallen so much that the German guards at the Bałuty Market frisked him when he was entering the square yesterday.

There's a new announcement signed by only Biebow that it's compulsory to bring in old junk and old rags.* In a word, there are changes going on in the ghetto, and nothing indicates that the war will come to an end soon. The Germans are moving forward again on the Russian front.

In the face of Nadzia's imploring, Podlaski has appointed her to a

---

* Over the course of the ghetto's history, hundreds of announcements produced in widely varying type by the ghetto's print shop were issued in the name of Chaim Rumkowski as the Eldest of the Jews. Collections of these notices are in the Yad Vashem and YIVO archives.

juvenile group, where she works for five hours a day. A ration of a kilo of carrots and half a kilo of beets was issued today, and Nadzia has already received it.

Unexpectedly, I received a one-time additional soup from Fuchs. I'm still treating my wounds and abscesses, which I can't get rid of. First of all, however, I'd like to get rid of the fever. Just to be of at least average health.

Biebow has also carried out a kind of purge in Rumkowski's secretariat on the Bałuty Market. The "Eldest" has completely fallen. He has fallen so much that the German guards at the Bałuty Market frisked him when he was entering the square yesterday.

Wednesday, March 10. Łódź.   Nadzia came to see me in the office in the afternoon. She persuaded me to go to a doctor to find out why I'm having this fever. At five o'clock I took off from work and went with Nadzia to Dr. Lustig, a very experienced Czech internist. He turned out to be an extremely nice and dedicated man. He examined me very carefully (5 RM a visit), and said he found nothing infectious. He was unable to determine where the fever comes from, but he didn't think it could come from the little wound on my leg. He told me to go to work, to check my temperature, on Sunday to go for a long walk, and to see him again on Monday. I have calmed down a little, but I'd rather not have the fever anymore. Nadzia is in seventh heaven.

The weather is very lovely, but politically it's worse and worse. The Germans are approaching Kharkov, and tension between the United States and the Soviets is building. The possibility of opening the second front in Europe seems out of the question. We are doomed to die in the ghetto.

Thursday, March 11. Łódź.   An official letter from the Gettover-waltung demanding the strict execution of all Biebow's orders has arrived at the office. However, as a result of various kinds of behind-the-scenes manipulations in the highest circles of the ghetto, the task of purging the young elements from the departments has been handed over to Rumkowski. At half past six, the "Eldest" came to our department with Sienicki in order to classify the employees in person. They didn't let us go home until late at night.

As Rumkowski was about to arrive, his portrait was again hung in Fuchs's office, though it had been taken down on Biebow's order! After the conference between the "Eldest," Fuchs, Sienicki, Andres, Uryson, and Franek (the chief of the former Personnel Department), all the clerks were called in for an interview. We entered the office one by one. The "Eldest" asked a few questions and told Sienicki to write down whether a given clerk should stay or be transferred to one of the workshops. Rumkowski had quite a long talk with me (in Yiddish, using the "Lithua-nian" dialect). He asked me about my age, former occupation, schooling, and family. (He seemed to know my family name.) When I told him that I had been the best student in school, he said that the Germans wouldn't care about that. Finally, he ordered Sienicki to write down that I should stay in the office. He transferred almost all the other youths to various workshops, however. He even gave some of them coupons to have holi-days in Heim [the rest resort in Marysin], and, in the case of one woman who fainted because he grilled her so much, he ordered that she immediately be given a loaf of bread, 10 dkg of butter, and 20 dkg of sugar. He nearly jumped up when young girls paraded around in front of him. Lunatics, perverts, and criminals like Rumkowski rule over us and determine our food allocations, work, and health. No wonder the Germans don't want to interfere in ghetto matters: the Jews will kill one another perfectly well, and, in the meantime, they will also squeeze maximum production out of one another.

I returned home before nine. Nadzia was scared, and the soup was cold. I keep having a fever. Tomorrow I will see a skin doctor for my scabs and skin irritation. Perhaps they are causing the fever.

Friday, March 12. Łódź.   I went to the doctor, and he has again prescribed the ointment for me. He confirmed that the fever most likely comes from the scabs.

Rumkowski and Sienicki toured various departments and made numerous purges everywhere.

The weather is lovely. 24°C [75°F] in the sun. In politics it's still pitiful. Although the Germans are indeed retreating on the northern and central fronts, they are moving ahead in the south and will take Kharkov any day. Nothing is happening in the west. They are bombing Germany a little, but they are not doing any real damage. Meanwhile, we are being finished off.

Saturday, March 13. Łódź.   Nadzia bought the rations today, so there is a bit of food to give us a dose of new strength. I limp again very badly because under my right knee I've got a lot of scabs with some matter under them. The fever has eased up a bit. I've noticed that I feel better outside, getting some exercise, than cooped up in a closed room.

Kharkov will fall any day. The Russians are said to have taken over Vyaźma. From the west, dead silence continues.

Sunday, March 14. Łódź.   All day I sat in bed and applied compresses to my scabs. Last night, as usual, the alarm sirens blew, but there was no raid.

A lot of work has supposedly been ordered from the ghetto again and another dark cloud has come over us: Ley,* the [German] minister

---

* Robert Ley (1890–1945) committed suicide in prison in Nuremberg while awaiting trial for war crimes.

of labor, the greatest anti-Semite in the German government, is expected to arrive. Even the Germans from the Gettoverwaltung are scared, and they are doing their best to arrange everything as smoothly as possible. Just to get by, just to get through as long as possible, just to come closer to the end of the war. The end, however, still seems far away.

Monday, March 15. Łódź. Last night there was an alarm again. In today's newspaper the Germans write that they have taken over Kharkov, but they also say the street fighting continues.

My scabs and skin irritations are not healing. I continue to have a fever, but I don't take my temperature because I no longer have a thermometer. I went to the doctor, but since I hadn't checked my temperature, he was unable to diagnose me. Later on I went to Mrs. Wolfowicz's. She promised that her son, Moniek, a director in the Housing Department, would intercede with Fuchs for one more soup for me, and that he would also try to do other things for me. Promises, promises, fools are taken in with fine promises. But what harm can they do to me? Maybe they will work out somehow.

Tuesday, March 16. Łódź. Yesterday 850 workers came from Germany (from an area near Poznań). They are going to be employed in demolition work. They are, however, in such a deplorable state that for now they can't be employed anywhere. They were in a camp that was literally a death house. Eighty to ninety percent of them died there. They were bullied in all sorts of ways; the work was inhumane, and the food was worse than in the worst periods here. They were beaten by the Germans and by over a dozen Jews, so-called *Gruppenführer* [German; group leaders] and *Unterlagerführer* [German; camp leaders]. As with us here, over there too the Germans found Jews who can finish off their own brothers quite effectively.

Wednesday, March 17. Łódź. I can't get rid of my scabs, skin irritation, or fever. I still walk like an invalid. Yesterday before I took off for home, Mrs. Milgrom, the wife of my boss and mother of my friend Lolek, came to the office. I complained to her about my lamentable condition and about the fact that I can't receive an additional soup in any way. Today it turned out that this kindhearted woman interceded with her husband, who called me into his office. He explained that, officially, he can't give me another soup because Fuchs holds everything in his mitts, but that he would try from time to time to give me another

ID card (the trick, though prohibited, is practiced by high-ranking officials) and so I would be able to have an extra soup. I have already received another ID card and have had two soups.

In politics absolutely nothing is known. Everything seems to have died or gone into a state of complete stagnation, worse than ever before. Even though there was an alarm last night and shots could be heard, it doesn't mean much yet. Our situation in the ghetto continues to look completely grim.

Thursday, March 18. Łódź.   [Anthony] Eden is in Washington, and they are conferring again, but we don't know with what possible results. The Germans are pressing forward again, and the bombing of Germany has stopped. For us, the situation is horrible. Every day is worse in the ghetto. The ration of potatoes in the workshop soup has been reduced to 15 dkg a bowl (the bins in Marysin are almost empty now). There are no new food rations. Extermination is approaching.

Friday, March 19. Łódź.   After a six-week break, a ration of meat (20 dkg) and sausage (15 dkg) has been issued. The Germans are again moving forward on the eastern front, while the conference in Washington is amounting to nothing. We can see no chance for any breakthrough in the present situation. Long months of torture are still ahead for us.

Saturday, March 20. Łódź.   Last night there was a big alarm accompanied by one explosion and several shots from an antiaircraft gun. However, the Germans have taken over Bielgorod and are moving forward. The last day of winter hasn't brought about any positive change in our lives.

Sunday, March 21. Łódź.   A lovely, truly springlike day. At eleven I went to the office in order to have soup, which one can again receive on Sundays if one comes to work. Milgrom let me know yesterday that he had created a small mix-up for me, increasing my salary to 90 RM, which is basically hard to do in the ghetto. I thanked him for taking care of me, and said the money would be very helpful.

Lolek Milgrom suggested that I give lessons at Podlaski's, but I didn't agree to it because the only compensation would be food and I probably wouldn't even get that. Anyway I don't have the strength to teach now.

After work, Nadzia and I went to "Aunt" Wolfowicz's. Later on, Moniek arrived. He told me to come to him tomorrow after two because he would try to arrange clothing and underclothes for us from Mrs. Wołkow, the chairman's secretary.

Monday, March 22. Łódź.   Heavy clouds are hanging over the ghetto. The Germans have demanded that all the workers who arrived in the ghetto in the last transport be turned over to them. In the evening the workers were taken to Czarnieckiego Street. They say that [other] prisoners were also rounded up with them. Rumors are already circulating about new deportations.

Hitler gave a speech in which he said that the situation is excellent for Germany again, that the Russians are being held back while the German offensive is in progress; he is not afraid of an invasion and has an extreme answer for enemy airplanes, etc., etc. In a word, the atmosphere is absolutely grim, and the situation is absolutely hopeless. Once again I have moments of melancholy and madness. There isn't a single person who believes in the war's end. These damned capitalist politics are bound to bring about the destruction of the entire world, and of us first.

My fever persists, and I still can't get rid of my scabs and the traces of skin irritation. My frostbitten toe is not healing either, and I have to drag myself around in clogs, which consumes half of my health.

In the afternoon I went to see Moniek Wolfowicz twice to find out if he had managed to secure anything for me, but he wasn't there. We are eating our last potatoes. I only hope that they will last until we can buy a new ration.

The weather is most lovely, truly spring. I really feel like living and surviving, but the horoscope looks poor here. Who knows . . .

Tuesday, March 23. Łódź.   I went to see Moniek Wolfowicz once again. He telephoned Mrs. Wołkow in my presence, and she told us to come to her tomorrow. Perhaps Nadzia and I will receive some clothing or a financial subsidy. Following Moniek's advice, I also wrote an application for a leave in Heim.

Wednesday, March 24. Łódź.   At noon I went to see Wołkow, but I couldn't get in. I will have to go again tomorrow at about ten or so. Lolek Milgrom let me know that Podlaski agreed to give me soup in return for my tutoring. In the evening I went to Podlaski's and agreed to tutor his son and daughter (one day, him; the other day, her). I will have a plate of soup at each visit. I had an opportunity to witness their supper. I didn't eat like that even before the war!

Meanwhile, I can't walk normally because of the scabs under my knees, which won't heal. My hand is a bit better. I have recently been working a little on *Alarm* again, but I can't do much. I still have a fever.

Thursday, March 25. Łódź.   This day went down in our memories as a day spent quaking in fear. At about eight o'clock, the Sonderabteilung policemen began stopping people and seizing them on the streets of the ghetto. As in the past, "hourglasses," the old, and the ones who couldn't produce their worker ID cards were taken. They were then gathered in the precinct houses and on Czarnieckiego Street, and selected into groups by a commission consisting of Jakobson,* [who is] the president of the court, the criminal police commissioner, and some other dignitaries. Some people have been let go, but many have been kept. Most probably it's again a matter of a deportation into scrap metal. However, in the ghetto nothing is known for sure.†

The action must have been organized in connection with the visit in the ghetto by Dr. Ley, the German minister of labor, the greatest anti-Semite in the Nazi government. Ley is said to have given a Jew-baiting speech in Łódź, the strongest ever. He came here to exterminate the Jews like bedbugs.

I came home at four because of rumors that they would seize people again in the evening. I don't look particularly well in my rags and clogs and with my anemic face. In politics there's nothing new. With food it's worse and worse.

Friday, March 26. Łódź.   Still nothing is certain. At night some people were taken from their beds, but the day has been calm. A number of the people who were detained have been released.

A ration for the next fourteen days has been issued. There are only 3

---

* Szaja-Stanisław Jakobson (1906–1944), a doctor of law, was deported in the final liquidation of the ghetto to Auschwitz, where he perished.
† Many of the deportees who had been brought in from Poznań and were scheduled for quick deportation back out of the ghetto had gone into hiding. To make up their quota of 1,000 persons, the Jewish Police began to seize people at random off the streets. The obvious capriciousness of such roundups, while involving far fewer people, seem to have terrified the population far more than the massive waves of tens of thousands deported, according to lists prepared under the auspices of the ghetto's Resettlement Commission.

kilos of potatoes, 4 kilos of beets and again only 10 dkg of oil, half a kilo of flour, 30 dkg of rye flakes, 45 dkg of sugar, 40 dkg of marmalade, 20 dkg of syrup, and a few other small things.

After work I went to the Podlaskis' to tutor. They gave me such a poor soup that I am considering quitting the whole affair. Meanwhile, I still can't get rid of my scabs and the wound on my toe. In politics there's absolutely nothing. Total silence.

Saturday, March 27. Łódź.   The Arbeitsamt-Getto [German; Ghetto Employment Department] will now issue new employment cards with a photo, signed by Biebow for all the workers in the ghetto. The forms for these ID cards, one of which I snuck for myself, have already been delivered to our office.

As in the past, "hourglasses," the old, and the ones who couldn't produce their worker ID cards were taken. They were then gathered in the precinct houses and on Czarnieckiego Street. . . . Most probably it's again a matter of a deportation into scrap metal.

Nadzia has received her ration: beets and even potatoes. Again, a dose of something to give new strength to our hearts. I went to the Podlaskis' to tutor again. The soup was not much better than the one yesterday, while they gobble up gingerbreads, meaty gelatin, and cutlets.

At the office for the third time I received a *Zusatz* (an additional soup) from Milgrom. He recently received a certain amount of the soup at his disposal, and he remembered me.

The weather's most lovely, simply charming, but in politics there's nothing new.

Sunday, March 28. Łódź.   In the afternoon I went to Wolman's. He let me read the introduction to a novel he had begun to write. When I came back home I thought I would faint. My legs were failing under me, and I could hardly walk. I also kept having a fever, and I can't get rid of the scabs and the wound from the frostbite. I look very bad. And here come deportations; more dark clouds hang over the ghetto.

Monday, March 29. Łódź.   In addition to Podlaski's little daughter, I have one more student, Radzyner's little brother. Now I will also get soup three times a week from the Radzyners. In the evening I also had a talk with Niutek, who is ill with the measles. He offered me a job translating one of Lenin's books from Yiddish to Polish. I took it willingly and will begin working on it in the coming days.

All the sick are to be gathered for deportation. There are rumors that the Germans have been halted on the Soviet front. Supposedly Tunis will be liberated soon, but the Allied invasion [of Europe] is still not mentioned (the German submarines must be working very well).

Today the clocks were set ahead an hour for daylight saving time. I earned an extra hour of office work.

Tuesday, March 30. Łódź.   I spent the day running around the city; as a result I could hardly move in the evening. At ten I went to see Mrs. Wołkow, but I couldn't get into her room before twelve. She remembered Moniek Wolfowicz's telephone call, and promised to settle the problem of shoes and clothing for Nadzia and me. Nadzia will also receive 30 RM a month, in addition to her weekly 5 RM, which, as a juvenile, she earns for working five hours a day. Mrs. Wołkow accepted my application for Heim, but she doubts whether anything will come of it.

After I left her office, I met Moniek Wolfowicz. It was a fortunate accident, since I was intending to go to see him. He told me that he had

had a talk about my situation with a desk officer in the Sonderabteilung, an old friend of my uncle's from Palestine, who promised to try to slip me into the ranks of the Sonderabteilung police.* My soul simply smiled at the thought. After all, that would enable me to get rid of my illnesses, infirmities, and incessant hunger. Moniek told me to report to Mr. Bursztyn from the Sonderabteilung and promised one more intervention with Mrs. Wołkow regarding my leave in Heim.

Because I was very anxious, at three o'clock I went to the Sonderabteilung. That Bursztyn man, however, wasn't there. So I dropped in on Wolman. He is writing scripts for several variety shows in various workshops. At four o'clock I once again went to the Sonderabteilung. I showed Bursztyn my graduation certificate and transcript from the *gymnasium* (I had them with me, since I had also shown them to Mrs. Wołkow). He must have been impressed by them because he told me to write an application and bring it in tomorrow in the morning. Perhaps something will be done. I went home full of hope and couldn't fall asleep for a long time. Admission to the Sonderabteilung is almost the only chance I have to save my health! For it to just come through!

A transport of the people who had been gathered last night, including the sick, was sent out. No one knows what will come next.

Wednesday, March 31. Łódź.   In the morning I gave Bursztyn my application. He told me to go home and wait for a response. My clogs have fallen apart completely, but I can't put on the tight shoes because of the wound on my foot. I have a fever and can't get rid of the scabs on my hand either.

A new ration of 5 dkg of cottage cheese and 4 dkg of margarine has been issued. Another scrap thrown to the dying.

Thursday, April 1. Łódź.   From yesterday's newspaper, which I read today, it appears that a new Soviet offensive has begun on the eastern front. In Tunis fierce battles are being waged. The Germans are also writing about battles that have been going on for several weeks with Communist bands in Croatia (today is the first time they're writing about it!). Berlin and the western part of Germany have been bombed devastatingly. New promises to the Soviets have been made from Washington, but nothing specific is known.

---

* This was a much-coveted work assignment, since these Special Department police officers oversaw food distribution in the ghetto.

There's been no reply from Mrs. Wołkow or from the Sonder-abteilung. I tutor everyday, and have also begun the translation of Lenin's *Imperialist War* from Yiddish to Polish. The translation is as smooth as silk. The weather is still rainy.

Friday, April 2. Łódź.   There are rumors that things in Africa will conclude any moment, and that an action is about to begin in the Mediterranean Sea.* Berlin is still being bombed heavily, and the Germans are in poor shape on the eastern front. We'll see what will come of this.

The weather is still rotten. I feel terribly bad. I have a high fever, but I'm continuing the translation of Lenin, and reading.

Saturday, April 3. Łódź.   In the afternoon I went to see Niutek to sound him out on my idea of joining the Sonderabteilung. He believes categorically that "none of our men" should join Sonder. Of course, his opinion will not influence me. He is very satisfied with my translation of Lenin. His younger brother is sick, so I don't tutor him, and don't receive any soup.

Sunday, April 4. Łódź.   My state of mind is worsening every day. The fever persists, and I look like a complete "death notice." I can't bring my irritated skin back to normal, either.

In politics there's still nothing new. The war is extending infinitely, and here I am with no more strength. Everyone in the ghetto is sick. TB is spreading unbelievably, and there is a great number of other infectious and noninfectious diseases. Nadzia has noticed symptoms of scabies on her body again. If things continue like this, I will go crazy. Oh, this horrible, endless hopelessness. No chance or hope for life.

Monday, April 5. Łódź.   I talked with Moniek Wolfowicz. We will meet at 3:30 tomorrow in front of Praszkier's apartment. Praszkier promised that he will give me something from the clothing in the storehouse that belongs "to him."

I witnessed Moniek's breakfast, which hardly differs from the breakfast of Fuchs or any other dignitary. Those in the ruling class in the ghetto are provided with everything in abundance. The division between classes in the ghetto has become complete. In hardly any respect can you compare the fate of a supervisor with the fate of a worker. The

---

* The Allies did, in fact, advance the war from Africa to Sicily and then to Italy.

workers are dying at a terrifying rate, while the ruling class lives in growing prosperity. The only way to survive the war is to join the higher classes, but that's impossible. As for my joining the Sonderabteilung, I haven't heard anything yet.

Tuesday, April 6. Łódź.   I went to see Praszkier, but didn't meet him. Through Moniek, he told me to wait for him in front of the Altschuhlager [German; Old-shoe Depository], where he was supposed to arrange boots for me, but as I immediately suspected, he didn't show up.

Wednesday, April 7. Łódź.   We received a summons from Wołkow to come to 1 Dworska Street. We were given coupons there for shoes and clothing. The translation of Lenin is proceeding quickly.

Thursday, April 8. Łódź.   Nadzia and I went to the Altschuhlager, where we bought two pairs of quite good shoes. However, we won't be able to receive them in sooner than ten days because they have to be repaired.

Friday, April 9. Łódź.   The weather is becoming colder. I can't get rid of the wounds under my knee. The frostbitten toe and the scabs are only a bit better. I also don't feel the fever so much.

   In the afternoon a new ration for the coming two weeks was issued, and it caused mourning in the entire city. There are no potatoes in it at all. Instead, there are 3 kilos of rutabagas and 3 kilos of beets. And this is supposed to be enough to cook for two weeks! My flesh crawls at the very thought of the hunger that awaits us. In politics there's nothing new.

Saturday, April 10. Łódź.   The weather is still like November. Everyone has a cold and a runny nose. Nadzia, too, has a bad cold. Hunger is worse than ever.

Sunday, April 11. Łódź.   I've noticed scabies on my body again. I think I will go crazy. Nadzia stayed in bed all day long because she is really sick. I had to cook and warm things up in the evening. The weather is still awful. No food is arriving in the ghetto.

Monday, April 12. Łódź.   Little Radzyner has already recovered, and today I had a lesson with him and little Podlaska. I will have three more bowls of soup a week again. Nevertheless, I feel hopeless.

Tuesday, April 13. Łódź.   In the afternoon Nadzia and I went to buy clothing. I found quite a solid coat and pants, and also pretty good underclothes for Nadzia and myself. Nadzia also found a dress.

The worst thing is that I have to deal with itching again. I apply sulfurized hydrogen water, but I doubt I will accomplish anything, except for some burns and abscesses.

Wednesday, April 14. Łódź.   I will be working in the bakery for three months!* The first person to tell me about it was Kogniczuk, my former schoolmate, presently a Sonderabteilung messenger. He brought a list of future "bakers" to the Bakery Department, signed by Gertler. Then, I met Moniek Wolfowicz, who confirmed that Chaim [Rumkowski] has received the list already, that I am on it, and that I will receive an assignment in the next few days.

I went home to tell Nadzia about it, but here I immediately received a dose of worry to balance my former joy. Nadzia has a terrible cold again, a cough, and probably a fever. She will have to stay in bed for a few days. I, too, feel sick.

I can't find out who put me onto that bakery list. In the afternoon a message came from Wołkow that my request (!?) for a job in a bakery had been approved and that I will soon be given a work assignment. Could it be that Moniek worked it out for me with Mrs. Wołkow? I will find out tomorrow. I just can't wait for Nadzia to recover so that I can completely surrender myself to satisfaction.

Thursday, April 15. Łódź.   It turns out that, indeed, Moniek had asked Mrs. Wołkow for a bakery slot for me, and she settled it favorably with the president "in a moment of his grace and good mood." Moniek has promised me that he will try to arrange a laundry coupon for us so that we can wash our clothes.

Meanwhile, I am completely sick, and I have a high fever. I bought a Bayer medication for the flu, fever and, cold, for Nadzia and me. Nadzia stays in bed, and I think she will remain there for another day or two.

Mrs. Deutsch came to see me today. She's been assigned to cook matzoth. It is very fortunate for her, since she looks as if she were dead. And she was in seventh heaven hearing about my probable bakery job. I

---

* This was also one of the most desired positions in the ghetto, since bakery workers ate their fill of bread on the job.

The certificate designating tuberculosis as the cause of Dawid's death on August 8, 1943.

think she is the most devoted friend I have in the ghetto, or anywhere else for that matter.

In the evening I had to prepare food and cook supper, which exhausted me totally. In politics there's absolutely nothing new. Again, out of impatience I feel myself beginning to fall into melancholy. There is really no way out of this for us.

Here the last of Dawid Sierakowiak's surviving notebooks breaks off. He died four months later of tuberculosis, starvation, and exhaustion, the syndrome known as ghetto disease.

The Photographs and Photographers

Two young men, very much committed to the emerging medium of photojournalism, were among the original population forced into the Łódź Ghetto. They proceeded to document life and death there through the course of the community's five-year history. The photographers, Mendel Grossman* and Henryk Ross, both born in 1913, were appointed by the ghetto's Jewish Administration—and provided with film, developing chemicals, and photographic paper purchased from the Nazis—ostensibly to document ghetto industry. But they worked incessantly to record a complete vision of their doomed community. They took thousands of photographs, capturing every aspect of ghetto life, and carefully catalogued, hid, stored, and distributed those images, so they would survive even if the photographers did not.

Did they anticipate that in future years false historians would attempt to deny that the Holocaust had occurred? Certainly they shared Dawid Sierakowiak's extraordinary dedication to create and preserve a lasting record of the ghetto's existence. Daring cameramen, they committed their lives to their mission. Ross, in an interview used in the broadcast supplement to the film *Łódź Ghetto*, enjoys telling how he was able to take photographs of a hanging in the ghetto from a clandestine vantage point in a nearby building, and how he then had to placate his nervous wife by burning a different roll of negatives, thus preserving the images of the hanging for posterity. One of those shots appears in this volume.

The photographers documented much more than Nazi crimes, preserving the rough textures of ghetto existence: children digging in garbage heaps for bits of coal; spirited young women smiling as they push fecal tanks to the outskirts of the ghetto. They brought to their task both the discerning distance of gifted photographers and the intimacy of their own captive lives in the unique community.

* For futher information on Mendel Grossman, see Mendel Grossman, *With a Camera in the Ghetto* (New York, 1977).

*Henryk Ross documents Mendel Grossman documenting a
deportation, probably in May 1941. Grossman kept his camera
discreetly out of sight in the hand case when he was not shooting.
The uniformed man at left is a member of the ghetto's own police
force. Photographs show about one unarmed Jewish police officer for
every hundred deportees assigned to accompany the Łódź Jews to the
trains. Germans did not usually participate in the deportations until
the day's quota of Jews was delivered to the railroad siding in
Marysin. Armed Germans then oversaw their boarding the trains.
Reflecting the complexity of the time, Grossman's and Ross's
photographs show the Jewish policemen sometimes carrying heavy
bags to assist individuals being sent out.*

Grossman kept shooting after he was deported from the ghetto in the final liquidation of August 1944. Only days before the Germans surrendered, his heart gave out on a forced march between German work camps. He was thirty-two years old, and still wearing his camera on a sling in his coat.

Ross survived, living out his life in a small house in Jaffa, south of Tel Aviv. He died in 1991, still in possession of nearly 3,000 negatives he had shot in the ghetto.

The photograph on this volume's cover was taken by a member of the ghetto's German Administration, probably in 1941. He was using color film that had recently been developed by Agfa. The 35-mm image, preserved as a glass-mounted slide, is part of a collection that contains as many festive snapshots of parties among the Germans as images of the doomed Jews in their ghetto. Strangely, a near duplicate of this photograph of thirty ghetto schoolboys exists in black and white among the archives of Jewish photographers' prints. The black-and-white picture was taken a moment before or after the color shot. A few of the boys' heads are turned away in the black-and-white version. There are several other pairings of nearly identical black-and-white and color ghetto photos. Grossman or Ross must have spent some time going around the ghetto, side-by-side with the German photographer, recording the same images but with a very different intent. The Nazi propagandists relished the way ghetto life dehumanized the Jews, while Grossman and Ross conveyed the enormity of both the Nazis' crime and humanity's loss by recording for posterity the very humanity and singularity of the ghetto dwellers as they lived their final days.